Handbook of
Teacher Training
in Europe

Issues and Trends

Edited by
Maurice Galton and Bob Moon

David Fulton Publishers
London

David Fulton Publishers Ltd
2 Barbon Close, London WC1N 3JX

First published in Great Britain by
David Fulton Publishers, 1994

Note: The right of the authors to be identified as the authors of their
contributions has been asserted by them in accordance with the Copyright,
Designs and Patents Act 1988.

© The Council of Europe and David Fulton (Publishers) Ltd

British Library Cataloguing in Publication Data

A catalogue record for this book is available from the British Library

ISBN 1-85346-228-4

Designed by Almac Ltd., London
Typeset by Action Typesetting Limited, Gloucester
Printed in Great Britain by Biddles Limited, Guildford

Contents

Contributors

Prof. Dr Friedrich Buchberger	Paedagogische Akademie des Bundes in Oberoesterreich, Linz
Prof. Maurice Galton	School of Education University of Leicester UK
Dr Len Masterman	University of Nottingham UK
Prof. Bob Moon	School of Education The Open University UK
Simon Newman	The Council of Europe
Daniel Premont	EIP
Monique Prindezis	CIFEDHOP
Mme Francine Vaniscotte	The European Commission
Dr J.H.C. Vonk	Vrije Universiteit of Amsterdam The Netherlands
Dr M.J. De Vries	Eindhoven University of Technology The Netherlands
Prof. John Dewar Wilson	Department of Education Victorial University of Technology Melbourne
Prof. E.C. Wragg	School of Education Exeter University UK

Introduction

Bob Moon and Maurice Galton

European co-operation around the theme of teacher education has increased significantly in recent decades. The Council of Europe has played an important role in bringing this issue to the fore through Standing Conferences of European Ministers of Education (Council of Europe, 1987a) and through numerous conferences and seminars (see, for example, Council of Europe, 1988 and 1990a). Other European and International Organisations have also played a role. The European Union (EU), for example, recognising that teachers represent the largest occupational group, has seen their status and training as pivotal in restructuring education, for lifelong learning and for the management of human resources in general (Smith, 1992). Teacher education has gained considerably from projects linked to programmes such as ERASMUS, COMETT, DELTA, TEMPUS and LINGUA (and looking to the future SOCRATES and LEONARDO). The information network EURYDICE has provided an information base to a developing programme of educational co-operation. The Organisation for Economic Co-operation and Development (OECD) and UNESCO have also both taken a number of initiatives in this area (see, for example, OECD 1990a, 1992; OECD/CERI, 1993).

European Associations of teacher educators have also played a significant role through annual conferences and specialist activities. The Association for Teacher Education in Europe (ATEE) with headquarters in Brussels, has produced a range of publications illustrative of such work. A major ATEE study of European teacher education systems (Buchberger, 1992a) updates and expands an earlier Council of Europe publication (Council of Europe, 1987b). The European Association of Teachers holds triennial congresses that address issues of concern to teacher educators and schooling generally. Other organisations and individual countries in Europe have also taken initiatives to promote co-operation around the theme of teacher education.

Co-operation, therefore, represents one of the first of a number of themes that now can be seen to characterise Teacher Education in Europe. And co-operation has been facilitated by structural transformations that have taken place in many European countries, within schools and subsequently in the forms and systems of teacher education. Neave (1987), for example, has spoken of the assimilation of: 'teacher education into the mainstream of university activity, thereby removing both institutional compartmentalisation and the apparent differences in status that came from remaining outside academics' (p. 7) and he goes on to term this a process of 'incorporation' that has progressed through a number of stages, leading in many countries to 'final formal incorporation into the university sector, stricto sensu'.

The harmonisation and democratisation of the structures of school systems have contributed greatly to this process. The development of common systems of primary and lower secondary schooling across Europe (Moon, 1993) and the widening of access to upper secondary and tertiary level education, has helped forge a greater sense of unity throughout the teaching profession. And this in turn has contributed to the recognition of the importance of all forms of co-operation.

A decade that marks the end of a millennium has focused increased interest on the challenges facing teacher education. Alongside the importance attached to co-operation a number of further themes can be identified, many of which are addressed in subsequent chapters. Four are identified here for preliminary consideration:

(1) the nature and form of government intervention in the control of schooling and teacher education;
(2) the expansion and democratisation of education in the post-compulsory years;
(3) the position and status of girls in schooling and women in teacher education;
(4) changing conceptions of pedagogy and the development of Information Technology in the schools of the future.

The role of government and teacher autonomy

The late 1970s and 1980s were associated with an unprecedented level of wholesale reformism in most European countries. This took many forms but in general represented an increased concern on the part of government to be seen addressing pressing problems within the school system. In many countries, legislated intervention came increasingly to frame the focus in which innovation was fostered in the school system and within the associated structure of teacher education. The introduction of a National Curriculum in England and Wales, for example, was quickly followed by highly prescribed regulations for initial teacher education. The wholescale restructuring, through a number of phases, of teacher education in France provides a further example, as has the debate in Finland where political uncertainties as to the place of teacher education within the university structure has echoed debate in other parts of Europe.

This increased exercise of governmental control in so many countries, whilst familiar to many of the countries in Central and Eastern Europe, often marked a sharp contrast with previous traditions. In the 1990s, however, there are signs that the momentum for central legislated reform is slowing. Roberto Carneiro (1993), a former Portuguese Minister of Education, has put this in graphic terms. He sees the last thirty years as characterised by wholesale reformism but he suggests we are witnessing the last laps of an era.

> Year after year, country after country, system after system, the educational establishment addressed reform as a necessary and mythical thrust. In a provisional balance and generally speaking, this value loaded approach − good governance was synonymous of engaging in bold programmes of global educational change − fell short of all the bright promises at the very outset. On the one hand actual outcomes remained far from expectations and on the other hand, the harsh realities of public finance trimmed down overambitious targets and cushioned triumphal trumpets. Finally, political cycles and voluntaristic *diktats* revealed themselves alien to school cycles and to the pulsation of real events down the ladder to the classroom level.

For Carneiro there is a need now to avoid the 'stop and go' broad cycle top down reformism in favour of a dynamic grassroots change strategy. To achieve this he endorses a combination of flexible conceptual level goal setting with a process of sustainable adaptation and innovation at the executive level. This, he argues, requires a wise devolution of responsibility in the decentralised selective innovation, thus providing far more rewards than mere central reformism.

This shift in the focus of strategic thinking is likely to reinforce the thrust of much of teacher education in Europe towards enhanced professional status and, within teacher education in particular, the broad acceptance of the need for teachers who can reflect critically on their practice to achieve an appropriate degree of autonomy in filling their professional role. The literature on this is now extensive and teacher educators in a number of countries have explored this theme. Anniki Järvinen and colleagues (1992) in Finland, following a number of research studies, suggested that by:

> developing a critical understanding of their work, teachers can be emancipated from the unquestioned habits, routines, beliefs and assumptions concerning their work and take charge of developing their profession. (p. 3)

Harnessing the concept of the critical professional to strategic decisions to devolve power and responsibility raises a number of questions for the form and style of teacher education, not the least because the context of such devolution has in itself undergone significant change. Whilst governments and communities may be prepared to give more autonomy to professional groups, such as teachers, the terms in which that is given may circumscribe the way such autonomy is exercised. Public expectations, for example, about accountability and some measure of the outcome of schooling, are unlikely to diminish in the years to come. The way teachers '*give account of their work*' will remain an issue of strategic importance and, therefore, of practical concern in teacher education. The balance of central, regional, school and teacher control and autonomy is of particular concern in Central and Eastern European countries where new definitions of the teacher role are emerging in the wake of wholesale restructuring of social and educational systems.

Education in the post-compulsory years

All European countries are experiencing high and increasing rates of participation in the post-compulsory sector. New forms of education and training are being developed and with an increased emphasis on vocational education. This emphasis is also influencing the final years of compulsory schooling where attempts to achieve a balance between the academic and vocational curriculum remains a current concern. The teachers necessary for the expansion of the post-compulsory sector and the more vocational orientation of the upper-secondary curriculum, have become a source of interest and concern at the European level. There has, for example, in many countries to be an increase in numbers and the extent to which these teachers should be prepared within the university framework, now commonly associated with most forms of pre-service training, is an issue of debate. In Denmark, the State Institution for Teacher Education (SET) provides both initial and in-service training for all teachers, including those in or intending to enter the technical and vocational sector. In Switzerland an international development centre has been set up to try and integrate teachers of further and technical education into the mainstream of teacher education. In Italy, however, no specific training for teachers in the technical and vocational areas is required (Council of Europe, 1988).

The evidence (Hostmark-Tarrou, 1988) suggests that in pre-service education there is a trend towards more general content and thus a developing convergence between these forms of training and the more established structure existing for teachers in primary and secondary education. The heterogeneous and fragmented nature of technical and vocational education and its existence partly within and partly outside the education system made improvements in pre-service training difficult. Hostmark-Tarrou noted that at the level of in-service training, the pace of technological change was posing particular problems requiring in some sectors forms of provision that would provide the complete retraining of certain groups of teachers.

The position and status of women in teacher education

Concern about the position and status of women in education has a long history in European education.

> Potestne esse femina quae dicter heroina, materia Epopoeiae?
> (Can the totality of the Epic, which embraces the world in unity and harmony and rises above every mere detail, admit a woman as protagonist?)

was one school question set for older children in the 1830s in Budapest (Mayris, 1986, p. 267). In the post-Second-World-War period there have been numerous international resolutions upholding the principle of equality of opportunity in education. The 1979 UN Convention on the Elimination of all Forms of Discrimination Against Women, for example, was signed by all European countries. In the 1980s, the Council of Europe initiated a project that explored national policies towards promoting equality of educational opportunity. This showed (Wilson, 1991) that the provision of higher level education for women has significantly increased since 1970 in most European countries and is fast catching up with the percentage of male participation. Within teacher education, however, certain patterns of participation represent a cause for concern. Wilson, for example (1991, p. 121), shows how at the lower levels of the education system teaching is becoming an increasingly feminised profession in many European countries. And she goes on to cite evidence (OECD, 1985) that institutions and/or areas of study can become devalued when the female participation rate rises. Equally, lower percentage representation in senior positions, particularly in secondary, tertiary and higher education is frequently reported. In many countries less than 25 per cent of secondary school headteachers and school inspectors are women, and in some cases the percentage is far smaller (Archer and Peck, 1992). In May 1990 the Council of Ministers of the European Community formulated draft conclusions on the promotion of equality of opportunity in education and particularly through the initial and in-service training of teachers. A number of teacher education institutions now include specific programmes towards such aims within pre-service and in-service courses.

The University of the Canary Isles in Spain, for example, has developed teaching materials and methods on an experimental basis (Castro and Mir, 1992). The Faculty of Education at Rotterdam Polytechnic in the Netherlands has pioneered the development of women only groups to change the attitude of trained women teachers towards their future career (Moermas and de Voogd, 1992). In England, as part of Sheffield Hallam University's research programme, a longitudinal study is being made of the impact of pre-service teaching on equal opportunities on subsequent career interests and attitudes (Boulton and Coldron, 1990).

The issue of gender is affecting teacher education in a variety of ways. It has become a subject of study in its own right (Britain's Open University, for example, has developed a masters programme credit on the issue) and it is increasingly recognised in the broader concerns of teaching and assessment. Most recently, for example, the influence of gender on formative and summative systems of assessment, both school based and in respect of national testing and examination systems, has been more widely recognised (see Gipps and Murphy, 1994), and is now forming a part of pre-service and in-service courses. The position and status of women, therefore, is likely to become an issue of increasing importance, not merely in terms of participation and representation at different levels within the education system, but also in terms of broad-ranging curricular and pedagogic education and training.

The challenge of new technologies

Over the last decade the impact of new technologies on teaching and learning, particularly in schools, has been vigorously debated. It is an issue that has excited high expectations and many disappointments. The ever-increasing flexibility of new forms of information technology, however, clearly offer significant possibilities for reformulating accepted practices of teacher – pupil interaction with consequent important implications for teacher education.

There are now clear signs that new forms of technology are poised to have a profound influence on the environment of educational institutions including schools. There is, for example, the increasingly wide gap between the world of work and education in terms of take-up and use of new technology. The pressures on the education system to respond to the so-called 'office revolution' will almost certainly increase. This is matched by the level of technology that is now associated with the home (the French minitel systems, for example) and it is difficult to see how schools could resist making some accommodation to these trends.

Perhaps more important, however, is the increasing congruence between the opportunities offered by new technologies and our contemporary understanding of intelligence and learning. The erosion of the ideas of general intelligence and the increased recognition of the concept of multiple intelligences (accepting that there is still much to be done in understanding the forms of this multiplicity) points towards a more differentiated approach to curriculum planning, organisation and, more significantly, assessment. Alongside this the constructivist agenda, that has had so much influence on learning theory, points to the significance of communication, language, interaction and feedback; individualisation but within a social context. Conventional strategies of teaching and learning are challenged by these analyses. New technology, in the forms and styles now evolving, provides a proliferation of resources through which, in part, a response can be made.

A recent report (OECD/CERI, 1992b) has indicated the technological and social trends that are likely to influence the education system in the coming decades. In summary this suggests:

for technological change

- across the board development of truly portable, inexpensive equipment (following developments in battery technology);
- speech recognition techniques that reduce or eliminate the need for keyboard skills;
- 'unwired' network connections from short-distance radio transmission);
- standardisation of software interfaces allowing different types of computers to exchange data over communication links;
- satellite distribution allowing the delivery of a mixture of sound, text, data, graphics and full motion video, probably with the capability of interaction from receiving sites using some or all of these media;
- integrated networks for electronic mail and for videotape systems.

The social and political trends which follow and stimulate technological innovation include:

- learning, the need to absorb and act upon new information, will characterise 75 per cent of all jobs;
- functional requirements of half of all jobs will change every five years (creating a permanent training need);
- mobility of working within organisations: up to a third of all workers may be changing or expecting to change their job at any one time;
- considerable increase in numbers of 'teleworkers', people who work from home using telecommunication links (up to 50 per cent of all workers for part or all of the week in some urban areas).

These developments and related trends, in whatever form they evolve, are already profoundly affecting our thinking about the future of education and the demands that future will make on teaching. New forms of technology within open and sometimes distance learning systems are playing an increasing role (and given explicit mention in the Treaty of Maastricht), particularly within the more school-focused forms of in-service training. The increasing significance of school-based experience in initial courses in some countries is fuelling the demand for technologically orientated and flexible forms of resources and training support. The form that any response takes to these changes represents one of the most important challenges for teacher educators today. Can new technology sensitise and humanise teaching and learning in a way traditional pedagogies have often failed to do? Do the new opportunities open up the possibilities of redressing some of the inequalities, injustices and unfulfilled achievements that exist across education systems? How can these new ideas be most appropriately integrated within the culture and institutions of teacher education? What new forms of co-operation amongst teacher education are opened up by the revolution in communications that these trends represent? All these are questions that pose important challenges for teacher education. This handbook brings together contributors from a broad section of

European institutions to explore issues such as those highlighted in this introduction. These same issues have also provided the focus of seminars and conferences in recent years. The major impetus for these events has come from the Council of Europe who have provided the catalyst for a number of studies in this area.

The handbook is divided into four parts. In Part One, Teacher Education in Europe, is set in its present context. Simon Newman, one of the Council's senior officers, sets out the work of the Council and explains its aims. Chapter 2 consists of a survey of present practice in European countries. This survey was carried out by Professor Friedrich Buchberger on behalf of the Association for Teacher Education in Europe (ATEE). Part Two examines a number of issues connected with the training of teachers and of teacher trainers. Most of these studies arose out of seminars or workshops set up by the Council of Europe.

The Council has also been active in promoting discussion concerning key issues of human rights in education. Some of these issues are dealt with in Part Three where there is also discussion on the impact of changes in technology, the media and of the new freedoms available to teachers now that they are free to work in various countries within the European Union. Finally, in Part Four, there is an attempt to look forward to the research base which will be necessary if teacher education is to become more effective across the whole of Europe. This is opportune, given that for the first time, the Fourth Framework, set out by the European Union following Maastricht, has included teacher training as one element for future research and development.

PART ONE

Teacher Education in Europe: Context

CHAPTER 1

The Council of Europe and Teacher Education

Simon Newman

This chapter describes aspects of the Council of Europe's work which are relevant to teacher education and training, and especially some specific recommendations on this topic.

Introduction: the Council of Europe and its work on education and culture

The Council of Europe was set up in 1949 in the French Rhineland city of Strasbourg, chosen to symbolise reconciliation between the French and German peoples. The Council's aims are to bring about closer European unity, to protect human rights and pluralist democracy, to promote awareness of Europe's cultural identity, and to seek common or convergent solutions to society's problems, thereby improving conditions of life for the individual. Today the Council of Europe has a membership of thirty-two European states. These include all twelve members of the European Union (which is, however, a completely separate entity) together with Austria, Bulgaria, Cyprus, the Czech Republic, Estonia, Finland, Hungary, Iceland, Liechtenstein, Lithuania, Malta, Norway, Poland, Romania, San Marino, the Slovak Republic, Slovenia, Sweden, Switzerland and Turkey.

The Council of Europe provides a forum for co-operation between its member states in a variety of fields including human rights, health, social affairs, education, culture, sport, the environment, local government, and justice, but excluding defence. It is governed by a Committee of Ministers which adopts recommendations to governments and international treaties known as 'European Conventions'. Ideas for the organisation's work often originate in the Council of Europe's Parliamentary Assembly, where representatives from the national parliaments debate the issues of the day, or in conferences of specialist ministers.

The Council of Europe's work on education, culture, sport and youth is based on the European Cultural Convention of 1954, which is open for signature by European non-member states. Thus the Parties to the European Cultural Convention include not only all the member states, but also Albania, Belarus, Croatia, the Holy See, Latvia, Moldova, Monaco, Russia and Ukraine. In addition there has been co-operation with such countries as Canada, the USA and Japan.

Government officials responsible for education and culture in the signatory states meet in the *Council for Cultural Co-operation* to adopt a work programme on education and culture on the basis of proposals by its four specialised committees: the Education Committee, the Culture Committee, the Standing Conference on University Problems and the Cultural Heritage Committee. Within the Council of Europe, the Directorate of Education, Culture and Sport is responsible for the administration of this programme. The activities in the programme are of two main types: *projects* and *service activities*.

Projects involve the study of a major theme or policy area over a period of usually four or five years, for example modern language learning, innovation in primary education, or the education of migrants. Often, experimental, innovatory schemes are chosen in the member states for comparative study. Experts come together to define a guiding philosophy and principles of good practice which may then be made into a recommendation to the member states.

Service activities are of a more permanent nature. For example, there is a Teacher Bursary Scheme, and the European Documentation and Information System for Education (EUDISED), which provides a unique pan-European database on educational research.

The 15th Session of the Standing Conference of European Ministers of Education

Much of the Council of Europe's specific work on teachers and their education stems from the 15th Session of the Standing Conference of European Ministers of Education, held in Helsinki in May 1987 on the theme: 'New challenges for teachers and their education'.

In choosing this theme for discussion, Ministers of Education recognised that teachers decisively influence the quality of education and the lives and future of young people. Hence, the Ministers agreed, it is vitally important to attract the best candidates into teaching and to help them to be effective teachers, able to meet the needs of the education system, to cope with the challenges facing them today and to equip their pupils to respond successfully to the challenges of the next century.

The pressures faced by teachers include:

- greater heterogeneity in the school population (a wider range of abilities, interests and backgrounds in the classroom);
- explosive growth in the quantity of information, and hence curriculum content;
- competition from alternative sources of information, especially the mass media, which may convey contradictory values;
- the introduction of new teaching methods, especially resulting from the advent of the new information and communication technologies at school;
- the opening up of the school to the outside world, confronting teachers with a variety of expectations and conflicting judgements.

Recognising teachers' need for support in dealing with such pressures, and anxious to improve the quality of education, the Ministers of Education meeting in Helsinki recommended a variety of measures, to be applied in each country in the light of its own situation (Council of Europe, 1987a, b, c; Hellawell, 1987). These included:

- improving the image of teaching as a profession and developing recruitment procedures so as to ensure that the best possible candidates are brought into teaching;
- placing greater emphasis on teaching practice and on the development of teachers' personal and social skills in their initial training;
- developing counselling services for graduates about to embark on a teaching career;
- viewing the initial and in-service training of teachers as an integrated whole, a form of permanent education;
- giving teachers greater responsibility for appraising their own work and for making good the shortcomings thus identified, e.g. through in-service training.

In addition, the Ministers recommended that the Council of Europe's Council for Cultural Cooperation should examine a number of issues relating to teachers and their training. Subjects taken up in reports and seminars for European policy-makers and practitioners since that time have included:

- the procedures used in different countries for the selection of candidates for teacher training and during initial training;
- the selection and professional development of trainers providing basic teacher training;
- the training of teachers in technical and vocational education;
- training teachers to teach children with widely varying abilities, interests and backgrounds;
- the newly qualified teacher: the induction period;
- the appraisal of teachers and teaching.

The main findings of each of these activities are summarised below.

6

Selection for teacher training

A report on procedures used in European countries to select candidates for admission to initial teacher training courses and for assessing student progress during training was commissioned from the National Foundation for Educational Research in England and Wales for discussion at a seminar held in Strasbourg on 29–30 May 1990 (NFER, 1990; Council of Europe, 1990b).

It is generally recognised that the development and implementation of effective criteria and procedures for student selection represent the first step in producing a high-quality teaching force. In this selection process, by far the greatest importance continues to be attached to formal academic qualifications. The precise requirements are established at national level in most countries although the training institution may add their own in some cases. Most countries prescribe a minimum qualification (e.g. certificate of upper secondary education) for teacher training which is provided nowadays mainly at tertiary level. Some countries set competitive examinations, some operate an entry quota system to establish the number of students who can be admitted to teacher training each year.

There is controversy over how far criteria other than academic ability can and should be taken into account in the selection process. Are there personal qualities that are associated with successful teaching – such as adaptability, creativity, self-confidence, empathy, ability to communicate effectively and to generate enthusiasm, aptitude for team-work, etc? Granted that some of these can be developed through training, it is argued that techniques for measuring the sorts of personal criteria that might be involved are insufficiently reliable and that it is notoriously difficult to predict which students will become good teachers. Some countries therefore put the stress on selection *during* training. Counselling and guidance are given in the first year, for example, at the end of which it is expected that students who are unsuited to teaching will have been identified by the staff of the training institutions and that such students will have recognised this for themselves. They are then offered additional guidance in choosing alternative strategies.

The main question in some countries with a shortage of teachers, however, is whether rigorous selection standards can be maintained in the face of heavy demand – a problem that was not satisfactorily resolved during the rapid expansion of schooling in the 1960s and early 1970s.

Training the trainers

At a seminar on 'The selection and professional development of trainers for initial teacher training' (Strasbourg, 27–28 March 1990), participants noted that very little attention has been paid so far to this category of staff whose influence on future teachers is crucial (ATEE, 1989; Wilson, 1989b; Council of Europe, 1990a). Participants identified some of the characteristics required of teacher educators and agreed that all those involved –

whether college-based subject specialists, experts in psychology or pedagogy, or school-based supervisors of teaching practice – should work together more closely to achieve greater harmony in objectives, motivations and assumptions. Beyond mastery of the specific discipline, the function of teacher educator requires the capacity to analyse and evaluate the learning process and behaviour of student teachers objectively. Teacher trainers must themselves exemplify 'good' teaching and must help trainees to overcome negative examples of teaching acquired during their own schooling. They must encourage student teachers to develop appropriate learning strategies independently, and also their capacity to assess their own needs.

The overwhelming importance of recent classroom experience was stressed as was the necessary interplay between theory and practice. The criteria for selecting teacher educators should be explicitly laid down, and formal on-the-job induction should be organised for new recruits.

One of the seminar recommendations was that the Council of Europe should sponsor university summer schools for teacher educators to allow them to explore such issues as qualifications, induction and professional development. Accordingly, a Summer School on Teacher Training Policies and Models in the Member States of the Council for Cultural Cooperation of the Council of Europe was held in Izmir, Turkey, on 21–26 September 1992 (Karagözoğlu, 1993).

Technical and vocational teachers

Those responsible for training technical and vocational teachers met in Strasbourg on 7–9 December 1988 (Hostmark-Tarrou, 1988; Council of Europe, 1988). Attracting high-quality recruits into teaching and teacher training in technical and vocational education was a problem for most countries, often because pay and conditions were better in commerce and industry. Several countries had therefore taken steps to improve the pay, pensions, working hours and status of this category of teachers. Some countries operated a 'pre-recruitment' system whereby teachers could be recruited without being fully qualified.

It was generally agreed that there should be stronger links between education and industry. More opportunities should be provided for both teachers and industrial employees to work alternately in industry and education. To move in and out of teaching was not necessarily a bad thing in a highly mobile society. This would in part overcome the problem of how to allow education to keep up with rapid change and specialisation in these fields and that of attracting good teachers in competition with commerce and industry. It would also make use of the knowledge and skills of people in transitional situations.

Since the twin objectives of technical and vocational education were to raise the standard of general education and to provide professional skills, teacher trainees should be given a more adequate general cultural foundation (mother tongue, modern languages, social sciences, etc). There should also be more emphasis on pedagogical skills. It was never safe to assume that competence in a vocational specialisation was enough to ensure effective classroom teaching, particularly in catering for the wide range of abilities and backgrounds characteristic of classes today.

The problem of how technical and vocational teachers could best keep their professional skills up-to-date became more intractable with the increasing pace of technological change. In the extreme case teachers had to be totally re-trained because the profession changed radically or even disappeared. One of the best ways to provide in-service training for teachers was to give them direct industrial or commercial training and experience. This also had the advantage of raising teachers' motivation and self-esteem. However, such industrial experience should not be too narrowly tied to a particular commercial product, and in-service training should be better linked with initial training. Teachers should be more involved in identifying their own needs and in negotiating provision to meet them. Too many in-service courses were shallow and lacked follow-up, and INSET should be provided in a more systematic and co-ordinated way.

On the question of assessment, it was felt that there was too little evaluation of the effects of training on classroom practice, and that teachers should be motivated and trained to assess their own performance.

It was agreed that more research should be done on the problems of this category of teachers and their education, to which relatively little attention had been paid so far. Furthermore, teachers should be trained in research, enhancing their leadership capacity in their own schools.

Mixed ability teaching

On 5–6 December 1990 the Council of Europe held a seminar on training teachers for teaching to a wide range of abilities, interests and backgrounds in the classroom. Research showed that teachers needed to develop the skills of teaching children as individuals, and that individualised or modular approaches might be effective. But this implied either a great deal of work for individual teachers or the need for more commercially produced teaching materials. The consequences for teacher training were that teachers must learn to widen the range of skills they had, a process that could be helped with good video materials and the use of new technology such as the micro-computer and interactive video-disc. Teachers must also learn to understand the many characteristics of individual children, including those related to their social, religious and ethnic background (Wragg, 1990).

Discussion at the seminar confirmed the trend towards growing diversity of the school population, and a wide range of practice in Europe in the grouping of children for classroom teaching. Some schools streamed according to ability, others put in the same class a very wide range of pupils from different social, religious and ethnic backgrounds as well as varying intellectual ability and academic attachment. Faced with growing heterogeneity in education, some countries were beginning to question current policies.

The importance of pre-primary education was stressed as correlating positively with primary school achievement and helping to overcome the problem of heterogeneity in primary schooling. Primary school teachers were in general better prepared for pupil-centred, mixed ability teaching (especially if recently trained and in countries where they were also trained to teach at lower secondary level) than their more specialised secondary colleagues.

Successful mixed ability teaching required teachers to see themselves as managers and organisers of learning rather than monopoly providers of knowledge. They also had to be highly motivated. The number of pupils in the classroom was a basic factor affecting teachers' capacity to cope with mixed ability teaching.

The greatest difficulty for teachers was to adjust their teaching to individual needs. They tended to address the middle range of ability, with the result that the gifted became bored and the slower learners could not keep up. Therefore teaching strategies had to be as varied as possible.

Teacher training should, in addition to providing the skills required for diversification of teaching strategies, be based as far as possible on classroom experience and analysis in a wide variety of situations. It should also provide as much information as possible on the social and cultural backgrounds of the range of pupils likely to be met. Subject studies should invariably be accompanied by study of didactic methods appropriate to the subject. In some countries initial training for all teachers now included how to deal with low achievers. Teacher trainers, as role models, should themselves adopt the strategies they wished their students to develop.

The importance of in-service training was stressed, especially for teachers with long years of service who might find it difficult to vary their teaching styles and strategies. However, it was difficult to get them to take part. One incentive might be increased status and pay for those with higher skills ('master teachers') (Delmelle, 1991).

The newly qualified teacher

The Council of Europe commissioned a study of measures adopted in the member countries to support and guide beginning teachers, who are often discouraged on their first encounter with classroom reality (Louvet, 1991). As might be expected, the situation varies considerably as between countries. In some there is a probationary period. Where there is such a requirement, the length varies but it is never less than a year. In some countries the main purpose of the probationary year is training, in others it is seen as an opportunity for both training and assessment, with varying degrees of emphasis. If the probationary period is seen as necessary for testing new teachers, however, this rarely leads to rejection for professional incompetence. Measures that exist to help new teachers to adapt to working life include help given by experienced school staff, university staff or inspectors. However, this supervision is often haphazard. In many cases support arrangements are too recent to have been assessed.

10

Teacher appraisal

The controversial question of assessment of teachers was discussed at a seminar in Strasbourg on 18–19 September 1989 (Wilson, 1989a, 1990; Council of Europe, 1989). Presentations were made on the situation in most European countries, particular attention being paid to Germany (Baden-Württemberg), Norway and the United Kingdom. The conclusions may be summarised as follows:

- The systematic, compulsory appraisal of individual teachers' performance is only one means of improving the quality of teaching and learning, along with many others such as the 'whole school' review or assessment of educational provision in particular areas;
- There is a wide variety of policies, practices and perceptions in Europe. Some countries accept compulsory, systematic appraisal of teaching performance, including classroom observation, while others reject it or are less interested, preferring other ways to improve quality;
- Insofar as countries are, or envisage, introducing appraisal, there is a need for clarity in the definition of terms. A fundamental distinction should be made between 'appraisal' involving the identification of ways (such as further training) to improve job performance, and 'formal assessment' for accountability or selection purposes at specific points in a teacher's career (notably for promotion). The criteria applied will differ accordingly;
- Appraisal need not necessarily result in further training. It might involve a change in responsibilities, confirmation that performance is in line with objectives, realignment of school policy, redeployment of resources, etc. The underlying purpose of individual appraisal is to improve the quality of education by encouraging individual insight into the effectiveness of job performance. It should result in positive reinforcement of teachers' professional status and image;
- For any country wishing to introduce appraisal, the criteria by which teaching quality should be judged should be fairly broadly determined above the level of the school (i.e. at central or regional level) but very specifically defined at school level (where it would be conducted) by school staff, education officers, inspectors associated with the school, etc. The criteria and principles underlying the appraisal process should be clearly understood by appraisers and appraisees in a preliminary dialogue designed to build confidence. It was expected that personal capacity, school context and institutional management would all be taken into account as factors in determining quality of performance in relation to objectives;
- Appraisal should include school leaders (headteachers, principals etc) as well as classroom teachers.

Teacher training is an integral part of many other aspects of the Council of Europe's work on education:

Teacher Bursary Scheme

Under the Teacher Bursary Scheme, member states admit teachers from other member countries to short national in-service training courses (Council of Europe, 1990c). In addition, four Council of Europe Teachers' Seminars a year are held at the Training Academy at Donaueschingen, Germany. Many of these have been devoted specifically to teacher training issues (Council of Europe, 1993a). So far, over 8,000 educationalists have taken part in the scheme, helping them to broaden their experience and cultural horizons and to establish links with teachers from other countries.

Modern languages

A Council of Europe recommendation to governments defined how teachers should be trained for the 'communicative approach' to modern language learning worked out by the Council of Europe's experts (Council of Europe, 1982; Girard and Trim, 1988). The idea is to get away from an over-theoretical concern with grammar to teaching how to manage the practical, everyday business of staying in a foreign country and making contact with the people who live there. This approach has been put across to the trainers of modern language teachers in a series of workshops. On the basis of an evaluation of these workshops, a consolidated report setting out a selection of teacher training methods and approaches was prepared (Trim, 1988). This continuing work has included the publication of such important material for teachers as *Communication in the Modern Languages Classroom* (Sheils, 1991).

More recently, the Council of Europe's Committee of Ministers has approved the setting up of a European Centre for Modern Languages in Graz, Austria, which will provide a forum and training for teacher trainers, textbook authors, and experts in curricula, educational standards and assessment methods. It will facilitate the exchange of information about new approaches and research in language learning and teaching.

Human rights, equal opportunities and intercultural education

A Council of Europe recommendation to governments on 'Teaching and learning about human rights in schools', adopted by the Committee of Ministers (Council of Europe, 1985) has lost none of its relevance at a time of multiplying acts of violence and terrorism, when intolerant, racist and xenophobic attitudes are re-emerging; and when disillusion is spreading among many young people in Europe affected by unemployment and continuing poverty and inequality in the world.

The recommendation contains practical suggestions for teaching and learning about human rights in schools – what the curriculum should contain, what skills and knowledge in particular should be acquired, what the school climate itself can contribute. The recommendation offers the following guidelines on teacher training:

The initial training of teachers should prepare them for their future contribution to teaching about human rights in their schools. For example, future teachers should be encouraged to take an interest in national and world affairs. They should have the chance of studying or working in a foreign country or a different environment. They should be taught to identify and combat all forms of discrimination in schools and society. And they should be encouraged to confront and overcome their own prejudices.

Future and practising teachers should be encouraged to familiarise themselves with:

- the main international declarations and conventions on human rights, and
- the working and achievements of the international organisations which deal with the protection and promotion of human rights, for example through visits and study tours.

All teachers need, and should be given the opportunity, to up-date their knowledge and to learn new methods through in-service training. This could include the study of good practice in teaching about human rights, as well as the development of appropriate methods and materials.

Of course there is an obvious caveat. Since human rights inevitably involve the domain of politics, the recommendation says that teachers should take care to avoid imposing their personal convictions on their pupils and involving them in ideological struggles.

One form of discrimination explicitly mentioned in the recommendation is sexism. An important Council of Europe objective is to promote equality between women and men and, again, this obviously has major implications for teachers and their training. The Council of Europe's findings result from an educational research workshop on sex stereotyping in schools held in Norway in 1981, a seminar held the following year in the Federal Republic of Germany on 'Sex stereotypes in schools: the role and responsibility of the teacher', and periodic reports on the subject to the Standing Conference of European Ministers of Education (Council of Europe, 1979, 1981, 1984a; Cels-Offermans, 1985).

It appears from research that teachers generally devote more time to boys than to girls in the classroom, the reason being that boys are more assertive in demanding attention. Teachers may not be aware of this. The best way of letting them examine classroom situations and their own behaviour is the use of videotapes during teaching practice and to discuss the results with the class involved.

Teacher training courses should in any case include a compulsory element on the problem of sexual bias in schools. Such training should include observation of attitudes, of language used in lessons, and of the contents of school textbooks. It is important to ensure that girls and boys are not steered prematurely into studies traditionally considered 'masculine', such as science and technology, or 'feminine', such as languages and literature. More effort should be made to recruit women teachers into traditionally 'masculine' subjects and positions of authority, and vice versa, since teachers can be important models for pupils, confirming or disturbing their ideas of the way society is organised.

In related work, a Council of Europe working party recommended that all teachers be trained for an intercultural approach to teaching in increasingly multicultural classrooms (Rey, 1986). Briefly, this means valuing and seeking to benefit from the enriching potential of cultural diversity. This concept was embodied in a recommendation to governments adopted by the Committee of Ministers in 1984 (Council of Europe, 1984b). Work has also been done on the training of teachers of gypsy children (Liégeois, 1987, 1994).

The European dimension of education

Building on past work on the European dimension of education (Shennan, 1991), and in response to the explosion of demand among educators all over Europe for basic information, appropriate teaching resources, and opportunities for training, contacts and exchanges, the Council of Europe is running a project entitled 'A secondary education for Europe'. Among other outcomes, this will result in a series of monographs describing experiments with the introduction of the European dimension into schools, specific teaching material for direct classroom use, and a guide to secondary education systems in Europe (Council of Europe, 1993b). The development of a network of school links and exchanges is a further aim of this project, which also draws on long experience with such activities as the European Schools Day Competition. The project was given strong backing by European Ministers of Education at the 17th and 18th Sessions of their Standing Conference (Council of Europe, 1993c, 1994).

Educational research

Finally, the 4th and 5th All-European Conferences of Directors of Educational Research Institutions (McAlpine *et al.*, 1988; Wilson, 1989) reviewed the latest research on teacher training, in particular in-service training, to which priority is given in most countries as a result of the ageing of the teaching profession, with little recent recruitment, and the increasingly rapid pace of change, especially in technology. One of the main ideas to emerge is that teachers should take more responsibility for planning, managing and evaluating their own training.

CHAPTER 2

Teacher education in Europe – diversity versus uniformity

Friedrich Buchberger

Teacher education in Europe – diversity versus uniformity

To give a first impression of the current situation of teacher education and training (TE) in Europe, let me introduce the article on 'Teacher Education in Europe' by two quotations from well-known experts in the field and by a comment on the importance of teacher education frequently made by experts as well as (education) politicians:

(a) The teacher education systems are almost all undergoing change of some kind or other at this time, undirected in any international sense, but with some identifiably common trends emerging. It is a period of great fluidity, with many difficulties for those engaged in the work, but interesting too, and the factors responsible for change are tending to operate [in] similar, if not exactly the same directions. (Bone, 1992, p. 61)

(b) This special issue of the *European Journal of Education* is concerned with a component of educational systems [teacher education] that, almost everywhere in Europe, is at the centre of controversy and uncertainty. (Eggleston, 1991, p. 195)

(c) Publications dealing with TE in Europe (e.g. Lundgren, 1986; Neave, 1992; Vonk, 1992) as well as speeches not only by education politicians (e.g. Mayor, 1992; Ritzen, 1992) frequently start by emphasising the prominent role teachers and TE ought to play in our society and its development. But in most European countries the diverse and complex field of TE seems to be full of contradictions,

contradictions, tensions and paradoxes (cf. Judge, 1990; Popkewitz, 1993a), and one of them lies in the fact that the intentions expressed are not always succeeded by appropriate action. This applies to policies concerning TE as well as to TE itself. Although there is wide-spread agreement that improvements of TE in all its subsystems (initial teacher education, induction, in-service education) are imperative (cf. Karagözoğlu, 1993; OECD/CERI, 1990, 1992), a host of both internal and external barriers (cf. Portmann, 1993) seems to hamper necessary innovations and reforms. Thus TE cannot always fulfil the prominent role postulated.

However, TE in Europe may be called a huge enterprise. More than half a million student teachers receive their initial teacher education and training (ITE) in more than 1,000 institutions at which more than 50,000 teacher educators and trainers are working. In-service education and training (INSET) has to be provided for more than 5 million teachers.

TE in Europe is organised in systems and models of highly heterogeneous natures. There are big differences both:

- between the different European countries (e.g. the enormous differences of ITE in the neighbouring countries of France and Switzerland; cf. Buchberger, 1992a) as well as
- within them (e.g. the different systems and models of ITE of the 16 Laender of Germany, Doebrich *et al.*, 1992, or the more than 150 different systems and models of ITE that may be observed in Switzerland; Badertscher, 1993; Furrer and Wanzenried, 1992).

Diversity seems to be a salient feature of TE (cf. Archer and Peck, 1990; Peck, 1993; Vaniscotte, 1992), although at the same time TE may be characterised by certain elements common to most of European countries. i.e.:

(a) There are some basic traditions which in many countries correspond to fundamental differences between the education of primary school teachers, lower and/or upper secondary school teachers and teachers for vocational, technical or commercial education (cf. 'the historic European schism between primary and secondary schools and the teachers in them', Judge, 1992. p. 1237).

(b) Some more recent leitmotifs (e.g. 'professionalisation', cf. Bourdoncle, 1993) have had strong influence on the development of most systems and models of ITE.

(c) Some curricular components seem common to most of the models of ITE.

(d) Most systems and models of TE seem to follow static conceptions of TE or a so-called 'rucksack-philosophy' (Buchberger, 1993a), which stresses the importance of ITE and disregards the need for a continuous professional development of teachers as well as the importance of INSET.

(e) In recent years trends towards convergence may be observed, which are mainly influenced by processes of a European integration or of policies of OECD.

(f) Some similarities or mutualities existing among different systems and models of ITE may be explained by influences some countries and their models of TE had on others in former days (e.g. the influence of the Austrian system of ITE of the Hapsburg monarchy on middle and south-eastern European countries; the influence of the former Soviet Union on TE of countries of the former eastern bloc; Mitter, 1984).

The different and complex systems and models of TE with their goals, contents, curricula and structures of organisation might be seen as (more or less tightened) conglomerates consisting of components of very different origins. The following components can be found in most systems and models of TE:

● education studies/studies in educational sciences;
● academic/subject studies;
● studies in subject matter methodologies/subject didactics; and
● teaching practice (Buchberger, 1993a,b).

A clear terminology has not been developed yet and these terms have different meanings in the different cultural contexts of Europe (cf. similar problems concerning the terms teacher education − teacher training). The importance given to these different components, the sometimes rather peculiar combinations of them (e.g. sequence, integration) and a set of interrelated features of an organisational as well as an institutional nature have led to this variety of systems and models of TE in Europe.

Diversity − some examples

This rich diversity may be demonstrated by giving the following examples which will focus on institutional and organisational features of ITE:

(1) ITE in most European countries is characterised by various segmentations existing between:

● different types of teachers (e.g. pre-primary, primary, lower/upper secondary, vocational education, special education) and
● the institutions at which (prospective) teachers receive ITE.

(2) The institutions of ITE are placed at different stages of the education systems. Although there seem to exist many open questions as regards categorisations of the sector of tertiary/higher education both within and between the different European countries (cf. Burn, 1992; Clark and Neave, 1992; Dalichow, 1992; Teichler, 1993), the following differences may be outlined:

(a) ITE for the pre-school sector may take place
● at schools at upper secondary level (e.g. Austria, most Eastern European countries),

- at colleges of ITE (e.g. Belgium/Flemish Community),
- at institutions of higher (vocational) education (e.g. The Netherlands) or
- at universities (e.g. Finland).

(b) A similar division applies to ITE for primary schools. In some countries (prospective) primary school teachers are educated

- at schools at the upper secondary level (e.g. Russian Federation, many Eastern European countries, most cantons of Switzerland),
- at schools at the post-secondary level (e.g. the Austrian Paedagogische Akademie),
- at colleges of teacher education (e.g. the Danish Staatsseminarium or Belgium),
- at institutions of higher (vocational) education (e.g. The Netherlands, Portugal),
- at universities of different natures (e.g. Spain on the one hand or Finland and Germany on another).

(c) While in all European countries ITE for teachers of academic subjects at upper secondary level is located at universities, the situation of ITE for teachers at vocational, technical, and economic schools ('an educational system within an educational system', cf. Neave, 1992) may be characterised by a host of very different solutions at an institutional level.

(3) Institutions at which (prospective) teachers are educated have very different patterns of organisation:

(a) In some countries ITE for teachers for pre-schools and primary schools is organised in schools at upper secondary level.

(b) There exist colleges of teacher education as single-purpose institutions (e.g. Austria, Belgium, Denmark).

(c) ITE may be part of institutions of higher (vocational) education (e.g. The Netherlands).

(d) At university level different patterns may be observed:

- ITE programmes may be organised in departments of teacher education run under the responsibility of faculties of education (e.g. Finland).
- There are also schools of education (e.g. Spain).
- Faculties of education may have responsibility for ITE (e.g. Czech Republic).
- In fragmented structures responsibilities for ITE are not always clear (cf. the situation at most German universities at which teachers receive the first theoretical part of their education).
- In some countries the responsibilities for ITE are split up into different institutions: the university is responsible for a first and mainly theoretical part of ITE; local school boards, pedagogical institutes and schools for a second and mainly 'practical' part (e.g. the Austrian model for the education of (upper) secondary teachers, Buchberger, 1992b; Germany, Doebrich *et al.*, 1992).

Different cultures of ITE may be seen in close relationship with different organisational patterns outlined.

(4)   The duration of ITE varies from very short courses (e.g. ITE for teachers in vocational, commercial and technical schools in most countries) up to programmes lasting five years and more (e.g. France, Germany, Spain).

(5)   The programmes have different organisation and structure:

(a)   In concurrent models the different components of ITE mentioned above have to be studied parallel to one another (cf. Figure 2.1, the B.Ed. route of ITE in England and Wales).

Figure 2.1 England and Wales: B.Ed. and PGCE routes

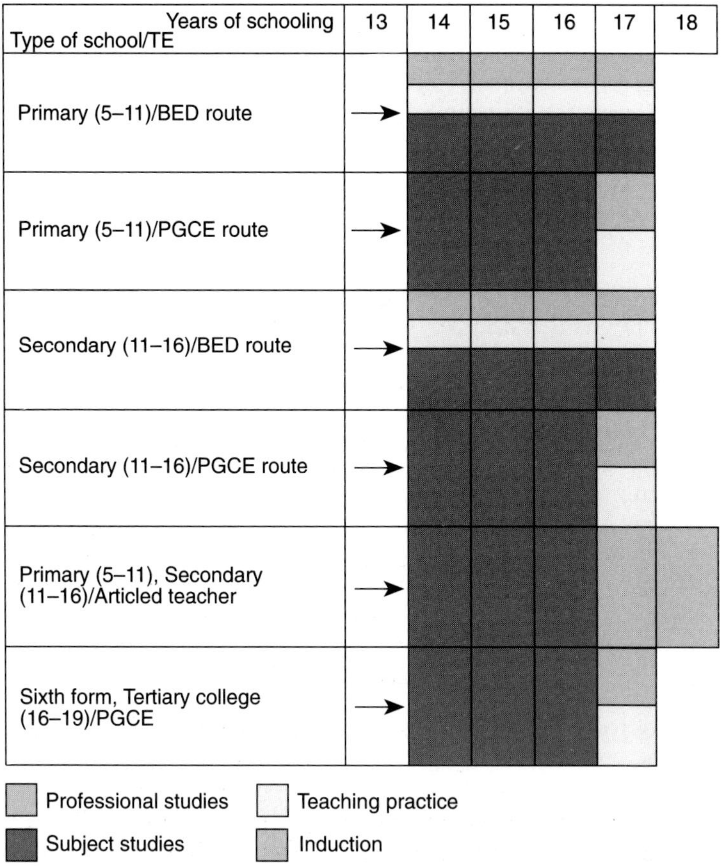

Years of schooling / Type of school/TE	13	14	15	16	17	18
Primary (5–11)/BED route	→					
Primary (5–11)/PGCE route	→					
Secondary (11–16)/BED route	→					
Secondary (11–16)/PGCE route	→					
Primary (5–11), Secondary (11–16)/Articled teacher	→					
Sixth form, Tertiary college (16–19)/PGCE	→					

▢ Professional studies   ▢ Teaching practice
■ Subject studies   ▢ Induction

Source: Hellawell, 1992, p. 344.

(b) In integrated models these components are not only offered at the same time, but in an inter-related way mainly focusing on professionally relevant topics and integrating 'theoretical' studies and 'practical' studies. Many programmes for the education of primary school teachers follow a concurrent model and a trend towards integrated and/or modularised models may be observed (e.g. Scandinavian countries).

(c) In consecutive models (prospective) teachers have to study academic disciplines/subjects (and sometimes the sciences of the teaching profession) first followed by professional studies and teaching practice (e.g. the English Postgraduate Courses in Education; cf. Figure 2.1, the PGCE route of ITE in England and Wales). But it is worth mentioning that in other consecutive models professional studies are offered first followed by studies in the sciences of the teaching profession and by studies of academic disciplines subjects (cf. the Zurich-model of ITE, Furrer and Wanzenried, 1992). Most models of ITE for teachers at (upper) secondary level are organised as consecutive ones.

(d) Modularised models of ITE offer clearly defined modules and it is up to the student teacher to decide in which sequence s/he will take the different modules. Some Scandinavian countries increasingly offer models of this type (e.g. Finnish developments in ITE for primary school teachers).

(e) A further distinction may be made between so-called 'one-phased' and 'two-phased' models of ITE.

- In one-phased models the successful completion of ITE at institutions of TE permits the (prospective) teacher to apply for a post at schools.
- In two-phased models (prospective) teachers first have to complete (mainly) theoretical studies at institutions of TE ('first phase'). This 'first phase' is followed by 'practical studies' at schools and special courses dealing mainly with (subject) didactics (e.g. the German Vorbereitungsdienst or the Austrian Unterrichtspraktikum). Local school boards and local pedagogical institutes separated from the university are responsible for this 'second phase'. A successful assessment of the tasks (prospective) teachers have to fulfil during this 'second phase' forms a necessary condition for getting the status as a fully fledged teacher. This 'two-phased' model as executed for example in Germany ends with a so-called second state examination/Staatspruefung and may be seen as an indicator of the importance the state attributes to teachers and teaching (and their control).

(6) The curriculum and content of ITE programmes vary considerably. The amount of teaching practice reaches from almost zero up to more than 50 per cent (cf. Schmidinger, 1993). The same applies to professional studies as well as to subject studies.

Figure 2.2 Germany: teacher training courses

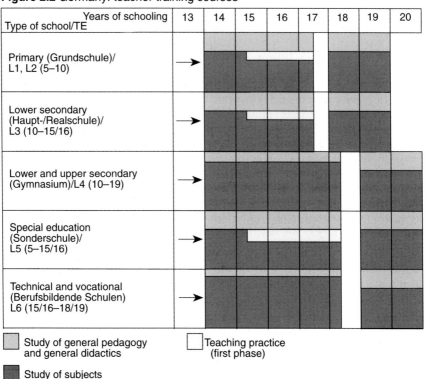

Type of school/TE — Years of schooling	13	14	15	16	17	18	19	20
Primary (Grundschule)/ L1, L2 (5–10)	→							
Lower secondary (Haupt-/Realschule)/ L3 (10–15/16)	→							
Lower and upper secondary (Gymnasium)/L4 (10–19)	→							
Special education (Sonderschule)/ L5 (5–15/16)	→							
Technical and vocational (Berufsbildende Schulen) L6 (15/16–18/19)	→							

Study of general pedagogy and general didactics

Teaching practice (first phase)

Study of subjects (including subject matter methodology)

Induction teaching (second phase)

Theoretical studies (second phase)

Source: Doebrick *et al.*, 1992, p.124.

(7) Institutions of TE are either strictly controlled by the state (e.g. by national guidelines or in some countries even by relatively narrow syllabuses) or have a relatively high degree of autonomy.

(8) Institutions of ITE may either have close links to schools, to the school system and to school improvement or they may be strictly separated from schools.

These institutional and organisational features outlined are only some of the many features in which systems and models of ITE differ at an institutional and organisational level both within and between European countries – and institutional and organisational features are only one of the many integral components of the complex (social) system of TE.

Common patterns and trends — some examples

A host of problem-solving processes in each of the European countries has led to the rich diversity depicted above. Three sets of interrelated factors might have contributed to it and these in turn may be used to explain some of the similarities among TE in Europe and some common trends:

(1) This diversity outlined mainly reflects the fact that problem-solving processes in the development of systems and models of TE have taken place

- under certain circumstances,
- at certain times,
- in particular (national) contexts, and
- have strongly been influenced by political debate.

It might be argued that theoretical and research-based argument as well as rational system planning or the expertise of those involved in TE have not always played the most prominent roles in constructing and developing systems and models of TE — and many of the recent problems of TE may be explained by this fact. As regards the situation in England and Wales, Judge (1990, p. 11) argues that 'TE in England and Wales is a product of history rather than of logic (although much has been achieved in the past twenty years to give it more shape and coherence)', and this statement seems to be valid for most other European systems and models of TE (cf. for reform practices of TE in eight OECD member states the comparative analyses edited by Popkewitz (1993a) and his metaphor of a 'social arena' and the various actors involved in it).

Close connections may be detected between:

- the development of nation-states and their (national) identities, and
- the development of systems of education and TE from the 18th century onwards. This applies especially to nations in continental Europe (e.g. France, Germany; cf. similar but recent developments in some new countries of the former Eastern bloc, Schleicher (1993) or in Iceland, Proppe *et al.* 1993). Such links may be seen as one main reason for the development of (nationally) different structures of education/schooling and the many different systems and models of TE in Europe that correspond in most European countries very closely with structures of schooling.

(2) Secondly it is possible to point to some long-standing traditions which

- consist of a blend of not always consistent (and sometimes hidden) assumptions, beliefs and opinions on the professional role of teachers and the acquisition of professional expertise (cf. Joyce, *et al.* 1981; Kennedy, 1990) and which
- have had strong influence on the development of institutional as well as curricular patterns of ITE.

Created in the 19th century such traditions may be made accountable for segmentations and divisions existing between different types of TE. They seem to be 'rooted in patterns of schooling, specifically in the sharp distinction throughout the last century and well into this between public elementary education on the one hand and secondary education provided only for a privileged minority on the other' (Judge, 1990, p. 11). Such traditions have had strong influence on the construction of systems and models of TE, and in many countries they still have even nowadays (cf. Judge, 1990, 1992 and recent developments in former Eastern European countries):

(a) ITE for teachers at primary level has been strongly influenced by a 'seminaristic' or 'ecole normale' tradition. The focus of this tradition is on 'practical' training (teaching practice, methodology) and devaluates the importance of both educational theory and academic/scientific knowledge. Categories like 'ethos' or the 'personality of teachers' ('Lehrerpersoenlichkeit') form integral parts of this tradition. In rather rigid learning environments (prospective) teachers should learn to 'model the master' and to acquire some basic skills of teaching (e.g. 'apprenticeship' model, 'sitting next to Nelly'). At an organisational level this tradition is closely correlated with concurrent models of ITE.

(b) An 'academic' tradition emphasises the high importance of theoretical scientific knowledge. (Prospective) teachers had to acquire scientific knowledge in academic disciplines (cf. the principle 'Bildung durch Wissenschaft'). It is assumed that this scientific knowledge and the competences and attitudes learned during the processes of its acquisition would enable (prospective) teachers to perform the tasks of teaching and of education competently. The importance of educational theory, methodology and teaching practice is devaluated or neglected in this tradition. ITE for teachers at (upper) secondary schools has been strongly influenced by this tradition.

(c) Other traditions may be detected in ITE for teachers of 'practical' subjects (e.g. music, sports), for teachers of vocational subjects or for teachers in special education.

(3) More recent leitmotifs (e.g. professionalisation, integration, universitisation) have played an important role in reforms and innovations of most systems and models of TE for more than 30 years.

All these factors outlined above have led to some broader and not always consistent patterns and trends detectable in many European countries (cf. Buchberger, 1993a,b,c,d; Neave, 1987, 1992; OECD, 1989, 1990), but it is worth mentioning that these patterns and trends have been challenged in recent years by new leitmotifs (e.g. quality, rationalisation, mobility):

(1) The duration of programmes of ITE has gradually been prolonged:

● This applies especially to ITE for teachers at pre-school/pre-primary level (cf. Pascal *et al.*, 1991). But in some countries (e.g. Germany) this sector is not a part of the school system and TE does not exist.

- The minimum duration of programmes for primary school teachers in countries of the European Economic Area is now three years and in these countries ITE now takes place in the post-secondary and/or higher education sector.
- Programmes of ITE for teachers (of general subjects) at (upper) secondary level organised by universities last a minimum of four years in all European countries.

(2) (New) systems of ITE have been introduced in many countries for teachers for the sector of special education and for vocational education/ vocational school system. The latter applies especially to ITE for teachers for commercial schools, while problems with ITE for teachers for technical schools persist in most countries. It may be worth mentioning that these problems have found relatively adequate solutions in countries of the former Eastern bloc (e.g. highly developed systems of ITE for vocational schools).

(3) The criteria for admission to ITE have been tightened. In most countries applicants to ITE for primary and secondary schools have to hold a qualified school leaving certificate of an upper secondary school which may be obtained after twelve years of schooling at the earliest.

(4) There is a trend towards incorporation of all ITE into the higher education sector and its universitisation although the patterns differ. The following stages of development may be detected as regards ITE for teachers of compulsory schools:

- Creation of schools at (upper) secondary level dealing with ITE in the 18th and 19th century.
- Establishing separate institutions for ITE at post-secondary level (e.g. colleges of teacher education, paedagogische Akademie, Seminarium).
- Linkages and/or incorporation of these separate institutions into the university sector (e.g. United Kingdom, Germany, Spain; recent developments in Ireland or Sweden).

This trend towards incorporation of all ITE into the higher education sector and its universitisation does not only apply to institutional features. Research and development, two central elements in this process, are becoming more important. As a result, progress in building up a scientific knowledge base for TE and teaching may be expected (cf. Coolahan, 1992b; Mialaret, 1992; Mitter, 1992b; Reynolds, 1989).

(5) Many programmes of ITE have received a higher amount of formalisation, standardisation and rationalisation, although a lack of explicitly defined goals for the professional education of teachers seems to persist in many countries (cf. Kennedy, 1990; Klafki, 1988). More specific components (e.g. specialised studies for different domains of learning (e.g. reading, social studies) and/or subject studies (e.g maths, foreign languages) have been infused into programmes of ITE for teachers at primary level. The relationship between programmes of ITE and (curricula

of) schools have been tightened, which applies especially to ITE for teachers at (upper) secondary level and to former decentralised systems of ITE (e.g. England and Wales, Norway).

(6) Many programmes of ITE now contain more professional elements. This means that both

- more studies in the sciences of the teaching profession (e.g. educational sciences, subject didactics/subject matter methodologies) and
- more practical components (e.g. supervised teaching practice)

have been incorporated into the programmes of ITE. This applies especially to ITE for teachers at (lower/upper) secondary level and in the sector of vocational education.

(7) In many countries segmentations between the education of different types of teachers and different institutions of TE have been reduced and the permeability between them has increased, but problems of ITE for teachers at lower secondary level still persist (e.g. Germany, Doebrich *et al.*, 1992; Portugal, Novoa, 1993).

(8) In most countries the importance of INSET and of continuous professional education has been recognised and (sometimes extensive) systems for INSET have been established (cf. Blackburn and Moisan, 1987; Hoeben, 1986).

It is debatable whether these broader trends and changed/changing patterns are

- only modifications following a 'more of the same philosophy' (cf. OECD, 1989, 1992; Wagner, 1991) and preserving a 'cult practice of teacher education' (cf. Houston, 1990),
- reflect incremental change (cf. OECD 1990) and effective adaptations to changed tasks and expectations (cf. Neave, 1987), or
- whether they do reflect substantial change in TE.

However, improvements and innovations of systems and models of TE seem to be indispensable (cf. OECD, 1992). In times of rapidly changing contexts of education, schooling and TE, even preserving the existing quality calls for permanent reforms and improvements. If one intends to enhance the quality of education, of school systems and of TE both permanent improvements and substantial reforms become necessary conditions (cf. Buchberger and Seel, 1985; OECD, 1992).

Describing and comparing systems and models of teacher education in Europe – some problems

In characterising the situation of ITE in Italy, Todeschini (1992, p. 187) has written that '(it) is not uncommon for Italy to appear as a country whose main peculiarity is to be full of peculiarities. Thus, to question about teacher education and training, answers could be very simple and/or awfully complicated at the same time, or virtually impossible' (Todeschini, 1992, p. 187). As outlined in the preceding paragraphs much the same seems to apply to the situation of ITE in Europe and descriptions as well as comparisons seem to be confronted with the problem mentioned by Todeschini.

Popkewitz and Pereyra (1993) cogently outline the many problems of comparative education in the field of TE (e.g. the necessity and neglect of 'theoretical entities'), criticise current practices in this area and speak of 'a missing and weak link' (p. 3). Then they define a set of criteria that should guide (scientific) comparative education in the field of TE. Following the distinction of a 'Science of Comparative Education' and 'International Reformative Reflection' developed by Schriewer (Schriewer and Holmes, 1992, p. 61) this overview on 'Teacher Education in Europe' may be seen as a contribution to the latter. As a contribution to 'International Reformative Reflection' it aims at

- defining the problem-space in a more open way and
- increasing problem-awareness by addressing some main issues of TE in Europe.

Nonetheless solutions to some fundamental problems of description and comparison ('which consists of interpreting and explaining; not just comparing', Popkewitz and Pereyra, 1993, p. 6) have to be coped with:

(1) The first problem consists of getting a reliable and valid data-base. This article is mainly based on

- descriptions of (systems and models of) higher education and TE contained in a number of encyclopaedias (e.g. Clark and Neave, 1992; Dunkin, 1987),
- official documents, texts and reports produced by different ministries (e.g. Council of Europe, 1987a; IBE publications on developments in education in UNESCO member states),
- reports produced by EURYDICE (e.g. Boreland-Vinas, 1991; Le Metais, 1990, 1991),
- reports prepared by experts for different OECD projects (e.g. Askling and Jedeskog, 1993),
- descriptions of and commentaries on TE in different countries produced by researchers and experts (e.g. contributions in the *European Journal of Teacher Education* or the *Guide to Institutions of Teacher Education in Europe,* Buchberger, 1992), and
- experiences the author could gather in participating in international projects in the field of TE.

Advantages as well as disadvantages and the relative quality of these sources are obvious. The analysis of different sources is to contribute to a high(er) degree of reliability and validity. In addition, it is worth mentioning that it has not been possible to collect reliable and valid data on all European countries (e.g. most of the countries of the former Eastern bloc). This implies that the descriptions and comparisons will mainly focus on the countries of the European Economic Space.

(2) A second problem concerns language. It seems that concepts and technical terms necessary to describe different elements and components in the field of (teacher) education have only been elaborated to a limited extent so far (e.g. terms to describe different curricular components of TE). At the same time identical notions have sometimes very different meanings in different cultural contexts of Europe (e.g. 'professionalisation' or 'university'). The author is very well aware of the fact that this problem has not been solved adequately in this paper either.

(3) A third problem relates to questions as to which levels of generality or specificity seem to be appropriate. Sometimes studies of systems and models of ITE are restricted to descriptions of some structural variables (e.g. institutions, admission criteria, duration of ITE, qualifications and access to the profession) and the authors make use of simplified diagrams to visualise them (e.g. Buchberger, 1993; Neumeister, 1987; Vaniscotte, 1989). This approach may have some advantages as regards a first orientation at a surface level, but descriptions of some structural variables and simplified diagrams cannot meet the rich diversity and complexity of TE in Europe. It seems to correspond to tendencies towards (over-) simplification and it may easily lead to inappropriate and misleading interpretations (cf. Judge, 1990, p. 1229: 'Patterns of schooling [and TE], although comparable at a superficial level, often embody widely different concepts of the purposes of that schooling, and therefore of the nature of teaching in public schools'). For these reasons this approach will not be taken and a presentation of simplified diagrams will be avoided, except in some cases to visualise some basic structures of systems and models of ITE.

(4) A (short) chapter on 'Teacher Education in Europe' has to restrict itself to a limited number of issues. Decisions have been made

- to focus on some general patterns and broader trends of the development of TE ('megatrends') and to give examples of the variety of patterns to be observed at an institutional and organisational levels;
- current changes and challenges as well as forces behind them will be analysed in the second part of the chapter;
- by focusing on ITE for teachers at primary and (lower/upper) secondary level some basic structures and main types of programmes will be described and analysed.

This selection implies that (many) other important issues necessary for a comprehensive understanding of TE in Europe cannot be discussed adequately (e.g. history of TE, mechanisms of social regulation, conceptions of the professional role of teachers).

Teacher education in rapidly changing contexts

In the past few years TE (ITE as well as induction and INSET) has again become a field of hot debate (cf. OECD, 1990). Productive unrest has become apparent. Significant changes and sometimes drastic reforms of teacher education are in a preparation phase or have been introduced recently in some (European) OECD member states (e.g. France, Italy, England and Wales) and in many former Communist countries (e.g. Bulgaria (Valchev, 1993); Russian Federation (Pivavarov, 1990; Ministry of Education, 1992); Ucraina (Lugoviy, 1992). Although the degree of problem awareness differs greatly both within and between the different European countries (cf. the analysis of Busch, 1990 at a European level; Bayer *et al.*, 1990 for the situation in Germany or Simola, 1993 for the situation in Finland) and some education politicians as well as educationists and teacher educators seem to follow a strategy of a 'muddling through' or one of problem suppression, there are many signals that TE has come to a turning point and that substantial reforms are necessary.

Productive unrest − some examples

Four selected examples of recent discussions and activities on TE will be presented briefly to underline this:

(1) Many educationists and politicians are convinced that far-reaching reforms of TE are imperative.

(a) Inspired by the concept of an 'open professionalism' (cf. Laderriere, 1990; Vonk, 1991) activities in many countries aim at increasing the quality of TE by professionalising it (cf. different meanings of this term in different cultural contexts, Bourdoncle, 1993 for the French context, Atkinson, 1993 for the British context, Kodron 1993 for the German context). Main components of a professionalised TE might be

- academic/scientific/theoretical studies in the sciences of the teaching profession (e.g. educational sciences, pedagogy, educational psychology, educational sociology, didactics, subject didactics or subject matter methodology) and in educational research aiming at the development of a professional problem-solving capacity,
- coherent and supervised practical clinical studies, and
- the integration of studies in the sciences of the teaching profession and clinical studies (cf. Buchberger, 1993a).

The reform of TE in France with the introduction of Instituts Universitaires de Formation des Maitres (IUFM) at the beginning of the 1990s (cf. Blondel, 1991; Zay, 1992) or innovations in some Scandinavian countries (cf. Askling and Jedeskog, 1993 or Kallos and Selander, 1993 for Sweden, Grankvist, 1992 or Hostmark-Tarrou 1991 for Norway, Haemaelaeinen *et al.* for Finland, Hansen and Proppe, 1992 for Iceland) work along this line. In 'A Nation at Risk', the USA, similar developments can be observed in many institutions of higher education dealing with TE (cf. Holmes Commission, 1986, 1990 and critical comments on it by Popkewitz, 1993b).

(b) At the same time and in sharp contrast both to traditional models of TE and to the approach of a professionalised TE outlined above England and Wales have introduced other forms of TE (e.g. school-based TE, articled teacher scheme, licensed teacher scheme) based on a minimum-competency concept (Laderriere, 1990; Vonk, 1991). A recent English document submitted to EURYDICE names the following principles for reform of ITE:

- a variety of different routes into teaching,
- schools should play a much larger part in ITE as full partners of higher education institutions,
- accreditation criteria for initial teacher training courses (cf. the use of training instead of education) should focus on competences of teaching (cf. Baker et al., 1993; Barton et al., 1993; Hellawell, 1992).

Similar activities have to be observed in some federal states of the USA with the introduction of alternative routes into teaching (cf. Stoddart and Floden, 1990). Although greatly heterogeneous in nature these forms of TE may be characterised by

- their focus on 'practical' training ('apprenticeship'),
- a disregard of (educational) theory and
- of (educational) research.

However, they have to be seen as a challenge as well as an attack against both traditional and professionalised forms of TE (cf. Buttery et al., 1990; Hillgate Group, 1989; Lawton, 1991).

(2)   The OECD pays special attention to problems of teachers and TE (e.g. the projects and reports on 'The Training of Teachers', 'Schools and Quality', 'The Teacher Today', 'Teacher Quality'). Main fields of interest are:

- quality and standards of TE,
- efficiency and effectiveness of TE,
- rationalisation of (teacher) education,
- recruitment for TE and the teaching profession,
- the teaching profession and conditions of service,
- INSET and the continuous professional education of teachers or
- co-operation of TE with schools and other social groups.

(3)   The Standing Conference of European Ministers of Education in 1987 revolved around the theme 'New Challenges for Teachers and Their Education'. The proceedings of this conference contain a set of important recommendations for TE (cf. Council of Europe, 1987c; Hellawell, 1987) and the Council of Europe has been asked for follow-up activities (e.g. analysis of policies and models of TE, Karagözoğlu, 1993; recruitment and training of teacher educators, Wilson, 1990; recruitment and selection of teachers, Newman, 1990).

(4)   Activities of the European Communities also have an impact on the development of TE:

(a) A change of the structures and organisation of higher education in general and ITE in particular seems to be necessary (cf. the 'Memorandum on Higher Education in the European Community', 1991 and the reactions to it; Kommission der Europäeischen Gemeinschaften, 1993).

(b) A European Dimension should be introduced into programmes of TE (cf. Beernaeri *et al.*, 1993; Commission of the European Communities, 1993 or the formula 'European Educational Space').

(c) The 'Mobility' of teachers has become an issue (Neave, 1991) and the recommendations for the recognition of diploma (cf. 89/48/EC and 92/51/EC) have an influence on the structure and organisation of TE not only within the European Communities (e.g. recent reforms of TE in Italy) and the European Economic Space (e.g. reforms intended in Austria or Finland, Buchberger *et al.*, 1994).

(d) Mobility programmes (e.g. ERASMUS) have brought new input into sometimes very rigid systems and models of TE (cf. Bruce, 1989; Miller and Taylor, 1992).

(e) Expert seminars aim at developing solutions for main problems of TE (e.g. 'Teacher Education and the University', Judge, 1992; 'Educational Research and TE', Coolahan, 1992b; 'The Professionalization of Teachers and TE', Bourdoncle, 1993; 'Quality in TE', Buchberger and Byrne, 1994).

Clusters of motives and forces

Four selected examples of recent activities and discussions on TE have been outlined above. What might be the reasons, motives and forces for these activities and discussions on TE? Six main and interrelated clusters of motives and forces which exercise and influence on the development of TE in most European countries will now be discussed in greater detail (cf. Buchberger, 1993a; Neave, 1991, 1992; OECD, 1990):

(1)   In our rapidly changing and dynamic society schools and teachers are confronted with increased, changed and new tasks and expectations, which emerge e.g. from changed structures of family and labour, changes of values, knowledge explosion, new technologies, internationalisation or multiculturality. As a consequence e.g. a restructuring of

- the contents of teaching and learning,
- curricula,
- methods of teaching and learning or
- a redefinition of the structure of organisation of schooling

are imperative. At the same time this calls for a redefinition of the professional tasks and roles of teachers and TE. Traditional, antiquated role conceptions (e.g. teachers as knowledge transmitters) have become obsolete and there are many cogent arguments in support of the proposition that they will have to be replaced (cf. Skilbeck, 1992).

It is being maintained that schools and teachers cannot deal adequately with these increased, changed and new expectations and tasks. Teachers supposedly have a lack of pro-activity and competence in dealing with changed and rapidly changing conditions of schooling and education. Their insufficient education is seen as one main condition for this unfavourable situation, although it is worth mentioning that in some countries teachers and schools might have adapted in a more appropriate way to changes than programmes of ITE did (cf. Judge, 1990, p. 9: 'A new urgency will thus be given to the antique problem of maintaining an effective relationship between the structures of teacher education and of schooling').

In reacting to this problem many countries have tightened the entry requirements for ITE, have prolonged its duration, have transferred ITE to the higher education sector, have made modifications of its curricula, or have established (sometimes extensive) systems of INSET (e.g. Spain, Morgenstern de Finkel, 1993). But it is debatable whether such policies are the adequate ones to solve the problems or whether substantial reforms with changed paradigms would be necessary (cf. Buchberger, 1993a, b; Hargreaves, 1990).

(2)   In many countries the political context and the political environment of school and TE are changing. Education, sometimes reduced to human resource development, is again winning a position as a political priority. Educational policy has become an integral part of broader (national) economic and social policies. It is argued that highly developed societies depend on an optimal development of the human potential of all its citizens. This calls for adequate investment in education and TE. There are the slogans 'A Quality Education for All' or 'High Quality Education and Training for All' (cf. Commission of the European Communities, 1991; OECD, 1992), but in (Western) European countries there is only broad agreement on the necessity of quality education, not on the number of citizens for whom quality education should be provided (cf. different policies in France, Germany or Scandinavian countries on the one hand and England and Wales on the other). In many countries this increased interest of national policy in education and human resource development corresponds with

- tendencies to rationalise and formalise TE,
- new structures of accountability, and
- a search for better quality of ITE as well as INSET and an increased quality control (cf. Van Vught and Westerheijden, 1993).

(3)   The past few years have also seen changes in the perception as to which tasks the state government and local administration should fulfil. Traditional structures of decision-taking and administration have come under attack both in countries following a so-called centralised system and in countries following a so-called decentralised system (cf. the many

problems connected with these far too simple concepts, Popkewitz, 1993). Autonomy, democratisation, devolution, deregulation as well as privatisation and private initiative on the one hand or centralisation on the other have become new formulae frequently used in many European countries. But these formulae have different meanings in different countries and cultural contexts. Autonomy, democratisation or deregulation may be seen as a next and necessary step in the development of democratic societies in which an increasing number of citizens will have to take increasing responsibility. Neo-conservative and neo-liberal ideologies or a 'New Right' (Elliott, 1993) see these formulae as programmes of a different nature.

Although highly heterogeneous in nature these changes of perception have implications for TE, its organisation, structure and curricula as well as for its administration, management and financing. Most European countries are nowadays following a policy

- of devolution and deregulation. The mechanisms of governance are changing from so-called 'rule-directed models' to so-called 'goal/objective/result-directed models';
- of reducing the responsibility and tasks of the (central) government/administration to strategical planning and management;
- of giving more autonomy to institutions of TE (e.g. Scandinavian countries, France, The Netherlands).

At the same time England and Wales have increased the responsibilities at a central level (cf. Elliott, 1993; Lawton, 1991). A trend towards convergence may be observed. Governments and ministries (of education) seem to take more responsibilities for the strategic planning of (teacher) education and fewer for administration and management, while at an institutional level responsibilities for the latter increase.

Economic thinking and economic rationality have an increasing influence even in the field of education and TE (cf. Wagner, 1993). They seem to dominate policies on education in general and on TE in particular in some European countries. New forms of financing TE have been introduced in some countries (e.g. 'lump-sum model' in The Netherlands) and institutions of TE have been made accountable for an optimal use of resources. TE − ITE as well as INSET − has become subject to market forces and an increased competition may be detected. In recent times this economic rationality, often reduced to fairly narrow criteria (e.g. problems with 'performance indicators') has had strong influence on the development of systems and models of TE in some countries (e.g. England and Wales, The Netherlands) and might influence (teacher education) policies of other countries in the near future (e.g. similar developments in Belgium, Finland, Sweden).

(4) The position of the teaching profession in European countries (e.g. the big differences in status, salary or conditions of work. Commission of the European Communities, 1988) as well as the situation of the labour market for teachers exert a strong influence on TE (cf. Archer and Peck, 1990; DSDE, 1993; Le Metais, 1990; Neave, 1992; OECD, 1989, 1990).

Some countries find themselves confronted with a shortage of teachers. This shortage may exist for all types of schools/teachers, only for some subjects (e.g. natural sciences, information technology, foreign languages) or only for particular types of schools (e.g. vocational, technical, commercial schools). Some experts predict a general shortage of teachers for the (near) future in most member states of the European Communities (cf. Neave, 1992). This calls for discussions on recruitment policies as well as on new definitions of the professional role of teachers and their education. New groups will have to be attracted to the teaching profession. Other forms of differentiation of the teaching profession apart from traditional ones (e.g. ITE received priority) might become necessary, at which criteria like different

- tasks (e.g. teaching – curriculum development – management – participation as co-operating teacher in ITE or as mentor in induction),
- responsibilities (e.g. teacher – head of department) or
- subjects (e.g. social studies – foreign languages – information technology)

are being taken into account (cf. the critical statements of Neave, 1992 on traditional forms of differentiation; Hargreaves, 1990; Holmes Commission, 1986).

Other countries (e.g. Greece, Ireland, Spain, most former Communist countries) are confronted with a surplus of teachers which frequently correlates with a very young teaching force. This calls for discussions on the selection of teachers. In addition these countries are confronted with the problem that all new tasks of school and education have to be achieved with a 'greying profession', which means that systematic efforts in INSET are necessary.

(5) Purpose, aims, structures and organisation of the higher education sector are rapidly changing (cf. Clark and Neave, 1992; Gellert, 1993; Teichler, 1988, 1993). And thus the following factors may be seen in close relation with these changes:

- (a) Highly developed societies depend on the optimal development of all their human resources (cf. human capital theories). This calls for (academic) qualifications at the best level possible and higher education for a large number of people.
- (b) In highly developed societies an increasing number of people has developed a strong demand for higher education. These two factors may be made accountable both for an enormous expansion of the higher education sector in most European countries and for its diversification in some (e.g. colleges, polytechnics, institutions of higher vocational education/Fachhochschulen, universities, research institutes).
- (c) In addition the speed of developments in technology implies that the higher education sector will have to take more responsibility for continuous education/training of a large number of people.

These general developments of the higher education sector will affect TE in many ways: in its institutional location (cf. the discussions in many countries whether ITE should be located at institutions of higher vocational education/Fachhochschulen or at universities; problems with the location of INSET and continuous professional education of teachers), its organisation, its curricula, and its student population.

(6) New results of conceptual and empirical research on TE may be seen as a sixth force in discussions on reforms of TE, although they often do not occupy the most prominent role (cf. the analysis by Popkewitz and Pereyra, 1993 on the social regulation of reform of TE). There are many new insights, which should not be neglected in TE policies and in developing new solutions. These are

- the concept of a reflective practitioner (Schöen, 1983),
- the programme of action research (cf. Elliott, 1993),
- the concept of reflective TE (Liston and Zeichner, 1991),
- Shulman's (1987) studies on the knowledge base of teaching,
- research on the professional development of teachers (cf. Fullan and Hargreaves, 1992; Kremer-Hayon *et al.*, 1983),
- studies on the professional expertise and its development (Dewe *et al.*, 1992; Kennedy, 1990),
- research on the effects of different models and techniques of TE (cf. Houston, 1990) or
- the experiences of concrete reform projects (cf. Doebrich *et al.*, 1981).

Research on teaching and TE indicates that in schools and in TE 'powerful learning environments' should be created, i.e. situations that elicit in students active and constructive processes of knowledge and skill acquisition, and that offer ample opportunities for interaction, communication and co-operation. In addition, students should be stimulated to set their own goals, and be guided in taking more responsibility for their own learning activities and processes. In other words, in powerful learning environments students and student teachers progressively become agents of their own learning activities and processes (cf. Buchberger *et al.*, 1994).

Teacher education as an open and dynamic system

In principle there exists wide-spread agreement that TE has to be conceived as an open and dynamic system (cf. Buchberger, 1993a, b; Churukian, 1993; Hargreaves, 1990; Holmes Commission, 1986; OECD, 1989, 1990; Petracek, 1989; Vonk, 1991) and that TE has to be a continuum starting with

- recruitment, and consisting of the following closely related elements
- ITE,
- induction,
- INSET/continuous professional education and
- further education.

TE has to support the professional development of teachers in all phases of their professional career. Despite this wide-spread agreement on dynamic conceptions of TE in principle, most systems and models of TE have been organised in accordance with static conceptions so far (cf. a so-called 'rucksack-philosophy', Buchberger, 1993a), where it is assumed that

- ITE is able to equip (prospective) teachers with most if not all competencies that seem to be necessary for them to fulfil the tasks of the teaching profession throughout a professional career;
- during a sometimes relatively short period of ITE prospective teachers are able to acquire all the knowledge structures and attitudes that seem to be necessary for permanent professional learning and development;
- where coherent measures for an induction into the teaching profession are not taken, and where
- INSET as well as further education might happen on a voluntary basis.

In most countries TE is split up into different and often unrelated subsystems:

- ITE,
- induction,
- INSET,
- further education,
- research and development,
- school improvement.

Realising TE as an open and dynamic system will have a host of implications which will sometimes involve a concept-reorientation for TE and the teaching profession, i.e.:

(1) It seems to be necessary to redefine the goals and tasks of each of the above subsystems and to define their contributions to the professional development of teachers more precisely.

(2) Goals, tasks and methods of ITE have to be defined with much more clarity. It has to be clarified which capabilities, competencies and attitudes necessary for permanent professional and personal development can be acquired during ITE (cf. Buchberger, 1992a; Hargreaves, 1993).

(3) A systematic and co-ordinated induction into the professional cultures of schools might be called a blind spot of TE. Although research on induction clearly indicates that many positive effects of ITE are 'washed out' when young teachers enter into schools, this has not led to systematic efforts in most countries. Most schools all over Europe have not developed a 'culture of induction' yet. Induction calls for the co-operation of ITE and qualified teachers at schools who have to receive special education and training to be able to take responsibility for this important task. Induction ('A missing link') might combine ITE and INSET and contribute to the

improvement of all subsystems of TE (cf. recent developments in England and Wales).

(4) A close co-operation between institutions of TE and schools might be seen as a key element for establishing and maintaining professional learning and development cultures at schools. Highly qualified and specially trained teachers at schools have to be integrated into the teaching practice component of ITE as well as into developmental research projects done there. Teacher educators and educational researchers need opportunities so that they can be actively involved in innovative work done in schools. Partnerships between institutions of ITE and schools have to be established (cf. the concept of professional development schools in the USA; Holmes Commission, 1990). Institutions of TE might be developed into resource centres and integrate ITE, INSET and school improvement.

(5) INSET will need more forms of school-based school-focused activities in which teacher educators co-operate with the staff of a school for a longer period of time on relevant themes and where all parties involved intend to improve the school and its problem-solving capacity.

(6) In many countries INSET is separated from ITE and the further education of teachers on the one hand, and from school improvement and research on the other. It is frequently controlled by representatives of the school administration. It is debatable whether these solutions can adequately contribute to the professional development of teachers and whether they might be called professionalised. More professional control of INSET by teachers themselves seems to be imperative (cf. developments in The Netherlands or in Sweden). INSET, educational research and development, and school improvement have to be integrated and to be brought under more professional control.

(7) In many European countries there are heated discussions whether INSET has to be voluntary or compulsory, and which incentives ought to be introduced for INSET. The following solutions may be mentioned here:

- Teachers may have a right to attend INSET for a certain amount of time (e.g. France).
- In another group of countries INSET activities are part of the working time of teachers and participation may be compulsory (e.g. Italy).
- Different forms of educational leaves do exist.
- Other countries (e.g. Switzerland) have a mix of compulsory and voluntary INSET.
- Participation in INSET may foster the career of a teacher and increase her/his professional status.

But, coherent strategies of staff development or human resource management are still missing.

(8) More attention will have to be paid to the further education of teachers. It could relate to such tasks of the teaching profession that so far

have been absent in most models of ITE (e.g. school management, curriculum development). In addition it will become necessary to equip teachers with those qualifications that seem to be necessary to deal adequately with new and rapidly changing tasks of the teaching profession (e.g. communication and information technology, multicultural education). But, the necessity of systematic as well as compulsory further education of teachers has been disregarded so far.

(9) A clear profile for teacher educators will have to be developed both for ITE and INSET. Although the quality and the effectiveness of TE largely depend on the competence and expertise of teacher educators there have only been limited efforts so far to professionalise this activity (cf. Lanier and Little, 1986; Wilson, 1990). Most teacher educators − professors and lecturers in the fields of education, subject didactics or the academic disciplines, mentors or co-operating teachers at schools responsible for teaching practice as well as teacher educators in the field of INSET − have never received training in appropriate methods of teaching/co-operating/ learning with adult learners and professional teachers, or in organisational learning and development (cf. Buchberger *et al.*, 1994).

(10) In many European countries the relationship between TE and educational research needs to be redefined. Like in all other (and not only academic) professions a close relationship between educational research and development and the teaching profession seems to be indispensable. But in most European countries (cf. as a counter example Finland) institutions of TE are separated from educational research and they neither have responsibility nor adequate resources for it. ITE as well as INSET will have to find a clear profile for educational research and development and an active involvement of teachers in it. This might be seen as essential for the improvement of all forms of TE. But it cannot be denied that some systems and models of TE have different opinions on this (cf. developments in England and Wales).

The conception of TE as an open and dynamic system as outlined here challenges traditional conceptions with their static rationale and their segmentations, but it poses questions that will have to be answered, no matter what the actual development and improvement of TE might be like.

Systems, structures and programmes of teacher education

In her thorough description of initial teacher training systems of the twelve member states of the European Union Le Metais (1991) restricts herself to

> general regulations governing [TE for] teachers of pupils of statutory school age and up to age 18 + in schools maintained or subsidised by the state. Teachers in nursery, technical or vocational schools and in special schools may hold different qualifications from, or in addition to, those employed in ordinary schools. Given the complexity of these

differences, regulations specifically governing the training of these teachers have been excluded. (Le Metais, 1991, p. 1)

On a country by country basis she presents descriptions structured under five headings:

- types of school,
- categories of teachers (most countries have more than one category of teachers, depending on the education received and/or on the type of school in which s/he may be employed),
- requirements for admission to teacher training,
- teacher training process (e.g. level, length and content of TE for each category of teacher),
- qualifications.

These limitations chosen may be interpreted as an indication of the many variables that have to be taken into account in comprehensive descriptions (and comparisons) of systems and structures of TE in Europe. Despite the facts that certain restrictions have been made and that Le Metais's descriptions have been prepared very carefully, the complexity and the rich diversity of systems of ITE are reflected in them only to a certain extent. Studies comparable to that of Le Metais (e.g. Buchberger, 1992; Vaniscotte, 1989) seem to be confronted with similar problems. Differences in structures of education and types of school (cf. EURYDICE/CEDEFOP, 1992), different categories of teacher (e.g. for different stages of school systems/age groups, types of school or for different subjects), and sometimes very particular types of ITE for different categories of teachers may be made accountable for this. In addition, a host of exceptions make the situation even more complicated.

Although the author is very well aware of the problems outlined above some basic structures of systems of TE in European countries will be described below. These descriptions will focus on institutional and organisational features of TE (ITE as well as INSET) and additionally they will deal with some selected elements of programmes of TE for teachers at primary and secondary level. Some simplified diagrams will be presented, which contain information on the types of school/age range of students, entry into ITE (years of schooling), the duration of ITE and the curricular models (e.g. sequence) and their components (e.g. the amount of different components in percentages). These diagrams were originally published in 1992 in the *Guide to Institutions of Teacher Education in Europe* (Buchberger, 1992).

Some basic structures of initial teacher education

Various criteria may be used for categorising systems and models of TE. Because of the close relationships between school systems, (I)TE and categories of teachers, an approach frequently adopted for categorisations at an organisational and institutional level uses criteria such as

38

- stages of the educational system (pre-primary, primary, lower secondary, upper secondary) and/or
- types of school (e.g. compulsory – non-compulsory, comprehensive – non-comprehensive, focus of education: general-academic, vocational, special education).

Although problems connected with this approach are obvious (e.g. different meanings of the term upper secondary level, different age ranges of these levels), it has been adopted here to describe some basic structures of systems of ITE.

(1) Taking the stages of primary level, lower secondary level and upper secondary level as criteria three main categories of systems of TE may be analysed:

(a) A first category of systems integrates the initial education of teachers for comprehensive schools (primary and lower secondary level), and provides different forms of education for teachers at upper secondary level (e.g. Denmark, Foldberg and Stenlev, 1992).

Figure 2.3 Denmark

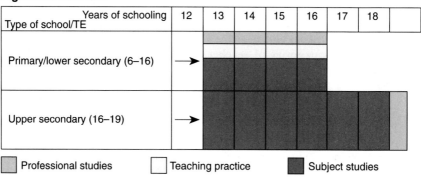

Years of schooling Type of school/TE	12	13	14	15	16	17	18	
Primary/lower secondary (6–16)	→							
Upper secondary (16–19)	→							

☐ Professional studies   ☐ Teaching practice   ■ Subject studies

Source: Foldberg and Stenter, 1992, p. 71.

The system of ITE in Sweden (cf. Andersson and Michaelsson, 1992) may be grouped into this category too, although there exist two different forms of ITE for teachers of comprehensive schools: one for grades 1–7 and another for grades 4–9 (cf. some recent developments to reintroduce separations between ITE for teachers at primary and secondary level, Kallos and Selander, 1993).

(b) In a second category of systems of TE different programmes are offered to (prospective) teachers at primary level and at (lower and upper) secondary level (e.g. England and Wales, Hellawell, 1992; France, Zay, 1992; Finland, Haemaelaeinen *et al.*, 1992; Ireland, Coolahan, 1992; Spain, Bordas and Montane, 1992). The programmes which sometimes consist of some components common to both forms of ITE are organised by institutions of higher education /universities. The duration of studies may be different (e.g. Finland, Spain) or the same (e.g. England and Wales, France).

Figure 2.4 Sweden

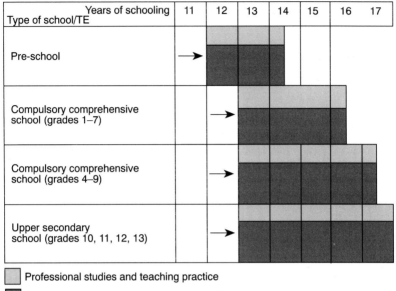

Type of school/TE \ Years of schooling	11	12	13	14	15	16	17
Pre-school							
Compulsory comprehensive school (grades 1–7)							
Compulsory comprehensive school (grades 4–9)							
Upper secondary school (grades 10, 11, 12, 13)							

▢ Professional studies and teaching practice

■ Subject studies and subject matter methodology

Source: Andersson and Michaelsson, 1992, p. 314.

Figure 2.5 Denmark

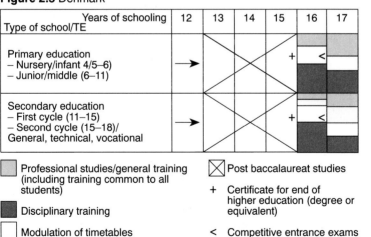

Type of school/TE \ Years of schooling	12	13	14	15	16	17
Primary education – Nursery/infant 4/5–6) – Junior/middle (6–11)				+	<	
Secondary education – First cycle (11–15) – Second cycle (15–18)/ General, technical, vocational				+	<	

▢ Professional studies/general training (including training common to all students)

■ Disciplinary training

▢ Modulation of timetables

▢ Practical training courses (and training course in industry for technical and vocational studies

☒ Post baccalaureat studies

+ Certificate for end of higher education (degree or equivalent)

< Competitive entrance exams

Source: Zay, 1992, p.105.

Figure 2.6 Spain

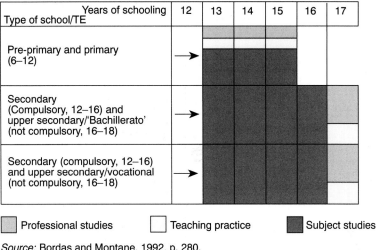

Type of school/TE Years of schooling	12	13	14	15	16	17
Pre-primary and primary (6–12)						
Secondary (Compulsory, 12–16) and upper secondary/'Bachillerato' (not compulsory, 16–18)						
Secondary (compulsory, 12–16) and upper secondary/vocational (not compulsory, 16–18)						

☐ Professional studies   ☐ Teaching practice   ■ Subject studies

Source: Bordas and Montane, 1992, p. 280.

Figure 2.7 Hungary

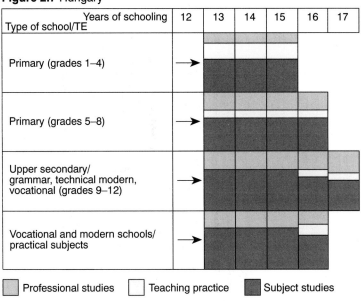

Type of school/TE Years of schooling	12	13	14	15	16	17
Primary (grades 1–4)						
Primary (grades 5–8)						
Upper secondary/ grammar, technical modern, vocational (grades 9–12)						
Vocational and modern schools/ practical subjects						

☐ Professional studies   ☐ Teaching practice   ■ Subject studies

Source: Lunyady and Kosa, 1992, p. 444.

41

Figure 2.8 Poland

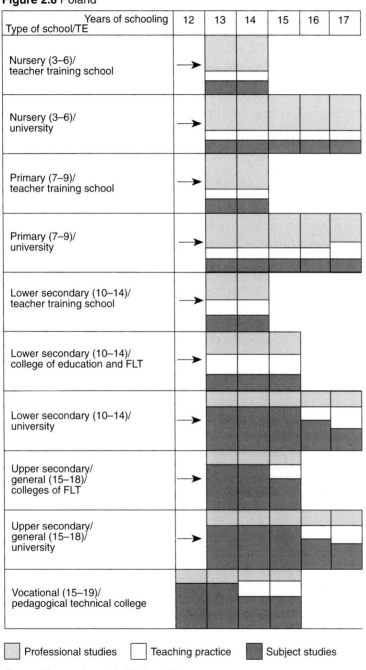

Years of schooling Type of school/TE	12	13	14	15	16	17
Nursery (3–6)/ teacher training school						
Nursery (3–6)/ university						
Primary (7–9)/ teacher training school						
Primary (7–9)/ university						
Lower secondary (10–14)/ teacher training school						
Lower secondary (10–14)/ college of education and FLT						
Lower secondary (10–14)/ university						
Upper secondary/ general (15–18)/ colleges of FLT						
Upper secondary/ general (15–18)/ university						
Vocational (15–19)/ pedagogical technical college						

Professional studies Teaching practice Subject studies

Source: Bleszynska *et al.*, 1992, p. 458.

(c) In a third category systems of ITE consist of the following structure:

- programmes for prospective teachers at primary level, and
- different programmes for different types of school as well as types of teachers at lower secondary level, which train either for the lower secondary level or the lower and upper secondary level.

Examples for this category are i.e. Belgium, Coppieters, 1992; Hungary, Hunyady and Kosa, 1992, Germany, Doebrich *et al.*, 1992, The Netherlands, Plate, 1992).

Other solutions may be found in countries like Norway (cf. Moerk, 1992), Portugal (cf. Valente, 1992) or former Eastern European countries (cf. programmes for teachers of different stages of the education system run parallel at teacher training schools at upper secondary level, post-secondary level and university level; Poland, Bleszynska *et al.*, 1992).

(d) TE for special education may be provided in widely differing structures. In some countries prospective teachers for special education receive their education in programmes running parallel to the education of teachers at primary and lower secondary level (e.g. Austria, Buchberger, 1992; Czech Republic, Cerna and Parizek, 1992). Special education may be an integral part of the education of primary teachers and specialisation studies are offered during these programmes (e.g. Finland). In a third group of models ITE for special education is provided as a post-graduate/post-diploma programme for teachers (e.g. The Netherlands). Very specialised forms of training are provided to deal with different groups of the handicapped (e.g. the blind).

(e) Some systems of TE are characterised by highly developed structures and programmes for vocational education. Some countries provide ITE for vocational subjects at lower secondary level (e.g. Belgium, The Netherlands). At upper secondary level three main structures may be detected: some countries have introduced special programmes for teachers of 'practical subjects' in the sector of vocational education (e.g. Austria, Germany, Czech Republic). Teachers for commercial schools at upper secondary level receive their education at higher education or university level (e.g. Germany), while ITE for teachers of technical subjects seem not to have been developed in most Western European countries yet (cf. the exceptions of France and The Netherlands or systems established in former Communist countries).

(2) As regards institutions at which ITE for teachers at primary level, lower secondary level and upper secondary level is provided, three main categories emerge:

(a) Some countries have incorporated all forms of TE mentioned above into the university sector (e.g. England and Wales, Finland, France, Germany, Greece, Spain). Despite this fact the programmes offered to prospective teachers for the different levels of the school system may vary not only in content and curricular structures, but in their duration. While the duration of studies is of equal length for prospective teachers at primary and secondary level in England and Wales or France, it differs in Finland, Germany or Spain (approximately one year of study).

Figure 2.9 The Netherlands

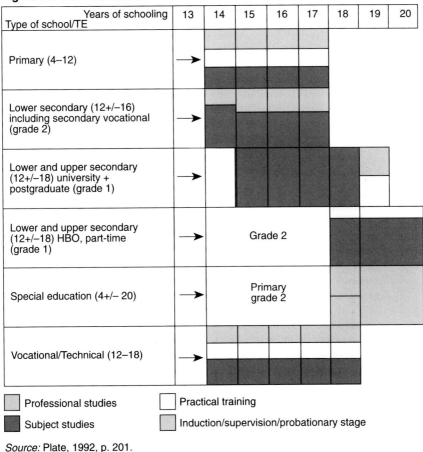

Type of school/TE \ Years of schooling	13	14	15	16	17	18	19	20
Primary (4–12)	→							
Lower secondary (12+/–16) including secondary vocational (grade 2)	→							
Lower and upper secondary (12+/–18) university + postgraduate (grade 1)	→							
Lower and upper secondary (12+/–18) HBO, part-time (grade 1)	→	Grade 2						
Special education (4+/– 20)	→	Primary grade 2						
Vocational/Technical (12–18)	→							

Professional studies

Subject studies

Practical training

Induction/supervision/probationary stage

Source: Plate, 1992, p. 201.

(b) A second category insists on separation between the different institutions at which ITE is provided for different types of teachers. Teachers for the primary level and some types of school at lower secondary level may be educated at schools at upper secondary level, at institutions at post-secondary level or at institutions of higher education, while teachers for other types of school at lower secondary level and at upper secondary level receive their ITE at university level.

(c) In a third category teachers for different types of school may obtain their teaching certificates at institutions located at different stages of the educational system and of different status and it is up to the (prospective) teacher where s/he intends to study (e.g. Bulgaria, Valchev, 1993; Poland, Bleszynska *et al.*, 1992).

(3) Some similarities and main differences of programmes of ITE have been outlined earlier and additional information is contained in the Figures presented. Three short items of information are now added.

(a) Many programmes of ITE for teachers at primary level may be characterised by a high degree of rigidity. An overload of subjects and topics to be studied by prospective teachers seems to correspond with rather inflexible programmes and overcrowded schedules and to inhibit independent professional learning (cf. Bruce, 1989). In reaction to this problem some systems of ITE have
- reduced the number of subjects to be studied by prospective teachers at primary school,
- introduced different forms of specialisation studies (for a limited amount of school subjects or learning domains), or
- modularised the programmes.

This applies especially to systems of ITE in countries where primary school lasts five years or more (e.g. Scandinavian countries).

(b) Most systems of ITE for teachers at upper secondary level follow a consecutive model. Although more studies in the sciences of the teaching profession and more teaching practice has been infused into these systems, substantial changes in their curricular structures have not been made. As regards the relationship between studies in academic disciplines at university and subjects to be taught at school the following may be observed: relationships have been tightened and curricula have been made more coherent. The most frequent number of disciplines that have to be studied (in relation to subjects of the curricula of schools) is two.

(c) In many models of ITE especially for teachers at primary level components of educational research and development (e.g. participation in research and development projects, preparation of a (masters) thesis) seem to be underrepresented. The Finnish or French systems of ITE, where prospective teachers are obliged to prepare a masters thesis may be taken as examples how this component may be integrated into programmes of ITE (cf. Coolahan, 1992b).

Structures and programmes of INSET

The recognition of the importance of permanent professional (as well as personal) learning and development of teachers and its relevance for school improvement may be seen as main reasons why all countries of the European Economic Area and most other European countries have made increasing investments into INSET and have established (sometimes extensive) systems for it since the late 1960s. Although the goals defined for INSET and the continuous professional education of teachers seem to be rather uniform across the different countries. INSET is organised in systems and models of greatly heterogeneous natures (cf. Blackburn and Moissan, 1987). These different systems might be seen as particular and complex mixtures of a set of variables, and seem to be a product of problem solving processes under particular conditions rather than a product of rational system planning or actions guided by theory. This nature of most systems of INSET does not allow the making of simple descriptions and comparisons.

(1) A recent document submitted by Spanish education authorities to EURYDICE may be used as an example to demonstrate goals and objectives of INSET as similar definitions may be detected in many other European countries (although priorities may differ widely). Over the period 1986/1990 Education Authority Teacher Training measures set out to achieve the following goals:

- to help to improve the school, seen as the primary permanent training nucleus, whose members are engaged in a common educational project;
- to provide teaching staff with professional resources that foster skills closely related with their teaching practice and to respond to the needs of the educational system and the profession;
- to create and foster teacher participation in the design, development and interchange of experiences within the context of training plans;
- to promote the updating of teachers scientific and educational knowledge;
- to provide specialised training for teaching staff in areas where such specialisations are lacking;
- to re-train teaching staff (vocational education);
- to devote special attention to the training of trainers.

INSET activities planned for the 1993/94 academic year will revolve around the following guidelines:

- Prioritisation of training for implementation of a new reform;
- consolidation of training structures and rationalisation of INSET networks;
- improvement in the quality of training;
- upgrading of the supply of activities carried out through co-operative agreement.

(2) Some important variables which account for the differences between systems of INSET in different countries will now be outlined mainly in the form of questions. Such differences reflect:

- the importance given to an educational system, its quality and permanent improvement in the educational, social and economic policies of a country;

- different conceptions of the role and the status of teachers;
- the importance given to a competent and committed teaching force and its conditions of service;
- economic conditions of a country.

(a) Who are the providers of programmes of INSET? Most countries have established particular institutes for INSET separated from institutions of ITE (although this separation is increasingly seen as problematic). The regional institutes for INSET in Italy (IRRSAE) and in the Laender of Germany or the teacher centres in Spain are some cases in point. Other providers may be universities (e.g. England and Wales, France), institutions of ITE (e.g. Iceland, Ireland, The Netherlands), teacher associations and trade unions or private organisations. Is there sufficient co-ordination between the organisations providing TE in general and INSET in particular? Is INSET co-ordinated with school improvement and curriculum reform? Does some form of competition exist between different providers (e.g. England and Wales, The Netherlands)?

(b) Who provides the resources for INSET? Is it central authorities (e.g. Ministry of Education, Austria), local authorities (e.g. Germany), municipalities (e.g. Ireland) or private organisations (e.g. some projects in England and Wales)? Which contributions do teachers themselves have to make? Is it a mix of sources?

(c) Who has control over content and organisation of INSET? Are decisions taken on a central level or at school level? What role do central authorities, the inspectorate, institutions of INSET, teachers or parents have to play, which one teacher associations and trade unions or communities, industry and commerce?

(d) What are the conditions for teachers to participate? Is participation a duty or a right for teachers, is it compulsory or voluntary? Although some countries have introduced some form of compulsory INSET (e.g. Finland, Sweden, most cantons of Switzerland) the introduction of coherent and systematic INSET that is compulsory has not really been achieved so far. When does INSET have to take place (e.g. during teaching time, school time, holidays)? Who has to cover the costs for the programmes and travelling/accommodation (the state, local education authorities, municipalities, schools, teachers themselves)? Does participation in INSET affect the career of teachers (e.g. Ireland, Spain)?

(e) Which types of INSET activities are available? Is it mainly short courses of sometimes heterogeneous natures? Are there coherent programmes at a local level and/or school-focused/school-based programmes (e.g. The Netherlands, Switzerland)? Are there coherent national programmes of INSET aiming at supporting curricular reforms (e.g. the five-year programme for the reform of primary education in Italy or the French programmes for introducing new information technology)? Do teachers have the opportunity to partake in programmes at universities or colleges to acquire new qualifications and diplomas (e.g. many Eastern European countries)? Do opportunities exist for sabbatical leaves, i.e. for programmes in foreign countries?

(3) Much literature is available that deals with INSET and the professional development of teachers theoretically and that presents examples of good practice in different (European) countries. Thus this literature permits making some generalisations as to conditions of effective INSET (e.g. Fullan and Hargreaves, 1992; Kremer-Hayon *et al.*, 1993, publications on the International School Improvement Project/ISIP of OECD). But, these cannot simply be applied to different national systems of INSET or transferred from one context to another. It is possible to talk of seven clusters of conditions of effective INSET:

(a) It is trivial to state that effective INSET calls for a well-developed infrastructure that is organised on principles of modern organisation theory. But the reality in many European countries clearly indicates that there are many problems and that basic requirements are not always fulfilled. There is a lack of resources, and responsibilities are not always clear. In a comprehensive study on the situation of INSET in the twelve member states of the European Union Blackburn and Moisan (1987) have identified many advantages in a system consisting of

- well-resourced institutions at a local/regional level with some permanent staff for organisation, administration and information, and with teacher educators. Under these conditions INSET can be provided for around 2,000–3,000 teachers;
- these local institutions (and networks) ought to be co-ordinated within networks on a larger scale that cater for some 50,000 teachers;
- additionally networks at school level or even within schools have to be established and some experts emphasise the prominent role headteachers ought to have in establishing these networks.

(b) The existence of a professional learning and development culture in schools might be seen as an important condition of effective INSET. It might contribute to the development of a 'corporate identity' of schools oriented on the concept of the 'problem-solving school'. The development of professional cultures depends very much on two factors. ITE that is highly professionalised is one of them. Appropriate conditions for the professional work of teachers form another (e.g. problems in England and Wales, Greece, Portugal). In addition these cultures need support by school authorities, parents, communities, and other external agencies (e.g. industry). So far only limited attention has been paid to the development of professional cultures within the different systems of education, while this is something common in successful companies outside the education sector.

(c) INSET has to be integrated into the improvement of particular schools and their staff development (cf. recent developments in England and Wales). This means a change of the focus of INSET activities from the individual teacher to the school. The recognition of this has led to an increase of school-focused and school-based INSET in many countries. This does not apply yet to coherent programmes of staff development in most countries.

(d) Goals, tasks and methods of INSET frequently are characterised by a lack of clarity and coherence. More coherence seems to be necessary in

- the strategic planning of INSET at a national level;
- planning at a local level and
- planning at the level of particular programmes.

An increased coherence and clarity might be seen as basic requirements for modularised programmes of INSET that correlate with greater effectiveness (cf. programmes of the Open University in the United Kingdom). It is worth mentioning that the evaluation of INSET in relation to defined goals is still a blind spot in many systems of INSET.

(e) In planning INSET it seems to be necessary to keep a balance between the different interests of central education authorities, local education authorities, communities, economy, parents and teachers. It is essential that teachers themselves should be actively and responsively involved in planning INSET and that they should be respected as professional partners in decision making by all partners mentioned above.

(f) INSET has to fulfil many tasks that are not always complementary. This calls for different programmes for the different goals of INSET, i.e. the transmission of information, training, attitude change, personal development, the acquisition of new qualifications, curriculum development, school development or organisation development. Coherent strategies are necessary to co-ordinate different programmes.

(g) INSET that focuses on concrete problems and projects seems to be very effective. Teachers (of a school or a small network of schools) co-operate (supported by external teacher educators) over a longer period of time on a project when trying to solve professional problems. Professional teachers are engaged in collaborative problem solving – one of the magic formulae frequently used to explain the prosperity of successful companies or of countries of the far east (e.g. the principle of 'kaizen'). School-focused/school-based INSET as well as organisation development might be seen as samples of this approach to effective INSET. The establishment of 'quality circles' in schools and the education system might contribute very positively to further improvements.

Concluding remarks

This chapter has described some general patterns and broader trends of the development of TE in Europe, presented examples of the rich diversity of patterns to be observed at institutional and organisational levels, and analysed current changes and challenges as well as forces behind them. A rich diversity seems to be a salient feature of TE in Europe, although at the same time TE may be characterised by some elements common to most of European countries.

More or less cogent arguments might be formulated in support of all of the different systems and models of TE outlined above – and indeed they have been put forward by those responsible for these solutions. But there is a lack of research on the effects and efficiency of these systems and models in relation to formulated goals and it seems that TE has not always been subject to rational system planning.

Many experts think that education and human resource development are megatrends of recent days and the near future. They argue that the prosperity of highly developed societies will depend very much on an optimal development of all its human resources. To achieve this, extensive investment into education will be a must. It will be imperative to invest better and more into the ITE as well as INSET. On the one hand it will be necessary to evaluate very precisely what has been achieved so far and what the real effectiveness of actions taken and the efficiency of investments made are; on the other hand substantial reforms and improvements will be necessary that use the knowledge as well as the technology available to a better degree than in the past.

Nowadays some European countries seem to be confronted with economic problems and budgetary constraints. This might be a temptation for some education ministries to take a strategy of a muddling through, to reduce investment in education or to take some form of problem suppression to deal with the problems mentioned above where pro-active action is imperative. But, did ministers of education of OECD-countries not say that 'the challenges of the 21st century will not be met in a spirit of more of the same' and that the 'OECD societies must transform themselves into learning societies' (OECD, 1992)?

It has been the intention of this chapter to sketch the problem areas and the main elements that systems and models of TE in Europe as well as policies on TE are confronted with and to present some input for problem solving, which can only take place under certain circumstances and in particular social contexts. In developing and constructing new solutions for TE, teacher educators as well as decision makers in many European countries have often been highly re-active (cf. Coolahan, 1991). It is to be hoped that this chapter might provide some input for more pro-active action in order to improve TE.

Acknowledgements

The author feels obliged to thank Brigitte Richter for her support in preparing the English version of the chapter. Yves Beernaert (Association for Teacher Education in Europe/ATEE) and Fernando Frechauth (EURYDICE) for their help in collecting reliable and most recent data for this chapter.

PART TWO

The Training of Teachers and Teacher Trainers

CHAPTER 3

Training Teachers to Teach Mixed Ability Groups

E.C. Wragg

Summary

There is a wide range of practice in Europe and elsewhere in the grouping of children for classroom teaching. Some schools stream according to ability, others put in the same class a very wide range of pupils, from different social, religious and ethnic backgrounds as well as varying intellectual ability and academic attachment. In training teachers for our rapidly changing society we need to look forward to the 21st century and consider such aspects as increased leisure, the demands for skill and the likelihood that people will work in teams. All these mean that both the process and content of education are important.

Amongst the most important issues in preparing to teach mixed ability classes are the questions of seeing the gifted and the less able as individuals, avoiding lessons aimed at or below the middle of the class; the effects of teachers' expectations; teachers learning to use a wide range of strategies, including more use of group work and individualised learning; whether subjects like mathematics and languages, which some argue are linear, lend themselves to mixed ability teaching; and the question of assessment of pupil progress.

Classroom research shows some of the needs for effective teaching of pupils of widely ranging ability. These are that teachers need to develop the skills of teaching children as individuals, that individualised or modular approaches may be effective, but that this involves a great deal of work for individual teachers.

During training teachers must learn to widen the range of skills they have, a process that can be helped with good video materials and the use of new technology such as the micro-computer and interactive video-disc. Teachers must also learn to understand the many characteristics of individual children, including those related to their social, religious and ethnic background.

Introduction

The question of how best to group children for teaching and learning has concerned generations of teachers and administrators in many societies. In some countries decisions about groupings are left to individual schools or to regions. In others there is a national pattern. In the United States and Sweden there have been mixed ability classes for much of the 20th century. In West Germany and the United Kingdom, on the other hand, a selective system meant that, until recently, the more able pupils were educated in separate schools. In England and Wales during the 1970s and early 1980s most secondary schools became comprehensive and non-selective, and so children of a very wide range of ability could be in the same class, as many schools introduced mixed ability groups, especially in the 11 – 13-year-old range.

There are several issues which arise from any grouping policy, and they have a considerable relevance to the training of teachers. These include:

- What criteria should be used to group pupils?
- What are the reasons for any grouping policy?
- Should gifted children be educated with others?
- Should disabled children be educated separately?
- What teaching strategies should be employed?
- What are the benefits and problems of any grouping policy?
- What are the resource implications, e.g. books and equipment?
- How is progress to be assessed?
- Is the policy suitable for all subjects/environments?
- Is a single pattern best?

How pupils may be grouped

When pupils are put into groups there are various choices open to those responsible for assigning them, although in small village or rural schools there may be only a single class. Some would argue that all groups are of mixed ability, even when classes are thought to be homogeneous, as children of apparently similar performance can be of different abilities. The most common sorts of groupings are as follows:

Streaming

A decision is made on children's *general* intellectual ability and academic performance. Pupils are then grouped with the most talented in the A class, the next most able in the B class and so on. The class stays together for all its subjects. The strongest argument put forward in favour of streaming is that it enables teachers to move at the appropriate pace since, in theory, members of each class are at a similar level. The arguments against are that some children are good at mathematics but not history, or vice versa, and that the transfer rate in streamed schools is often low. This second point is particularly important in large schools. Research in England (Jackson, 1964) showed that the transfer rate from one stream to another during or at the end of the academic year might be as low as 3 per cent, which meant that pupils put into low streams might have little chance of moving up to higher grade classes.

Setting

In this case pupils are grouped according to their *specific* ability in each subject studied. Thus someone might be in Set 3 for mathematics, Set 2 for science and Set 1 for French. The strongest argument in favour of setting is that, since all pupils should be at a similar level in each subject, the teacher should be able to move them all forward together at the appropriate rate. The chief argument against is that the process may be too competitive if children are constantly striving to be in the highest set of each of several subjects, and may fragment the school day, with pupils unable to get to know their fellows because they are always with different people.

Banding

In order to overcome the criticisms of setting and streaming some larger schools split their pupils into broad bands of ability and then assign pupils to a class within a Band. Thus a secondary school with an eight class intake might decide to have three classes in Band A for high achieving pupils, three classes in Band B for children of average ability, and two classes in Band C for low achieving pupils. The main arguments in favour of broad banding of this kind are that the question of transfer is not as important, because a pupil in the lowest Band only has to take two steps to get into the highest Band, and also that it is the best compromise between streaming and mixed ability teaching. The main argument against is that children may still be labelled as being made of gold, silver or bronze, and that this may be self-fulfilling, that is, a pupil in Band C will see himself as third rate and therefore have low aspirations.

Mixed ability grouping

Some schools put children of all abilities into the same class. There are few truly mixed ability classes, because very often children with severe mental or physical handicaps have been taken out of the mainstream school system altogether, and may be educated in special schools, hospitals or at home. Nonetheless there can be a very wide range of ability in the same classroom, with a future Nobel Prize winner sitting alongside someone who can barely read. The main arguments for mixed ability classes are that it is good socially and intellectually for children to mix with others of different ability, backgrounds and interests and that it avoids premature labelling. The principal arguments against are that it is extremely difficult for teachers to handle such a range within the same class and that they will, therefore, most likely aim their teaching at the middle of the ability range, confusing the slower children and boring the clever ones. In selective schools like the gymnasium, or the grammar school, there is often talk of 'mixed ability' classes, but in reality these are more like the 'banding' system described above, since the whole ability range is not involved.

Other criteria for grouping

Streaming, setting, banding and mixed ability grouping are broad overall strategies for assigning pupils to classes, but there are other criteria which can figure in the operation. These include the following: age of learners (children are often grouped by age, but at the Sutton Centre in Nottinghamshire members of some classes range from 14 to 83 years old), friendship, physical features (e.g. children of same height and weight working together in PE lessons), social class factors (private schools, 'uptown' and 'downtown' schools), and religious/ethnic/language factors (Catholic and Protestant schools in Northern Ireland, children of immigrant workers, or 'Gastarbeiter', Moslem schools, Welsh language schools). Personality and learning style have sometimes been explored as grouping criteria.

There is also the question of single sex or co-education. Some supporters of co-education have suggested that, since girls are said to be at a disadvantage when educated alongside boys, there should be separate classes for girls in subjects that are traditionally regarded as 'male', such as mathematics, science and technology. Another matter is the question of vocational education and whether pupils heading for the same adult occupation should be educated together. The question of pre-vocational education has become an important matter throughout Europe during the last decade, raising questions for the education of older pupils about whether future doctors and lawyers should be educated together with or separately from future electricians or hairdressers.

The major issues affecting teacher training

When planning teacher training courses it is necessary to incorporate a set of concerns which are closely related to any discussion of the teaching of children of widely varying backgrounds, interests and abilities. These include such topics as expectations, the education of very able and very slow learning pupils, classroom organisation and the numerous contexts in which teaching and learning take place, including the many subjects and topics which are taught.

Aspirations for the future

Alvin Toffler, the American futurologist, said that all education was a vision of the future and that if we have no vision of the future we will be failing the nation's youth. Given that pupils in school today will only be in their twenties when the year 2000 comes, it is quite clear that they will spend most of their adult lives in the 21st century. Trainees must learn to develop a picture of the future.

Visions of the 21st century are mixed and will vary from country to country and from one predictor to another, but certain key developments are probable. These include the likelihood that people will have different working patterns from those of their parents and grandparents; that they may change jobs or need retraining several times in their working lives; that many will have more leisure; that with increased automation, fewer may work in factories and more in service industries, including recreation and leisure; and that people may find themselves working as members of a collaborative team.

If these predictions come true there are several implications for school and for the whole of any country's education system. One is that it will not be sufficient to acquire knowledge alone, for much of this will be outdated before long. In order to be up-to-date pupils must also learn how to learn, for they may have to retrain and indeed be lifelong learners if home and family life become more important.

Another is that, if people are to work collaboratively as members of teams, or to work more in service than manufacturing industries, the ability to get along with others, often with different talents, is vital. Thus the *process* of education becomes important, not solely the *content,* so that if pupils work together on a project in school, they are not only learning knowledge, skills, attitudes and behaviour, but also how to share ideas, help others, take responsibility, find things out for themselves, rather than wait to be told. These are all vital skills for people in our increasingly complex bureaucratic and technological society, and this wider view of the purpose of education is important to bear in mind when considering research evidence on the effects of schooling.

The gifted and less able

There is no single definition of 'giftedness' or 'slow learners'. Some see giftedness as being something possessed by the top 2 or 3 per cent of the ability range, others argue that many children can be gifted in one particular aspect, like music or language learning, but not necessarily be in the top group for all subjects. The same kinds of argument are put forward at the other end of the scale. 'Slow learners' can be seen as those with the most severe learning handicaps or, it is sometimes argued, most people have some kind of learning problem, whether it is learning to swim, drive a car or understand algebra.

One concern, therefore, in many countries is whether children at the extremes of the ability range should be educated with the rest. In some countries there have been attempts to integrate even quite severely disabled children, such as the blind, the deaf, the physically disabled, into mainstream schools, and opinion is divided whether integration or separation is preferable. Those who support integration say that the benefits to children to be educated in a 'normal' environment can be considerable. Critics argue that scarce facilities, like purpose-built equipment and expert specialist teachers, are simply scattered thinly over several schools instead of being concentrated in one properly equipped institution.

With gifted pupils the arguments are also diverse. Some believe that it is simply not possible to stimulate the cleverest children if they are surrounded by others of average or below average ability. Others claim that it does a disservice to bright pupils to segregate them, that their presence helps raise standards for other pupils and that if, as often happens, they are one day put in authority over their fellow citizens, they ought to understand how ordinary people learn and function. Learning to understand wide diversity in children is an important task for teachers during training.

Expectancy

A notion which is often mentioned in discussion about the training of teachers for mixed ability groups is that of expectancy. There is some evidence and a much stronger belief, that children may, to some extent, live up to what teachers and parents, and indeed society as a whole, expect of them. Thus if a group of pupils are labelled 'low achievers' or 'exceptionally clever', this becomes a self-fulfilling prophecy, with those bearing a positive label feeling buoyant, paying attention in class, striving to achieve even better results, and those with a negative label losing interest, believing school to be a waste of time and dropping out at the earliest opportunity. One of the most frequently mentioned criticisms of education is that of too low expectations, especially amongst teachers working in difficult circumstances, perhaps in inner city schools, and themselves feeling demoralised. It is also a widely made criticism of the teaching of children from certain ethnic, religious or social backgrounds.

Teaching strategies

Many teachers with substantial teaching experience have acquired fairly fixed teaching patterns. This is not surprising when one considers the research evidence which shows that many teachers take part in as many as 1,000 or more interpersonal exchanges in a single day, asking someone a question, reprimanding a pupil, giving an explanation. Even teachers with only five years' experience may have engaged in over a million such exchanges, with many repeats of favoured teaching strategies (Jackson, 1968).

When faced with new challenges, or with children from very different backgrounds, therefore, some teachers may find it difficult to modify their predominant teaching styles and strategies. For example, if someone used to teaching clever pupils suddenly finds herself with slower learners, she may not immediately be able to choose the right vocabulary, give suitable examples or analogies, or be able to adapt to the much slower rate of learning she encounters, and both teachers and pupil may become frustrated.

Teaching children from a wide range of the ability spectrum requires all the traditional teaching skills plus new ones. Teachers need to be able to address the whole class, organise smaller and larger group activities and also to have the skill to create and monitor individual activities. If a class of 12 year olds is studying Roman civilisation in Europe there is no point in giving exactly the same assignment to a very clever pupil and a very slow one. Yet not all teachers can demonstrate the versatility needed, and this raises important questions both about re-training experienced teachers and about inducting beginners.

One of the greatest difficulties faced by trainee teachers with mixed ability classes in many countries has been the shortage of suitable text books and work schemes. In the United States, where heterogeneous classes have been the norm, many courses are conceived in the form of graded units, so that one pupil might be working on Unit 3 but a quicker pupil might have reached Unit 6. Most European teachers, in the first instance, have to use a single class textbook and create their own materials.

School subjects

There are different problems in different subjects for teachers facing a wide range of pupil abilities. Some teachers believe that learning subjects like mathematics or a foreign language is a linear process, in other words, if you have not yet mastered A you cannot proceed to B. This means that shortly after commencing study of such subjects the class may already be spreading out in such a way that the brilliant pupils are racing ahead and the rest will never catch them. Other teachers claim that all subjects, even mathematics and foreign languages, can be taught to mixed ability groups, provided the organisation of learning is properly structured.

A related subject issue is the question of stereotyping, whereby some subjects, like physics and technology, are seen as traditionally 'male'. Trainees need to look specifically at factors in school which may affect sex stereotyping, like textbooks which feature only male scientists, or classes who never have a female science teacher. A similar point will be made by the community leaders of ethnic minority groups. They will point out that there are no pictures of African or Oriental people in many European textbooks, that some schools do not understand Asian religious festivals, aspects of diet or that Asian girls may not be allowed by their parents to do dance or bare their legs for physical education lessons. In science lessons food tests may commonly deal with potatoes or meat, but less likely with rice, mangoes or other tropical or non-European foodstuffs. The contributions of non-Europeans to mathematics and science may be neglected, and the history syllabus may have little to offer pupils not from the majority culture or religion. All these are important matters for discussion, though not for easy solution, because opinion divides about whether minorities should be allowed to protect and sustain their own culture or be pressed into full integration with the home country or majority culture.

Assessment of progress

With a narrow band of pupils in any class the assessment procedures are much more straightforward than when one has to teach a wider range. A system of appraisal of progress based solely on numerical marks or ABC grades can soon demoralise those who always get low marks. Sometimes teachers seek to combine their assessment methods with a recognition of pupil effort, so that a slow learning pupil might achieve D for the actual piece of work but A for effort. This is a particular problem when pupils reach the stage where they take national or regional public examinations. If the school has been 'generous' and given high grades to slower pupils, they and their families can receive a shock when the results of the public examinations are known. If, on the other hand, the pupils' work has been strictly graded in realistic preparation for the public examination, then the lower achievers may have lost interest.

Compensatory or enrichment education

One way of justifying children of mixed ability being kept together for some of their school time is to offer some kind of enrichment or compensatory classes. Slower pupils, those with a specific learning difficulty or children who have missed school through illness, may have special remedial lessons, often in smaller groups. Gifted pupils may also be taken out for extra demanding enrichment work which goes beyond what happens in normal class time.

Both these forms of special treatment are widespread, but they are not necessarily uncontroversial. Critics would argue that, for slower children, such extraction may be embarrassing, clearly identifying to the rest those who are not so clever. Supporters contend that most pupils are quite clear who is clever and who is not and that it is only fair to try to meet the special needs of those who are not being fully satisfied in normal lessons.

Research evidence

A great deal of research has been conducted into mixed ability teaching, and the work on classroom processes is particularly relevant to teacher training. Professor Martin Roeder of the Max Planck Institut in Berlin studied how teachers cope with individual differences in the classroom. He found that only 20 out of 389 lessons observed contained any group work. He comments that a high amount of drill practice tends to keep high achievers back without much benefit to low achievers (Roeder, 1990). However, his research has not replicated the findings of some American and Swedish research which suggests that, when teaching mixed ability classes, teachers may aim at a 'target' or 'steering' group of children in the lower half of the ability range (Lundgren, 1977). A report from what used to be East Germany in 1989 of 5,000 lessons showed that 80 per cent of the ablest pupils had nothing to do for up to ten minutes per lesson (Mescheder and Steinhüfel, 1989).

In England the Teacher Education Project (Wragg, 1989) at the Universities of Exeter, Nottingham and Leicester reported in 1984 on a study of 40 comprehensive schools, most of which had mixed ability classes in the early years. Amongst problems described most frequently by teachers were those of teaching the most and least able in a mixed ability class. In 90 per cent of lessons observed, where group work was employed, each group was given the same task. Difficulties most frequently cited by teachers included the most able pupils finishing their work before others, being bored and feeling held back by slower children. They also found it difficult to cope with the poor reading ability of the lowest achievers who were not always able to read the instructions for the assignments or comprehend the textbooks and also has a short attention span and found difficulty with writing. In 1,638 classroom transactions observed the most frequent category was 'managing' which occurred in 54 per cent of cases and 'informing' which occurred 42 per cent of the time. Only 4 per cent of these were described at 'stimulating'. It was also found that teachers of mathematics and modern languages were least in favour of mixed ability groups.

Yet studies in different countries report very high amounts of whole class teaching with most pupils doing the same assignment. The Teacher Education Project mentioned above found that, when clever pupils finished their work early, they were usually given more of the same by the teacher, rather than enrichment work. If a highly able pupil finished ten mathematics problems before anyone else, then it was likely that the teacher would ask him to do another ten of the same kind, rather than move on to a higher level.

If whole class teaching cannot meet all the demands for greater participation and a better recognition of individual differences, then teachers need to know how to use group work effectively and understand the dynamics of small groups. Research has found fairly consistently that small group size can result in higher satisfaction from participants, more spoken contribution from them, and, when the group is cohesive, a high degree of commitment to it. The evidence on achievement, however, is mixed and there is no clear cut advantage for either whole class groupings or small groups (Bridges, 1979).

A great deal of attention has been given by investigators to gifted and less able pupils, and the international literature is far too large to summarise here. Definitions of 'giftedness' or 'retardation' are not internationally agreed, so different writers use different means of determination. Giftedness can also be multi-dimensional. Some children have immense natural talent and intelligence, but may not use them, so they do not necessarily score high on achievement tests. Certain pupils may be called highly able because they absorb vast amounts of information rapidly, but others may be unusual in the way they apply knowledge. Some Nobel Prize winners, for example, have enormous talent in a relatively narrow field.

There is little evidence that many schools take any particular steps to identify potentially gifted pupils. Sometimes they say they have none at all. Most experts in the field advocate the use of several sources of information, not just a single IQ or achievement test score. American research (Passow, 1985) suggests that the use of IQ scores alone can lead to a serious underestimation of giftedness. In the early 1970s the advisory panel to the United States Commissioner of Education (Marland Report, 1971) suggested three important characteristics of a curriculum for highly able children. These were a differentiated curriculum that promotes higher level intellectual activity; teaching strategies appropriate to the curriculum context and learning styles of brighter pupils; special resource rooms, classes and seminars. All these are achievable within a general mixed ability programme, though the more that separate provision is offered, the less likely classes are to be truly mixed ability. That is why many schools compromise by having more able pupils taken out for only a part of the day or the week. The question of educating the most talented in a mixed ability framework remains one of the most problematic issues.

Similarly the literature on low achieving pupils offers mixed messages. One of the hopes of mixed ability grouping was that such pupils would be helped by the more able and would also acquire a wider circle of friends, but there is no clear cut research evidence that this universally happens. One British researcher found little change in friendship pattern in mixed ability classes, with pupils still tending to choose friends of similar intelligence and social standing to themselves, a finding borne out by studies of married couples which show a high correlation between partners on intelligence and social class criteria, a process known as 'associative mating' (Ford, 1969). Evaluations of enrichment or compensatory programmes for slower learners have often suggested that these need to be sustained over a long period of time (Bell, 1970; Solity and Raybould, 1988). There is little point in taking slower pupils out of mixed ability classes for a very short programme. It seems more effective for structured help, either in a remedial class or in the mixed ability group, to be sustained over a longer period.

Since the aspiration of many educators is that mixed ability teaching should enable each child to fulfil his potential, there has been a great deal of consideration of the question of individualised instruction. This can take several forms. The teacher may create individual assignments for each pupil, though this can be immensely time consuming; use may be made of commercially produced unit or modular courses, with each pupil picking his way through the modules at his own pace; with modern technology, such as the micro-computer, the video cassette, the interactive video-disc, there may be programmes available which pupils can take at convenient times of the day, provided, of course, they are properly equipped work stations in the school where such technology is available.

Recent work at the University of Amsterdam, in Holland, has reported a good success rate for pupils working on programmes based on the notion of mastery learning, that is, following a diagnostic test, being able to study units of learning which allow children to master one concept or principle before moving on to another. He reports that 95 per cent of pupils approved of the programme and that several below average children moved up the average level on a national mathematics test.

Researchers have often concentrated on such aspects as the type of goals being prescribed in individualised instruction, the learner's level of ability, how many pupils one teacher has to deal with, what sort of equipment is available, teachers' professional competence and how broad the ability range is that they have to cover. Sometimes two or more teachers work together as a team, so that one takes responsibility for overall management and the others are able to work with individuals. This needs a great deal of organisation and professional skill to be effective. Several examples of the mastery learning approach are reported, not only in Europe, but in countries like Korea, Indonesia, Brazil, Australia and the Lebanon.

An experimental school in Indonesia uses a system of pre-testing. Before pupils begin a new topic they take a test which determines whether they start the unit immediately or do preparatory tasks to put them in a position to commence learning. Units take between two days and two weeks and involve whole class activities as well as a great deal of individual work. A test of learning at the end of the unit determines whether pupils go on to enrichment activities or do remedial work to reinforce the basic concepts (Soedijarto, 1976).

In the United States in the 1960s the Keller Plan, (Keller and Sherman, 1974) named after its originator, psychologist Fred Keller, and also known as Personalised System of Instruction, spread through hundreds of schools. It, too, was based on 'mastery learning' principles but used pupils as well as teachers to monitor other pupils' learning. Many of the evaluations of the Keller approach were favourable, but they were often conducted by supporters and enthusiasts. One meta-analysis of 75 studies of the Keller Plan showed that, in a typical Keller Plan class, the average final score was 74 per cent compared with 66 per cent in matched mixed ability classes taught in a more traditional manner (Kulik *et al.*, 1979).

More effective teacher training

Many countries in Europe now have a mature teaching force with a majority of teachers being 40 years of age or more. This carries with it both advantages and disadvantages. The major advantage is that there are many experienced teachers available to help with new developments, but the main disadvantage is that, in a busy professional career, with thousands of interpersonal exchanges every week, longer serving teachers may find it more difficult to change their teaching styles and strategies. The evidence from large-scale research studies, reports from commissions or school inspectors (HMI, 1978) as well as individual case studies (Ball, 1981), suggests that too little change may have occurred when schools switched from some form of streaming to mixed ability grouping. Many teachers merely carried on with the old-style strategies which were not necessarily appropriate to the new situation, what is sometimes called 'innovation without change'.

There are several clear implications of this both for the training of new teachers and of those already in a teaching post. However, this poses a problem for those countries which do not have a proper structure for initial and in-service training. Surveys of European provision shows a wide range of practice (Marklund, 1990). In initial training, for example, there are countries which have full-time training courses lasting up to a year for graduates and up to four or more years for undergraduates. There are other countries which have little such structure, and in some countries it is possible for graduates to teach without any training at all. Even where training is provided there are countries where it is entirely theoretical and does not involve a supervised period of practical teaching in a school. The same applies to in-service training. Surveys show that some countries have elaborate in-service provision in universities, colleges, teachers' centres, or school-based programmes, while others have little other than self-help groups of teachers who voluntarily come together for mutual support and encouragement.[1]

Teaching styles and strategies

A great deal of attention must be given to teaching styles and strategies. Teachers need to develop a variety of strategies, not solely teach the whole class as a single unit every day. Amongst the skills they need are to master the following:

- Plan and prepare effectively for a wide ability range.
- Use whole class teaching judiciously and where appropriate.
- Be able to manage small group work.
- Be able to design or administer individual assignments.
- Find ways of extending and enriching the work of more able pupils.
- Understand the difficulties of slow learners and plan accordingly.
- Recognise children's individual differences not only of ability, but also of their personality and religious, cultural and social values.
- Assess and record pupils' progress effectively, using means appropriate to their individual situation.

The development of portable television cameras is a most helpful tool for teacher trainers. First of all training videos can be made of classrooms where teachers are known to be teaching mixed ability groups successfully. It is important here for a wide variety of such home-made or commercially produced videos to be available covering many situations. Science teachers like to see science lessons and foreign language teachers want to see language lessons, so that they can identify with what they see.

Another valuable use of the portable video camera is to be able to film teachers while they are at work, and then play back for discussion what has been captured on video. Few teachers have had the opportunity to watch themselves at work. Although classes of pupils are at first self-conscious when a video camera appears in a classroom, in countries and schools where the video camera is widely used, it soon becomes an accepted feature of classroom life.

Many teachers, however, will not be able to see themselves on video, and there are numerous ways in which they can learn some of the skills of teaching mixed ability classes more effectively. What is needed for experienced teachers is a set of good quality training materials which will enable them to modify their teaching strategies. The Teacher Education Project, for example, produced workbooks[2] with such titles as 'Class Management', 'Teaching Slow Learners in Mixed Ability Classes', 'Teaching Bright Pupils in Mixed Ability Classes', 'Handling Group Work', 'Effective Questions' and 'Explanations and Explaining'. These provide a structure for pairs of teachers to work together to improve each other's teaching, or for a teacher or tutor to work with a trainee. This might involve identifying a bright pupil or a slow learner and then investigating his progress and designing appropriate work for him.

Resources for teaching and learning

One of the most frequently occurring criticisms of teachers of mixed ability classes is that they often fail to match the work to the individual child, to stimulate the more able or to find tasks which not only accommodate but extend the slower pupil. The problem here is that it is extremely difficult to match every single assignment to the level of achievement of twenty or thirty different pupils. Whenever a teacher changes over to mixed ability teaching, the amount of preparation time needed invariably increases.

Furthermore, there are often insufficient commercially produced courses which are suitable for classes of widely varying ability and this means teachers either spend hours preparing a collection of graded or individual worksheets, or they simply use the existing textbook, whether it is suitable for a broad spread of abilities or not.

One useful approach is the adoption of modular courses. A module has been defined as, 'a self-contained and independent unit of instruction with the primary focus on a few well defined objectives. The substance of a module consists of materials and instructions needed to accomplish these objectives' (Creager and Murray, 1971). Consequently modular courses consist of a series of interlocking, individual units, some versions perhaps slowly paced, others moving at a faster rate. Each unit will have a statement of purpose, a description of what the pupil should be able to do at the end of it, sometimes a diagnostic pre-test which will tell the teacher what the pupil already knows or can do, the actual materials and text needed, and sometimes a post-test which will reveal to the teacher and the pupil what has been learned. Within the modular framework it is possible to design courses which are interesting and stimulating, though badly designed modules can be dreary and uninteresting. Many users report that they were able to teach more effectively with modular courses than under the previous system, though the amount of work involved converting to that approach can be formidable. Dieter Antoni of Klagenfurt,[3] for example, reports that in an experiment with two groups of 300 pupils, after undergoing individualised instruction, fewer pupils had to repeat a year.

With the development of certain new technologies the individualisation of learning should become easier. The micro-computer has already been shown to be a most useful tool for learning, and it may be especially helpful for slower learners who have fallen behind and need enrichment work, or for clever pupils who can go on to higher level individual work. The interactive video-disc, still in its infancy, also has considerable potential because of its phenomenal storage and retrieval power, its use of moving film, still picture and screen text, and the rapidity with which we can reach any point on it. The compact disc version of interactive video-disc may be even more useful. Unfortunately neither the micro nor the interactive video-disc is widely spread in many countries, and it would be worth considering schemes such as the one in the United Kingdom, which put at least one micro-computer into every primary and secondary school in the country.

Understanding individual differences

In order to teach children of widely varied backgrounds, it is necessary first to understand them both as individuals and as members of a culture. This is especially important when the teacher himself is not a member of the social, ethnic or religious group to which the pupil belongs.

In Belgium, the Bureau Pedagogique de l'Enseignement Catholique[4] has produced materials both for teachers and pupils to help see children as individuals. Units aimed at teachers and students in the Ecoles Normales have titles such as 'Migrants' or 'Immigration, École et Société'. An assignment for a pupil in a 'questionnaire exploratoire' invites him to consider his own motivation by commenting on an imaginary pupil: 'Paul a appris sa leçon. Il e été interrogé et a obtenu 7/20. Il est découragé et se dit que la prochaine fois, il y consacrera moins de temps.'

Teacher training courses, whether for newcomers or for the experienced, need to make teachers aware of cultural differences, individual learning styles, and the fairness or unfairness of opportunities available to different pupils. It has often been shown that girls are less likely to succeed than boys in such fields as technology, science and mathematics, that children from lower social groups may have a poorer chance of success than those of equal ability from higher social classes, and that certain ethnic minorities may feel that the educational system is biased unfairly against their children. These are all illustrations of the greater sensitivity which teachers need to address if the children in their classes are to stand a chance of being treated as individuals.

Finally teachers need to reflect on why they are teaching a mixed ability class. The system may, of course, have been imposed on them, perhaps against their will. In this case their support must be elicited, for if they are hostile then the change will not work properly. If they look at the aspirations for introducing a change to mixed ability classes, and even if they have been teaching mixed ability classes for some time it is still worth considering certain basic presumptions, they may find that there is hope for better individualisation, improved discipline, a wider social range of friends for pupils, with a better understanding of each other and so on. A study by Carolyn Evertson in the United States showed a lower level of pupil co-operation in mixed ability classes. Teachers thus need to ask themselves whether these objectives are being achieved in their own classroom, for if they are not then this would be an example once more of innovation without change (Evertson *et al.*, 1981).

The 19th-century training notion of the 'normal school' and the 'normal master' are out of place in the sort of pluralist society in which many people live in the late 20th century. There is no single agreed 'norm' in teaching, especially not in teaching classes of mixed ability. Teachers need to be able to handle a wide variety of styles, to decide what makes sense with individuals or groups, to select and structure content and choose their teaching strategies wisely. If teachers are to teach mixed ability classes skilfully they must be trained to be sensitive to individual differences, to prepare interesting tasks and assignments, to use resources and modern educational technology wisely. High-quality training at both the initial and post-experience phases are, therefore, absolutely essential.

Notes

1. For example, twenty teachers in Vienna have met regularly to inform each other about education of an informal basis under the heading 'Selbstorganisation'. By contrast the United Kingdom has thousands of organised and informal in-service courses run by universities, polytechnics, colleges, teachers' centres, teacher unions and school inspectors.
2. P. Bell (1981) *Teaching Slow Learners*; E.C. Wragg (1981) *Class Management and Control*; T. Kerry (1981) *Teaching Bright Pupils in Mixed Ability Classes*; T. Kerry (1981) *Effective Questioning*; G. Brown and N. Hatton (1981) *Explanations and Explaining*; T. Kerry and M.K. Sands (1981) *Handling Classroom Groups*. All published by Macmillan, London.
3. D. Antoni, *Zentrum Für Schulversuche und Schulentwicklung*, Universitätsstrasse 70, Klagenfurt, Austria.
4. Bureau Pédagogique de l'Enseignement Catholique (1987) Rue Guimard 1, Brussels.

CHAPTER 4

Appraisal of Teachers

John Dewar Wilson

Introduction

Given contemporary social, technological and economic pressures it is not surprising that most countries want to improve the quality of teaching and learning in their education systems. Teachers would appear to have a crucial role. But what are the means to assist teachers to maximise their effectiveness? In some countries appraisal has been suggested as one potentially important tool. What does appraisal involve, how is it organised, and what is its relationship to the professional development of teachers? A further question is what kind of professional development improves the quality of children's learning?

This chapter addresses the above issues and draws upon background papers and process of a seminar organised by the Council for Cultural Cooperation of the Council of Europe, and held in Strasbourg in September 1989. It first summarises practice in thirteen European countries. Then it distinguishes between terms used almost interchangeably in country reports – evaluation, assessment and appraisal. It identifies three models of appraisal – inspection, peer review and line management. The meaning of quality in school level education is discussed in terms of system and institutional goals and quality of individual performance as a teacher. The relative strengths and weaknesses of each model for contributing to the dual goals of professional development and enhanced quality of educational functioning are considered finally.

Background

Appraisal was discussed by the Standing Conference of European Ministers of Education in Helsinki in May 1987. It was resolved that 'teachers should learn to appraise their own professional performance', and 'an important role of inspectors and school leaders ... should be to provide support and advice. Those called upon to undertake any appraisal should be specifically trained in evaluation techniques and made aware of the fact that appraisal forms an integral part of staff development work in schools. Appraisal should be both positive and constructive, and teachers should be given the opportunity, through in-service training, to improve their professional skills'. The resolution 'recognised that there is no hard and fast measure of good teaching' and that 'appraisal should not be based on narrow educational objectives alone such as academic achievement, but should take account of more general aims such as success in fostering the personal development of pupils, and in equipping them to take an active, responsible and constructive place in society'.

Interpretations of appraisal in different countries

Country reports in 1989 indicated that a number of countries had, or were evolving, systems for what is variously referred to as the evaluation or assessment or appraisal of teachers. In this section a brief account, based on the English version of the text, is provided of the different approaches then in use.

In *Belgium* education is a community responsibility. The conditions of employment of teaching staff in schools organised by the Communities are laid down by royal decree. The regulations contain an important section on teacher assessment – 'signalement'.

In *French community* public sector schools assessment of teaching is the responsibility of the Ministry of Education's school Directorate and of the Inspectorate. The latter's responsibility is to appraise (sic) and counsel all teachers, especially with a view to their in-service training, on the basis of central directives, and to evaluate (sic) the schools themselves to ensure that the curriculum is being implemented.

Grant-aided schools constitute the bulk of the system and teacher-advisers are employed by education authorities to provide teachers with guidance and counselling.

For *Flemish community* schools assessment (sic) is compulsory for all teachers on permanent contracts. Its purpose is to determine the value, aptitude, efficiency and merits of the staff member. Each has an assessment file which contains (1) reports on the work of temporary staff and probationers, (2) assessment notification slips, and (3) inspectors' reports.

Reports on temporary staff must be drawn up by the headteacher at the end of a period of temporary service. Reports may also be drawn up by the inspector after a class visit. The teacher may be assessed as giving 'total' or 'partial' satisfaction, or 'not giving satisfaction'.

Probationer teachers automatically obtain a permanent contract at the end of one or two years of probation, provided they have given satisfaction. The headteacher draws up the report at the end of the probationary period; inspectors also visit and report. Recommendations are: permanent appointment, extension of the probationary period for one year, and dismissal.

Reports on tenured teachers are drawn up at the end of each school year by the headteacher. In the absence of any changes since the previous report, the assessment is automatically extended for a further year. Teachers are assessed: unsatisfactory, good, very good, exceptional. Two successive 'unsatisfactory' assessments lead to dismissal.

After each visit the inspector draws up a report on the work of teaching staff. This document includes, firstly an analysis of the lesson observed and the teacher's professional and relational skills and, secondly, professional advice. The assessment scale is the same as for assessment notifications slips.

Assessment influences selection and promotion. Only good teachers are permitted to take part in selection and promotion tests. Finally there is an appeals procedure for teachers who disagree with their assessment.

In *Cyprus* appraisal is on-going over the teacher's career. It is a means to identify development needs and to match them with development opportunities. Every two years inspectors write reports appraising (sic) teachers on a numerical scale on four aspects: professional qualifications, efficiency, organisational and administrative abilities, and human relations, conduct and participation in out-of-school activities. Reports are based on information given by teachers about their qualifications, years of service and other activities. They also take into account a report written by the school principal, as well as teachers' personal records. The inspectors use this information to identify approaches to assist teachers to improve their work. These include: offering general guidelines on teaching and special guidelines for particular subjects; organising demonstration lessons by experienced teachers; exchanging views with teachers; organising seminars; suggesting relevant supporting teaching material; co-operating with teachers on probation.

In *Denmark* assessment (sic) occurs at entry to teaching, within training, on application for first teaching post and at the end of probation. Thereafter no formal assessment or appraisal takes place.

In *Eire* inspections of primary schools occur every four to six years. Following a meeting with staff there is classroom observation, discussions with individual teachers, and a further meeting to consider a draft report. The aim is accountability and staff development. In post-primary education evaluation (sic) is not so formal or elaborate.

In *France* schools are inspected by the national inspectorate to check that they are following instructions issued by the Ministry of Education, and to safeguard the independence of teachers (government servants) from local authorities. The inspectorate also observes individual teachers at work in the classroom, writes reports on their performance and awards numerical marks – the 'note pedagogique' – which are important for salary purposes and for progress in the career. The report is drafted for the appropriate authority, and a copy given to the teacher. In a changing context the Ministry has, in recent years, put more emphasis on the autonomy of the school, and the responsibility of its staff to set goals, and to seek through inservice training to realise them. School staff, under the leadership of the headteacher, have been encouraged to self-assess (sic) the extent to which they have fulfilled these objectives, and inspectors have played a role as external assessors. Another approach has been to undertake appraisal (sic) of the education system as a whole, using statistical methods covering nationally representative samples. This is carried out by the General Inspectorate and the Directorate of Assessment and Forward Planning; the aims are to ascertain how much influence teachers have on pupils' results, and what effect training has on teachers.

In the *Federal Republic of Germany* each Land has its own education system. In *Baden-Wurttemberg* in 1989 regulations existed for a line management appraisal system on a quinquennial basis. Teachers would be assessed on seven criteria; special subject knowledge, psychological understanding, verbal skills, knowledge of pedagogy, ability to discuss and achieve purposes, resolution, commitment and co-operation with others, and leadership. No grades would be given but teachers would receive a profile of comments, essentially on a four-point scale − weak, ordinary, better, outstanding. The process would begin with self-appraisal (sic) and would involve classroom observation (on two occasions) and discussion between teacher and appraiser. The profile would be communicated to the authorities, and might be taken into account for promotion or in handling complaints from parents. This process would also be used with teachers seeking confirmation as fully qualified staff.

The system had not been introduced, partly because of opposition from teacher unions, but partly also because teachers are civil servants and it would be necessary to introduce a similar system for all including, for example, the police. The intention was to pilot it first on administrators.

In *Iceland* there is no regular formal assessment, although committees dealing with special problems sometimes carry out formal investigations and evaluations of teachers and teaching in a particular subject or stage. Schools are expected to draw up 'school-based plans', based on National Curriculum guidelines, and these give teachers opportunities for self-evaluation (sic), as well as one criterion for appraisal. The country memorandum noted:

> Given the different circumstances teachers in different schools are faced with, it becomes very hard to find a common, fair and useful criteria to assess teachers and their work. The main policy is, therefore, to improve other factors which seem to affect the quality of teaching.

This is done nationally through providing funds for school innovations so that expert assistance may be obtained, providing resources to the Teachers Association for in-service education, innovations and professional development, developing national diagnostic tests to help teachers adjust school work to individual pupils, and evaluation of the need for production of educational materials.

In *Italy* there is no comprehensive system for assessing the productivity of teaching; nor is there a system for the appraisal of teachers that can be used to assist their cultural and professional development or to improve their teaching. A 1982 Act requires formally qualified teacher trainees to accomplish a 'year of training' by serving in an educational establishment. During this period they are monitored by a tutor and required to attend a seminar consisting of 30 hours of study and specialisation; they then have to present a report to the school's appraisal (sic) committee on their teaching work and their activity in the seminar. This committee consists of corporately elected teachers, two or four in number, depending on the size of the school, and is chaired by the director.

Subsequently, in the course of their professional careers, teachers cease to be subject to the judgements of the committee. They are simply obliged to carry out their duties like any other state employee. There is therefore only one form of disciplinary appraisal, applicable when a teacher breaks the law. While there is an inspectorate of 600 persons, it does not evaluate the educational system as a whole in any organised and consistent manner. In order to examine particular aspects and features of education, the Ministry of Education may enlist the services of private organisations.

Where teachers' in-service training is concerned, numerous activities are conducted by the staff of the Ministry and the 'Provveditorati agli Studi' (provincial level) and by the regional institutes of educational research, experimentation and retraining (IRRSAE). There are also two national schemes, one concerning training in information technology for teachers in higher education, and the other for the requalification of primary school teachers. However, there is no common appraisal (sic) scheme for these activities.

In *Malta,* where the 'odious' term 'inspector' has been replaced by the more acceptable 'education officer', a line management appraisal model exists. Its objectives are to help teachers to define their particular needs, individually and as a group, and to improve their practice. Appraisal helps ensure that in-service training and development matches needs of individual teachers and their schools, thus improving educational quality by making the system more responsive. By assisting the process of staff development appraisal reinforces the professional independence of individual teachers and their responsibility in the classroom. There is continuous dialogue between appraiser (head of school in consultation with the subject education officer) and appraisee (the teacher) prior to the assessment, with outcomes recorded on a Performance Rating Sheet. In cases of disagreement, a cooling-off period of one month is stipulated.

The teacher is appraised on: (I) Performance of Duties, (II) Personality and Character and (III) Discipline.

Performance of Duties includes knowledge of section and department, quality of work (accuracy, neatness and presentation), output, dependability to perform work without supervision and to meet deadlines, method (approach to work), oral and written expression, mental alertness (quickness of comprehension), and resourcefulness and judgement (ability to overcome difficulties, to plan with ingenuity and drive, and to present new ideas). Personality and Character includes personal attributes such as general appearance, attitude towards the public, relations with colleagues, leadership i.e. organising ability, delegation of duties, control of staff, supportivenes of staff and tact. Discipline includes respect for authority and adherence to regulations.

Each aspect is rated A (very good), B (good), C (satisfactory), D (not satisfactory). The final report is sent to the Assistant Director of Education of the Section for Endorsement. Another part of the appraisal form consists of a declaration by the teacher that the report has been discussed with him and that (a) s/he agrees or (b) disagrees with specific ratings for stated reasons. In case of disagreement a request may be made for the case to be considered by a Reviewing Panel. The Staff Association may then be involved. The last part consists of Remarks by the Reviewing Panel.

In *Netherlands* individual school boards formulate personnel policy including appraisal. Much interest has been expressed but little is known of what has been implemented.

In *Norway* teachers are evaluated (sic) formally in terms of their competence as teachers only in the stage of initial training, or in the first two years of service. The evaluation is made by those who train and certify. Thereafter, it is assumed that they are professionals who can take responsibility for their own continuing development. No one − not even the headteacher − has the formal right to inspect and evaluate the performance of any fully qualified teacher. Teachers' unions do not accept any specific appraisal policy for teachers. The aim of government has been to encourage schools and teachers to accept responsibility for the quality of their own performance, to self-evaluate the extent to which they are fulfilling objectives of National Curriculum guidelines in relation to local needs and conditions, and to develop the professional quality of their work. As part of this emphasis on organisational development teachers are encouraged to collaborate with peers and to open their teaching to others for appraisal. School authorities have also been given considerable budgetary freedom within a context in which national government is concerned to establish how far standards in schools are being maintained and where development needs to be promoted.

Various competence programmes have been introduced. At the local level, school-based evaluation projects have been initiated by schools themselves, or in collaboration with local advisory bodies and personnel; at the regional level training programmes for advisory personnel in school-based evaluation have been initiated by regional school authorities alone or in collaboration with teacher training institutions. Many of the school-based evaluation projects emphasise experimental learning and a collaborative innovation strategy. Appraisal of teaching and social relations in schools will often be an integrated part of these projects which are stimulated by a democratic philosophy of school evaluation. These projects serve

74

the professional development of teachers rather than managerial control.

The Ministry of Education initiated a project on national evaluation and quality in education in which appraisal is a major interest. The aim is to try to combine such assessment with a systematic programme for in-service training of teachers. Looking at appraisal in terms of Figure 4.1 below, the emphasis in Norway is on internal (school-based) self-appraisal for professional development, although with the assistance of certain external guidance and teacher centres. Any radical move towards external assessment for performance measurement would be resisted.

Figure 4.1 The Norwegian conception of appraisal

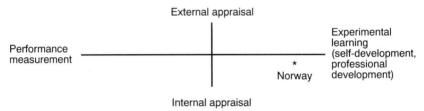

In *Portugal* formal assessment occurs only within initial and in-service training, based on co-operation and dialogue between all concerned.

In *Switzerland* responsibility for education lies with 26 cantons and there are 15 different education systems. Assessment occurs at the beginning and end of teacher training. Some cantons have an induction system. There is little assessment during teachers' careers; cantons co-operate in the evaluation of school systems, rather than of teachers.

In *England and Wales* teachers are formally assessed over initial training and during probation, but not subsequently. Schools as institutions are evaluated through inspection by Her Majesty's Inspectorate, but the published reports of inspections do not mention teachers by name or make comments on the performance of individuals. Government in England funded an initial feasibility study on appraisal in one local education authority in 1985–86.

In 1987 extensive piloting was undertaken based on principles set out in a report of the Appraisal Training Working Group of the Advisory Conciliation and Arbitration Service (ACAS, 1986). In April 1989, centrally funded pilot work on staff appraisal in further education was also initiated.

In the English model appraisal is viewed

> not as a series of perfunctory periodic events but as a continuous and systematic process intended to help individual teachers with their professional development and career planning, and to help ensure that the inservice training and deployment of teachers matches the complementary needs of individual teachers and schools. (ACAS, 1986)

The appraisal system piloted is in Figure 4.2. Two parties are involved: a representative of school management (appraiser), and the individual who is being appraised (appraisee). In primary schools the appraiser would

Figure 4.2 Phases of compulsory (formal) appraisal for England preparation, review and follow up in current job

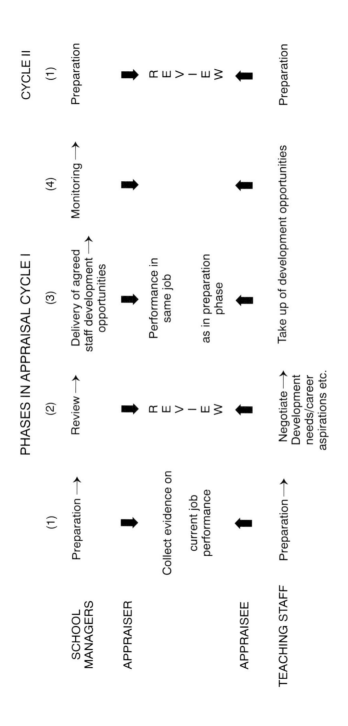

normally be the headteacher, in secondary the head of department or a member of the management team. The process is cyclical. In phase 1 of a cycle both parties prepare. Preparation includes the appraiser observing the appraisee's performance as a teacher in the classroom. Phase 2 is the review, where an interview allows both parties to explore the evidence, review satisfaction/dissatisfaction with current role performance, negotiate the appraisee's development needs in relation to quality of current job performance and longer-term career aspirations, and agree to plan for development. Phase 3 is the provision by school management, and take-up by the appraisee, of these development opportunities. Phase 4 is monitoring, informally, by the appraiser, of the appraisee's response to development opportunities. Responsiveness is part of the evidence taken into account in the second appraisal cycle. Both parties receive training for appraisal; promoted staff are usually both appraisers and appraisees.

Government has powers to require the 400,000 teachers employed in around 25,000 locally maintained schools to be appraised. It has encouraged voluntary implementation of appraisal rather than making it mandatory and a system is operating in a considerable number of areas.

In *Scotland*, which has its own educational system, and where trainee teachers and probationers are formally assessed, piloting of appraisal, also on an internal school-based line-management model, was undertaken on a voluntary basis in 1988/89. A consultation paper was issued by government in February 1989. National guidelines were issued in 1990. Education authorities have drawn up local schemes of staff development and appraisal for approval by government. The appraisal process includes job descriptions, interviews between teacher and appraiser, the evaluation of classroom performance, the production of written reports, and an attempt to meet identified needs through in-service training and other means to staff development.

One of the envisaged outcomes of the appraisal process in the United Kingdom is the provision of better founded reports for those assessing candidates for promotion.

In some federal units of former *Yugoslavia* teachers were formally examined at the end of a two-year induction period. This examination consists of observation and analysis of a model lesson, connected to an examination on teaching methods of the subject in question and on school legislation. Fully qualified teachers could be 'inspected' by external 'school counselling' bodies, but the terminology indicates the changing conception (and debate) about the role of external agencies. Within schools directors were expected to supervise teachers (including observing them teach) and to promote their development through counselling and offering in-service training opportunities. At the time of the break up of the Federation, training for the elected (non-permanent) post of school director was just being introduced.

Views of teachers' representatives

Country reports reflect central government perspectives. The views of teacher associations are also important.

The World Confederation of Organisations of the Teaching Profession (WCOTP, 1988) saw evaluation of teaching

> as a means to allow teachers, individually and as a group, to define their particular needs in terms of staff development and practical experience, and to reinforce the professional independence of individual teachers and their responsibility in the classroom.

It rejected the notion of using evaluation evidence for purposes of 'merit pay', or to encourage competition between teachers.

The report argued for teachers in schools engaging in 'collective appraisal of the effectiveness of the educational programmes and the methods and materials in use and in the analysis of the problems encountered', but stipulated that this should not be at the expense of more traditional forms of evaluation, and that additional funds should be made available by education authorities for the purpose of collective appraisal. Quality pre-service training was required to equip teachers to exploit resources, to self-evaluate, and to interpret and act on the results with a view to promoting their own professional development.

At the 1989 seminar the spokesperson for the International Federation of Secondary Teachers (FIPESO) reported that the organisation was not opposed to teachers' accountability to society. Teachers' organisations understood appraisal in terms of professional development designed to produce more progress and satisfaction for teachers in their jobs. But employers, whatever their endorsement of this objective, would naturally tend to use appraisal as a method of control.

Terminology

Evaluation, assessment and appraisal are terms used almost interchangeably in the above reports. Clarifying the different meanings attached to each is not easy because the terms are not always conceptually distinct, and even experts in English-speaking education systems may use them interchangeably.

Evaluation is the umbrella term. It refers to the process of designing and implementing approaches for collecting and interpreting evidence on the quality of educational institutions, programmes and the mechanism which sustain them. Thus inspection of a school is an example of an evaluation. Some writers, especially in USA (e.g. Millman and Darling-Hammond, 1990), also use the term to describe the quality of functioning of individual(s) in the full range of roles played within an organisation, but that use is confusing in the opinion of the present writer. Evaluation evidence contributes to judging the effectiveness and value of educational organisations and the means to improve them. Evaluation may be undertaken by external agents (such as inspectors) or by internal agents (such as school managers or a group of teachers) or by a combination of both. It is, of course, common to read of teachers being urged to self-evaluate their own work; invariably this means collecting evidence of the effects of their work with pupils in the classroom.

Assessment is a component of evaluation. It refers to the process of collecting evidence of the performance of an individual in a specific role, or on a specific task, by using one or more techniques and coming to a judgement about the meaning of that evidence. The assessment process may be informal or formal; it may be done by others, or by the individual on his own, or it may be done by both parties co-operatively. Formal assessment is undertaken for a specific purpose, such as granting tenure at the end of the probationary stage of entry to teaching, and is deliberate. Informal assessment is on-going and casual.

All teachers and prospective teachers are formally and individually assessed at some point in their teaching career. The most common points are:

- selection for initial teacher training;
- credentialling at the end of teacher training;
- selection for first or subsequent teaching post;
- credentialling for tenure/full membership of the profession.

Assessment also occurs where a teacher seeks a promoted post, or where complaints about professional conduct lead to questions about dismissal.

In addition, in some systems, such as France and Eire, teachers are formally assessed on their classroom performance from time to time, by inspectors or headteachers who issue reports on the quality of their work.

Figure 4.3 sets out these assessment points in terms of the stages in a teacher's career and related research issues.

Teachers may justifiably be assessed by management at these points. They are situations in which the individual has offered himself for specific role (i.e. trainee point B), member of staff (D), or member of promoted staff (F); or a decision is required on the individual's suitability for membership of the profession and/or entry to the next stage of the career process (credentialling at the end of training (C) or granting of tenure (E).

Formal assessment of applicants for entry to teacher training, of student development, of the system for establishing suitability for tenure, and for promotion have all been much criticised over a long period. WCOTP (1989) found no common systematic procedure for handling promotion. Studies in UK (Wilson *et al.*, 1985; Morgan *et al.*, 1983) indicate that those managing formal assessment often rely on implicit criteria which may be partial, undeveloped and undefined. In addition, the evidence collected may not relate to the criteria and the process of decision-making is often haphazard and partial. Consequently many formal assessment procedures do not pass standards of professional scrutiny.

Formal assessment tends to be most formative or development oriented within initial training, or immediately after, when tenure is sought. Those who are perceived to be not ready for tenure may have their probation extended. Development activities may be prescribed for them, and for tenured teachers whose competence is in question. Bridges (1987) has shown that 'weak' teachers often do not respond to the help offered.

Appraisal, as the term is understood in English-speaking countries, is

Figure 4.3. Points in the career at which teachers may be formally assessed

Stage Research Issues for Teacher Assessment

A — Image of teaching and recruitment
B — Process of selection into training
C — Student development in training
D — Process of selection into teaching
E — Development in probation
F — Assessment for promotion
G — Appraisal

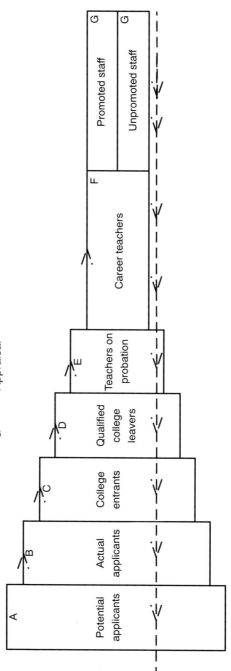

> Predictive aspects of teacher assessment
< Evaluative evidence on teacher assessment

formal assessment of the on-going work of an individual. It is practised in commercial, industrial and public service organisations (Long, 1986). Different models exist but typically it is conducted 'in-house' on an annual basis, by line-managers, and involves staff at all levels. Performance of tenured staff in the current role is reviewed, over the period since the previous appraisal. The aim is to identify, in a changing work context, individual goals for the year ahead, and to review career options within the organisation. Appraisal systems reflect the philosophy of the organisation. They are more central to managerial and quality improvement process in some organisations than in others. Training in appraisal, for both appraiser and appraisee may be provided. Policies differ, too, on use of appraisal to determine merit pay, promotion and dismissal.

Models of appraisal

In the light of the above appraisal of teachers may now be defined as the process of systematic review of quality of current role performance of a tenured (i.e. presumed competent) staff member, in the context of personal and system development needs. On this definition three models of appraisal would appear to exist in Europe at the present time viz: inspectorial, peer review and line management.

The inspectorial model involves an official, of experience, and presumed competence, appointed by a central agency, having the right to observe a teacher at work, grade his performance, and offer advice for development. The model permits 'checking up' − perhaps once every four years or less often − on whether the teacher is carrying out directives set nationally, or teaching 'competently'. The teacher is viewed primarily as a deliverer of central curriculum policy. Although inspection of individuals is usually set in the context of whole-school inspection the emphasis is on the individual working with other independent professionals.

In the peer review model appraisal is voluntary and undertaken on an internal, informal basis. Staff as a collegial team accept their collective professional accountability for meeting expectations defined variously by central government, local school managers and the community, and reinterpret these in such a way as to provide quality learning experiences for students. In the process of realisation of these plans there is opportunity for each individual, in planning, delivering and assessing the programme, to offer his practice for observation, analysis and constructive criticism by others in the team. The development and implementation process may be aided by external consultants as part of innovation, but its direction and outcomes lie in the hands of staff themselves.

In the line management model appraisal is a tool of management − nationally, locally and at institutional level. It is conducted by staff according to centrally determined guidelines, which may be modified for local needs. It is hierarchical and compulsory. It focuses on current practice and aims to identify the development needs of the individual, balance these with organisational needs and match them to available opportunities.

Criteria of quality

Any of the models of appraisal described above may contribute to professional development of teachers, but professional development is an appropriate goal only if it results in improved teaching and learning. Accordingly it is necessary to define quality and to consider the contribution of appraisal to its enhancement.

Laderriere (1990) suggested that in the 1970s there was international consensus on the profile of qualities and tasks expected of teachers. Teachers were expected to pay greater attention to the individual child's overall development; to identify pupils' needs and learning problems; to dialogue with pupils to improve their knowledge, counsel them, and present the learning plan clearly; set, analyse and review curriculum goals, develop and adapt curricula and teaching methods in the context of 'action research'; assess results achieved; co-operate closely with school staff (e.g. team teaching), with parents and the community; take part in training activities, and contribute to planning and management of the school/system on the basis of their experience. Although it remained valid this profile had not yet been generally implemented.

One explanation could be teachers' own perceptions of their development needs. Observation in classrooms in USA led Goodlad (1984) to criticise schools for weak pedagogy and curriculum. But neither teachers, parents nor the students themselves suggested that teaching was to blame. 'All three groups tend to view the misbehaviour of the young as pervasive, existing as a condition apart from efforts, including teachers', to control it' (p. 74). Few teachers saw themselves as 'not adequately prepared' to teach and most agreed with the statement that 'most of the teachers in this school are doing a good job'.

In a study of Scottish secondary teachers' attitudes to and involvement in professional development Cumming *et al.* (1988) contrasted 'self-starters' – teachers keen to exploit the local 'structure of development opportunities' and willing to trial new approaches to practice – with 'reluctant starters', who took the view that their teaching could only be 'better' if they had more resources, time and motivated pupils. Cumming argues that management's job is to contrive conditions which cause 'reluctant starters' to see again problems or dilemmas of teaching. Conventional in-service training – often of poor quality – does not influence their attitudes and behaviour, and the authoritarian stance of some management may inhibit frank discussion of development needs. Cumming draws attention to models of promoting development through coaching (Joyce and Showers, 1988) and consultancy, which can result in collegial support for development.

School context and management have been shown to play a critical factor in the effectiveness of schools (Hopkins, 1987). Elsewhere (Wilson, 1988) it has been argued that the quality of the individual teacher's work reflects two factors: the match between qualifications, training and the demands of the job, including support at school level, and 'personal capacity' to realise and display the skills, bending and flexing to particular pupils at a specific time. Individual teacher quality reflects the teacher's capacity to plan, deliver, and reflectively evaluate the optimum programme for the individual learner.

Models of appraisal, teachers' professional development and quality of teaching and learning

The different appraisal models reflect different conceptions of how to promote professional development in teachers. In this section the strengths and weaknesses of each are considered, and the extent to which they promote qualitative improvement in schools.

As a means to professional development the inspectorial model suffers obvious disadvantages through being externally imposed, denying teachers' status as professionals, underlining the isolation of the teacher in a team of individuals, and interposing between school management and staff. Logistically, too, it is difficult to expect follow-through and impact when inspections occur years apart. While external consultants can play an important role in professional development the conditions for their success are that they have been invited in, are not perceived as a threat, and have highly developed consultative skills which are deployed in intensive, sustained interactions (Dalin and Rust, 1983). Inspectors do not satisfy the first two of these conditions, and cannot meet the last. In some countries they are being retrained as consultants. Inspectors can of course be an influence for good in terms of both individual development, through sponsorship of able, ambitious professionals, and system development. It is of interest that in some systems, such as in England, the number of inspectors has been reduced drastically in recent years as employing authorities and schools have gained more responsibility for monitoring and promoting teacher development.

Peer review makes teachers as a group in each school continuously responsible for quality. It assumes that teachers will exercise this autonomy responsibly and set themselves exacting and continually higher professional standards. The 'reluctant starter' is the responsibility of colleagues. The model assumes that teachers are sensitive to the representations of different interest groups, can develop mechanisms to filter these, and have the professional skills to develop practice, or are willing to bring in outsiders to assist them. It leaves open the door for complaints from teachers about the quality of their professional training to equip them for these roles, and the level of resourcing of schools, though such concerns are not unique to this model. It leaves unanswered the means by which the community will be satisfied with the standards reached in a particular school, or at national level how standards across the system as a whole are to be defined and monitored. Evidence from the effective school literature indicates what can be achieved when a team of staff, with appropriate external support, are motivated to achieve; the challenge of the peer review model is to demonstrate that all schools could achieve this.

The line management model aroused opposition in England and Wales when first proposed because it was associated with 'weeding out' incompetent teachers. The model can be construed as individualistic, hierarchical and bureaucratic in that line managers appraise individual staff members to a pattern largely laid down from above, but these features may be less obtrusive when the system applies to all staff — including headteachers. It is, however, undeniably episodic in frequency, and expensive of time spent training participants, undertaking the process, and providing meaningful staff development opportunities. Evaluation of piloting has demonstrated returns, however (Bradley, 1989). These include increased reflection, better morale, better in-service education and training opportunities, and more thoughtful career development. Implementation has developed relationships and practice within the school. Specific improvements to teaching include liaison with other teachers over pupils and work schemes, classroom organisation and management of pupils, use of materials, resources and displays, and use of alternative teaching strategies and approaches. Four in five of those surveyed claimed that appraisal had helped them develop their skills, and three in four that it had assisted them significantly to improve pupil performance. The evaluators raise the question of whether such effects could be maintained when appraisal was institutionalised. The factors identified with successful implementation — an open school climate, suitable training, commitment by the headteacher, clear understanding about responsibilities, a well-presented and well-managed process, and a deliberate implementation strategy — might apply to any model of appraisal, or indeed reduce the need for appraisal at all. The system has less impact where there is no confidence in the appraiser, targets are vague, the process is too 'cosy' or the system is poorly managed.

Other means to promote teachers' professional development

Other means to teachers' professional development and school quality exist besides appraisal. These include thoughtful recruitment and selection policies; radically different pre-service training (borrowing from experience in industry, the armed forces etc); developed personnel policies for promoting and retraining teachers, inducting them into new roles, and managing their careers on a 'whole profession' rather than an 'individual school' basis; enabling schools to compile descriptions of their effectiveness on the basis of the views of all the interested parties, and developing partnership between constituencies within education, and especially teacher unions so that the profession accepts responsibility for the quality of its members and the service they provide.

Conclusion

The underlying purpose of appraisal is to improve the quality of education by encouraging individual insight into the effectiveness of job performance. It should result in the positive reinforcement of teachers' professional status and image. What emerges is that a wide variety of policies, practices and perceptions on appraisal exist in Europe. Some countries accept compulsory, systematic appraisal of teaching performance, including classroom observation, while others prefer other ways to improve quality.

Perhaps it is reasonable to conclude, as did the Seminar, that the criteria by which teaching quality should be judged should be fairly broadly determined above the level of the school (i.e. at central or regional level) but very specifically defined at school level by school staff, education officers, inspectors and others associated with the school. Personal capacity, school context and institutional management are factors which determine quality of individual performance in relation to the defined objectives. Individual teachers are ultimately the agents of the quality of learning experiences in their own classrooms. Whatever the means to assist them continuously to reflect on and develop their practice the criteria and principles underlying the process should be clearly understood by appraisers and appraisees alike.

CHAPTER 5

Teacher Induction: The Great Omission in Education

J.H.C. Vonk

Introduction

The large majority of new teachers experience their first year of service as problematic and stressful. They do not feel sufficiently prepared for their job as teachers, and their transition from initial training to the profession often resembles an on-going confrontation with problems they did not expect and cannot solve due to a lack of adequate training.[1] Many beginners experience the induction period as a 'praxis shock'.

In nearly all European countries, the systematic induction of teachers into the profession has been a neglected area in education and teacher training, despite the massive numbers of beginning teachers that have left the profession within their first three years of service.[2] In some European countries, such as the United Kingdom, the concern for induction has waxed and waned. In the 1960s and early 1970s, for example, there were a number of policy initiatives with respect to teacher induction, some of which have generated research and improved (in-service) training practice. Related to that, the major reviews that covered induction were published in the late 1970s (Bolam *et al.*, 1977; Tisher, 1980; Veenman, 1984). In the late 1970s and early 1980s, however, because of the continuing fall in pupil numbers, and, as a consequence, the increasing oversupply of teachers at all levels during the last decade, teacher induction became of minor interest. Bolam (1987, p. 746) reports that there is not much evidence of deep concern with respect to teacher induction in most (European) countries. In spite of the fact that the professional rhetoric in the UK and other countries of the EU has been reasonably consistent, government action has not.[3] That rhetoric can be found if we follow the deliberations of the *Standing Conference of Ministers of Education in Europe Helsinki, 1986* (Council of Europe, 1987c) on improving the status and the quality of the teaching profession. It was expected that teacher induction would gain renewed attention in a number of countries in Europe, but no major initiatives have been undertaken since the early 1980s, either on the political level or on the research level. Another example of that rhetoric is offered by the Final Report of the EC conference *The Teaching Profession in Europe* (October, 1991), in which neither the concept 'induction' nor any related actions are mentioned, and in which teacher professional development is approached from a purely bureaucratic-managerial point of view.

Not only policy makers are to blame for the lack of interest in teacher induction. If we take a closer look at the efforts of the profession with respect to the induction of new colleagues, we have to establish that, apart from a limited number of exceptions,[4] in most schools systematic and well-thought-out induction programmes are almost non-existent. During induction most beginners (with some exceptions) experience that they are left to fend for themselves. They rarely find support or help from colleagues (mentors) or from the school management, and if they find support, it is mostly inadequate and of little help. This is the more true because most teachers spend the major part of their time isolated from their peers, and, as a consequence, beginning teachers do not receive, as is natural in other professions, on-going direction and assistance from more experienced colleagues (Huling-Austin, 1990). Besides, from the first day, beginners have exactly the same responsibility as their colleagues with many years of experience and students, parents, colleagues and management often expect them to act accordingly. Many beginners fail to meet these expectations, and the drop-out during the first three years of service can sometimes reach up to 60 per cent (Ooms, 1991). Conclusively, we establish that currently induction is still no part of the culture in most schools.

Over the last few years, however, there has been growing attention towards the improvement of the quality of teaching. Related to that, also the improvement of the quality of school management and staff development has come into focus, and in that context the induction of beginning teachers tends to become an issue of concern once more. Approaches will, however, differ from those used in the past. Times have changed − we live in the post-modern era[5] − and nowadays the belief in the existence of a set of standardised effective teaching behaviours is over. The same is true for the central role of supervisors who had the responsibility of keeping up the desired teaching standards in the schools through strategies such as clinical supervision and the like. Teacher development has become oriented more towards the development of the individual teacher in a given school environment (Christensen and McDonnell, 1993). In this context school management not only has to perform administrative leadership, but also 'educational leadership' (Glatthorn, 1990), the latter being a condition for good management of a school organisation. These leadership modalities promote the enhancement of the quality of the individual teacher's performance as well as that of the school organisation as a whole. Effective educational leadership will be crucial for the development of more autonomous high-quality schools. However, we do not see the responsibility for this leadership function restricted primarily to the position of school leaders but as a function of the school as a whole (Glickman, 1990). If we consider teachers as autonomous self-directing professionals (Vonk, 1992a, p. 47), everybody in the school organisation can be challenged to take responsibility for it. The school management's major task is to facilitate and monitor proper execution of this function. In this context, effective induction of teachers in a certain school depends heavily on the extent to which the educational leadership function is implemented in that particular school. Because beginning teachers are most in need of direct and personal assistance, the existence of a mentor system is crucial in this context.

The aim of this contribution is to highlight the basics of an induction programme − i.e., the development of a support system for beginning teachers aimed at their professional development − which is based on the principle of the mentor-protegée relationship. We see this type of programmes as a vital part of effective educational leadership and staff development in schools. Essential for the realisation of such programmes is the training of mentors. As a consequence, we focus on the various elements of that training in this contribution, and pay attention to the characteristics of the professional development of beginning teachers in more detail. Although, in our opinion, teacher induction covers the first five years of teaching, we will restrict ourselves to the induction during the first year of teaching. The following issues will be highlighted in this chapter.

- The concept of teacher induction.
- The concept of mentoring.
- The mentor's knowledge base.
- The mentor's interpersonal skills base.
- The mentor's technical skills base.

This contribution is mainly based on the author's research since 1980 into the professional development of beginning teachers during their first five years of service (Vonk, 1982, 1984a, 1989a; Vonk and Schras, 1987) and on the expertise (based on a developmental research approach) he gained from a large number of in-service courses for beginning teachers (Vonk, 1989b). The second source is his theoretical and practical expertise gained from the training of mentors of beginning teachers, i.e. senior teachers who are responsible for mentoring their beginning colleagues (Vonk, 1992b).

Teacher induction, the concept

We define *teacher induction* as the transition from student-teacher to self-directing professional. The process of becoming a teacher is developmental in nature and teacher induction can best be understood as part of the continuum of the process of teacher professional development (Letvin, 1992) which can be described as follows.

If we look upon teachers' careers as a coherent whole, from initial education and training to retirement, it will be obvious that throughout their careers, based on their personal life experiences and their formal and informal professional experiences, a continuous and coherent set of changes is taking place in their ideas about the profession and in their professional way of thinking and acting. These changes are both qualitative and quantitative in nature.

Figure 5.1 Continuum of the process of teacher professional development

Initial training → induction → self-directed professional development

Although the term development connotes internally guided rather than externally imposed changes, professional development is considered to be the result of a learning process which is directed at acquiring *a coherent whole of the knowledge, insights, attitudes and repertoire that a teacher needs for the everyday practising of the profession* – often indicated as the teacher's professional knowledge base (Vonk, 1991a). In essence, teacher development is self-directed development; i.e., teachers have to develop their own individual style of teaching.

In a number of studies (Burke, 1987; Levine, 1989; Vonk, 1989a; Burden, 1990; Fessler and Christensen, 1992; Huberman, 1992) the different phases in teacher professional development have been investigated. We distinguish the following phases in a teacher's career.

- the *pre-professional phase*,[6] the period of initial education and training, aimed at developing teachers' starting competencies;
- the *threshold phase*, the first year of teaching, aimed at helping novices to survive under the new conditions and to start developing a professional identity and an appropriate repertoire of actions;[7]
- the *phase of growing into the profession*, generally the period between the second and seventh year of service, is aimed at helping teachers to expand their knowledge base and repertoire of actions;
- the first *professional phase*;
- the *phase of reorientation towards oneself and the profession*, sometimes indicated as the mid-career crisis;
- the *second professional phase*;
- the *phase of winding down*, the period before retirement.

Induction concerns the first two phases in the process of teacher professional development after initial training: the *threshold phase* and the *phase of growing into the profession* (Vonk, 1991a, p. 65). The importance of teacher induction both for beginners and schools is that it contributes to avoiding unnecessary tension and (future) malfunctioning. A good start definitely influences a teacher's abilities and willingness to change in a positive way. Our own research[8] indicates that teachers who have been left to fend for themselves in their first year of teaching generally develop a strongly survival oriented repertoire of actions, sometimes indicated as 'survival kit'. This type of repertoire results from a 'trial and error' approach and from pressure brought on by circumstances. Because of time constraints beginners hardly find time for reflection and if they do, they lack a solid *orientation base*:[9] they do not know what to reflect on (McIntyre, 1993). As a consequence, such a repertoire offers very few points of contact for expansion and further development. Changes in that repertoire demand great effort on the part of those teachers because these changes could lead to a loss of control over their classes and therefore result in renewed unrest amongst students or in class control problems. This is something that they definitely wish to avoid. Adequate mentoring, however, can help teachers to develop an open-minded attitude to change and will result in a more flexible repertoire of actions.

The concept of mentoring

The last two years, under growing pressure to develop more school-based initial teacher education programmes, a number of books on mentoring have appeared in the UK and the USA (e.g. Wilkin, 1992; DeBolt, 1992; McIntyre *et al.*, 1993; Caldwell and Carter, 1993). Most of these books are collections of papers in which different concepts of mentoring are presented. Most of these concepts consider mentoring as a method for transferring practical knowledge to the teacher trainees. We, however, define mentoring as 'a dynamic, reciprocal relationship in a work environment between an advanced career incumbent (mentor) and a beginner (protegée) aimed at promoting the career development of both' (Healy and Welchert, 1990). Beginning teachers' interest in the relationship is the help they receive from an expert in acquiring a professional identity and their development from novice to self-developing professional. Mentors' interest in this relationship is that, in order to be able to help beginning teachers effectively, they have to reflect continuously on their own repertoire of actions. The latter nearly always results in improvement of that repertoire. Apart from that, in particular for older teachers, the mentoring relationship means practising 'generativety'.[10] Essential in this definition, however, is the reciprocity. The mentoring relationship contributes to the professional development of both participants, i.e. it promotes the quality of their professional practice.

Apart from being a qualified teacher with excellent classroom management skills, an expert in the subject he teaches and in the subject methodology concerned, a good mentor has to have the following personal qualities: open-mindedness, reflectiveness, flexibility, listening skills, empathy, creativity and a helping attitude. Those responsible for mentoring beginning teachers must meet a number of prerequisites.

The first is a *knowledge base*. Mentors need to understand the nature of the process of professional development of beginning teachers, the nature of problems beginners experience and what the cause of those problems are, and finally, they have to have insight into the essentials of the teacher's professional learning process. The second is an *interpersonal skills base*. Mentors must master a wide range of interpersonal behaviours and know how these behaviours affect their protegées, and what type of behaviour is appropriate in what situation. Third, mentors must master a wide range of *technical skills*: counselling, observing, providing feedback, providing instruction, evaluating.

It will be clear that mentors have to be carefully selected: not all teachers meet the prerequisites mentioned above or have the abilities to develop them. After selection they will still need substantial training to be able to act effectively as a mentor. In the following section attention will be paid to the description of the content of the mentor's knowledge base in more detail, since that description automatically includes an analysis of the problems of beginners.

Mentors' knowledge base

A mentor's knowledge base includes three elements. First, knowledge of and insight into the process of teacher professional development in general, and into that of beginning teachers in particular. Second, knowledge of and insight into the nature of the problems beginning teachers experience, into the ways these problems may arise and evolve over time, and into strategies to help beginners to cope with these problems. Third, an important mentor task is to help protegées to develop their own practical theory – the integration of (academic) theory and experiences, therefore, they need insight into the process of learning from experiences.

The professional development of (beginning) teachers

Teacher professional development is not a simple, spontaneous process, but the outcome of a complex interaction between individual teachers and the various environments in which they are participating (Lacey, 1977; Vonk, 1984b; Zeichner and Gore, 1990; Hargreaves, 1992). The nature of a (beginning) teacher's professional development is a function of the interaction between person-related[11] and environmental[12] factors. This process, which cannot be envisaged separate from its environmental context, has the following characteristics.

- Professional learning is based on continuous reflection on one's everyday experiences in a certain context. The frame of reference for that reflection consists of one's practical and theoretical knowledge (Calderhead, 1988; McIntyre, 1993).

- Professional learning is a lifelong process. Teachers are continuously confronted with new situations and challenges that give opportunities to learn (Burke, 1987; Fessler and Christensen, 1992).
- Professional learning does not take place in isolation but in the context of a particular school. Consequently, the individual teacher's professional development and staff development are inextricably linked. This means that teacher development also depends on the extent to which educational leadership functions are performed in the school (Fullan, 1991, p. 315).

Teachers are often considered to be reflective practitioners (Schön, 1983, 1987), and their professional learning is mainly triggered by a confrontation with new phenomena, with dissatisfaction in their current practice or with an experience of cognitive dissonance. Related to changes in a teachers repertoire or in the curriculum, Burke (1987) describes three subsequent stages in a teacher's learning process: the orientation stage, the reorganisation stage and the integration stage.

> *The orientation stage*: In this stage teachers are confronted with change and both the necessity of that change and the impact thereof on teachers' every day acting in the classroom is discussed. Based on the outcome of this discussion, teachers take a decision whether to cope or not. This stage is mainly concerned with preparing teachers for the intended change.
> *The reorganization stage*: If teachers are prepared to adapt to the change, they have to gain new knowledge and repertoire or to develop a new perspective on their already existing knowledge end repertoire. This stage is mainly concerned with learning and instruction (INSET).
> *The integration stage*: In this stage of the learning process the newly acquired knowledge and skills have to be integrated into every day classroom practice. This stage is mainly concerned with mentoring, peer-coaching and the like.

For mentors it is important to know what sort of questions and problems of beginners they will encounter when mentoring novices. Every experienced teacher will say: 'I know!' Research shows, however, that the mind works selectively, and in particular when one's experiences as a beginner are concerned. In general, only particular events or a general feeling of (dis)satisfaction or stress are remembered. This is obvious because once a beginner has tackled a certain problem it is no longer regarded and remembered as such. Apart from that, it appears that many teachers have scarcely any knowledge or insight into the actual causes of the beginner's problems. Therefore, we will first describe the various aspects of a beginning teacher's developmental process and after that the nature and the causes of many of the problems they face.

Characteristics of the threshold phase

This period in teachers' careers primarily concerns the first year of teaching, i.e. the period in which they make the transition from initial training to the profession − crossing the threshold − and in which they are confronted for the first time with all teacher responsibilities. Related to that, beginning teachers have to learn to use themselves as instruments. In this period the beginner's repertoire of actions is determined mainly by 'survival' and getting to know the various aspects of their profession. In this phase, teachers are mainly concerned with the recognition of their role as educator by themselves ('I' as a teacher) and by their students, colleagues and the school management. The pursuit of recognition[13] is one of the most important moving spirits behind the way beginning teachers act in the classroom. We identified that beginning teachers' feeling of being recognised by their pupils and relevant others is one of the criteria that marks the end of the threshold phase in beginning teachers' professional lives (Vonk, 1984a).

Figure 5.2 Dimension in beginning teachers' professional development

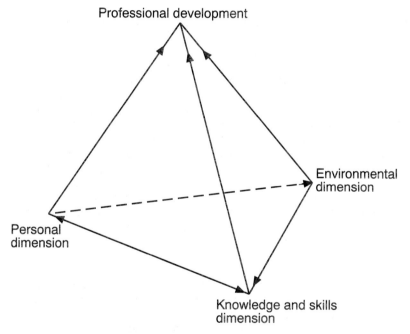

Apart from finding one's place in the school, the problems reported most frequently by beginners in this period come in the following categories: classroom control, organisation of teaching and learning activities, subject matter and materials, handling the differences between students, testing, dealing with parents, dealing with students who show problem behaviour

(Vonk, 1984a, Veenman, 1984). Vonk restricts his research into the problems of beginning teachers to secondary school teachers while Veenman mainly focuses on primary school teachers. It is obvious that in secondary education problems with subject-matter are more dominant than in primary education, while contacts with parents are more important in primary education. Nevertheless, there are many similarities. It is important for mentors to understand both the origin and the nature of the problems of beginning teachers. In order to analyse the problems of beginning teachers we distinguish three different dimensions in the experiences of beginning teachers which result in their professional development during the process of their induction into the profession: the personal dimension, the environmental dimension, and the professional knowledge and skills dimension (see Figure 5.2).

The personal dimension   An essential characteristic of being a teacher is that in teaching-learning situations teachers always use themselves as instruments. As a consequence, in education the teacher as a person is always at issue. Many beginners experience this as very confrontational and frightening; in particular because the majority of them is still in the transition stage from adolescence to adulthood. For many of them, becoming a teacher means growing to maturity under high pressure: they have to develop a new perspective on themselves − *I* as a teacher − and to learn how to develop professionally. In the beginning, for example, most beginning teachers do not have the slightest idea how they will behave under pressure or in situations of great stress; for every failure they tend to blame only themselves, and they do not make a distinction between personal and organisational problems, etcetera. They have no experience in this regard and therefore have to develop new behaviour to cope with these situations and sometimes even to adjust their self-image. Besides, their beliefs about 'good practice' and their pedagogical values are being questioned, which might result into a painful process of adaptation to more realistic, i.e. practice oriented beliefs. Finally, because beginners are in transition from novice to self-developing professional, many of them have to learn to be autonomous, flexible, empathic, and to accept diversity between students, and to have an eye for individual differences. Apart from these qualities they already have to be good organisers, interaction oriented and verbally skilled.

The environmental dimension   As argued before, beginning teachers develop professionally in a particular school context. They have to adapt to an existing school or departmental culture, and to the beliefs that exist in that school/department about the aims of education and about 'good teaching', appropriate teacher performance, teacher-pupil relationships and the like. That process of adaptation is often indicated as teacher socialisation.[14] If we take a closer look at the situation of beginning teachers in schools, it can be characterised by confrontations with:

- *new responsibilities*: from the first day and the first lesson on beginners are responsible for the classes they teach. These responsibilities are exactly the same as those of teachers who have been teaching for twenty years.
- *a school environment in which various teaching cultures exist*: each school, each department has its written and unwritten rules, and one is supposed to adhere to these rules (Hargreaves, 1992). However, beginners are not familiar with either the written or the unwritten rules of the game in their new school, they usually discover them by painful experience. These rules are so obvious to the existing staff that nobody explains them in advance.
- *expectations concerning the way in which one functions*: colleagues, school management, pupils or students and parents, all have their expectations about the new teacher. Beginning teachers are expected to meet these expectations. The problem however is that most beginners do not have the slightest idea about what these expectations are, and if they do, they do not know how to cope.

The above mentioned confrontations compel a beginner to *reorient* himself with regard to his own ideas about '*I* as a teacher' and his knowledge and skills already gained – what worked well during initial training will not always work in the new school environment. Apart from this, many novices have to make a change from identifying themselves with the student role to that of the teacher role. This reorientation and the resulting role change are combined with feelings of uncertainty and stress. Furthermore, the organisation and physical resources of a school, and perhaps more significantly the beliefs that are not only held and valued within the institution (written rule pattern) but have become embedded within its many taken-for-granted practices (unwritten rules), inevitably exert a powerful influence upon the novice teacher (Calderhead, 1992). In particular in situations in which beginners do not receive any support, they experience the first months of their induction rather as a *rite of passage* than a valuable learning experience. Although the process of adaptation to the new school environment is interactive in its nature, we found three major adaptation strategies. First, those teachers who felt familiar with the existing school/departmental culture simply adopted that culture. A second group of teachers adapted strategically to the culture of the school/department, because they felt they first had to show their colleagues and pupils they were able to function in the existing culture before changing their teaching approach. The last group did not agree with the existing culture and decided to follow their own pace. The members of the last group only survived if they had considerable frustration tolerance.

Practice shows that, no matter how well a novice teacher has been prepared for the transition from initial training to real practice, crisis situations nearly always arise. In short, beginning teachers must learn how to handle those new responsibilities, how to behave as a teacher and how to attune their perceptions about 'good teaching' and their ideas about the teacher's role (philosophy of education) to reality and to keep in harmony with their own personality.

In this context *the pedagogical aspects of teaching* are of great importance. Schools tend to have a mission which includes a philosophy about 'good education' in the broadest sense of the word. As well as being a practical and intellectual activity teaching is also a pedagogical endeavour. Teaching involves caring for young people who are on their way to adulthood – 'becoming a person' (Van Maanen, 1991), and preparing them for participation in society, and trying to influence the way in which they relate to each other and to real life. Growing-up includes changing the way of looking at things, changing connections, altering affinities, criticising established notions, distancing oneself from what was close and familiar, developing one's own set of values, or supporting a new cause. Pupils' growth becomes visible in the establishment of new relations to the world outside and inside (p. 33). Teachers influence that process, first, because value judgements are implicit in all teaching acts – not only the teacher's individual values but also the systems' values – the hidden curriculum, and second, on various occasions parents might ask teachers for pedagogical advice.[15] Van Maanen argues that pedagogical influence is situational, practical, normative, relational and self-reflective (p. 15). Schools need to offer young people a caring and supportive environment, not only because caring teachers and caring schools tend to reproduce a caring orientation in the students themselves, but also because a caring school climate sponsors the conditions for personal growth itself (p. 35). Sergiovanni and Starratt (1993, p. 50) also emphasise commitment to the ethic of caring as an important dimension of professional virtue. They plead for a shift from viewing teaching as a technical activity involving the execution of validated teaching strategies towards viewing teaching as a professional activity involving concern for the whole person.

However, although in theory many beginning teachers consider the pedagogical aspect of teaching as very important, they report not to know how to deal with it. They are hardly aware of the implicit values of the system they represent. Apart from that, today, in most mainly instrumentally oriented teacher education programmes this crucial element of the teacher's job is greatly neglected.

Professional knowledge and skills dimension   The professional knowledge and skills a beginning teacher has to develop concern three sub-dimensions: pedagogical content knowledge, classroom management skills and finally teaching skills.

Pedagogical content knowledge   In general novices have an elaborate academic background. They do no expect to meet problems with subject matter. Quite soon, however, they experience that they do not master their subjects at 'school' level.[16] Because beginners have major problems in translating their academic knowledge into school knowledge, they have to *reframe* their subject knowledge base. Publications by Shulman (1986) and Wilson *et al.* (1987) have resulted in a number of studies concerning the changes in novices' understanding of the subject knowledge they teach. Many beginners spend considerable time during their first two years of service on re-learning the subject matter (Vonk, 1984a). In order to teach a subject a teacher needs both breadth and depth of professional knowledge, i.e. a rich factual knowledge base with many interconnections which represents a much more thorough understanding than one achieves as a learner. If we take a closer look at beginning teachers' professional knowledge, we see that they draw on sources of knowledge which can be identified as: content knowledge, pedagogical content knowledge, knowledge of aims and purposes, knowledge of learners, and knowledge of educational contexts, settings and governance. Shulman (1986) suggests that these sources of understanding, of which beginning teachers' pedagogical content knowledge is the most important element, make the process of pedagogical reasoning and action possible.

Pedagogical content knowledge comes from three sources: (i) The *discipline perspective*: which is based on a breadth and depth of content knowledge, i.e., understanding the organisation of concepts and principles in the discipline (basic to the subject matter to be taught) and the strategies the discipline uses to discover new knowledge as well as the development of strategies and materials to enable learners to understand those concepts and processes. (ii) The *pupil perspective*: which concerns a rich factual knowledge base with many interconnections, such as, the knowledge of analogies, similes, examples and metaphors by which to explain the subject matter to the pupils, as well as knowledge of pupils' pre-conceptions, experiences in every day life, and difficulties that are commonly experienced by pupils, and that may help teachers to communicate effectively with their pupils. (iii) The *general methodology perspective*: which concerns knowledge of the different ways topics can be taught and the pros and cons of each approach, which is also an essential part of teachers' pedagogical content knowledge (Gudmundsdottir and Shulman, 1987). Ashton (1990) sees pedagogical content knowledge as the integration of pedagogy and content knowledge. It is this pedagogical content knowledge that distinguishes the veteran teacher from the novice.

All in all, this type of knowledge represents a much more thorough understanding of the subject matter than one achieves purely as a learner. Mentor activities aimed at improving the quality of teaching (i.e. the development of beginning teachers' professional knowledge base) should focus on broadening beginning teachers' pedagogical content knowledge. This means the presentation of content and methodology from all three perspectives mentioned above, simultaneously.

Classroom management skills Research shows that most beginning teachers have poor classroom management skills, i.e., they are not able to organise their lessons in such a way that on *on-task* working climate emerges and can be maintained effectively. They have problems with reacting adequately to unrest and discipline problems, because they have no overview of what is happening in the class and lack an adequate set of classroom rules and, if they have established such a set, they do not know how to maintain it, and finally, they do not know how to deal effectively with those who break those rules (sanctions).

One of the major origins of beginners' problems is that they are not familiar with the complexity of the classroom in which they have to work (ecology of the classroom). Classroom teaching is one of the most difficult modes of teaching. One teacher is brought together with 25 to 30 students in one room, and that group is expected to be engaged in activities that will lead to externally defined objectives as they are laid down in the curriculum. For the beginners this 'learning' environment is characterised by: multi-dimensionality, simultaneity, immediacy, unpredictability, publicness and history (Doyle, 1986). The main question for them is how to manage a group in such a complex environment. A mentor has to consider in what way he can help, support and advise a beginner to function properly under these stressful conditions.

Basic to good classroom management is the development of skills to monitor a class effectively. The ability to monitor effectively is based on two important teacher qualities: *focal attention* and *classroom knowledge* (Doyle, 1979). Focal attention is that limited part of teachers' information processing system that allows them to select important information[17] during classroom teaching and to react to it consciously. Beginners have to learn to direct their (focal) attention to that part of the information, coming from the class as a group, that is important to keep their students on-task. This part of teacher repertoire in particular has to be routinised. To achieve this it is important for beginners to develop a conceptual framework of their classes as soon as possible, i.e., what kind of reactions from each student may they expect on teacher's actions, which students do well and which do not, who is co-operative and who is not, etcetera. This *classroom knowledge* is a prerequisite for flexibility in focal attention, and therefore for effective classroom management.

Teaching skills At the start of the threshold phase beginning teachers experience numerous problems with ordinary classroom teaching. Although they have learned a number of teaching strategies, both in theory and school-practice, they still seem to lack effective classroom teaching skills, such as: the skills to structure the teaching-learning environment in order to tackle the time-on-task problem, to vary the learning activities which last a limited amount of time, to monitor individual students' progress, etcetera.

Conclusively, the whole situation in which the beginning teacher operates can be characterised as a *difficult control situation*. For beginning teachers who have several different classes it is problematic to act adequately under those circumstances. At the same time, it appears that the concept of the teacher's role they developed during initial teacher education scarcely offers them a basis from which to tackle the difficult control situation (Vonk 1984a, pp. 11−14 and p. 109).

Once beginning teachers have crossed the threshold by overcoming the obstacles of the threshold phase,[18] they enter the phase of 'growing into the profession' − the following five years of teaching. In this phase they usually focus on extending and/or improving their repertoire. Many teachers seek and try our new materials, methods and teaching strategies (Vonk and Schras, 1987). Most teachers find their job stimulating, and they are looking for opportunities to expand their repertoire. Those teachers, however, who had traumatic experiences during the threshold phase often tend to keep their distance from any possible change. They show little interest in improving or extending their repertoire and prefer to follow the survival strategies they developed during the threshold phase. Those who are eager to extend their repertoire in this phase are open to suggestions and willing to attend workshops and conferences.

Learning from experience

If one conceives beginning teachers as professionals in the making, it follows that the development of their own practical knowledge base takes a central position in their learning.[19] In this process systematic reflection on their experiences is crucial. Without this reflection beginners cannot build up a flexible repertoire. However, the beginning teacher's learning process differs from that of a student-teacher. During initial teacher training acquiring theoretical knowledge and insights dominates gaining practical experience. The learning environment is structured from simple to complex, and many, if not all, learning experiences are planned in advance. The learning environment of the beginning teacher is, on the contrary, mainly determined by what happens in the classroom and he only learns from the (practical) experience during those lessons. He learns by doing. A beginning teacher, however, runs the risk of drowning in his own experiences. A mentor can offer effective assistance in structuring the multitude of experiences and how to reflect on them. Mentoring can thus be considered as a means to help beginning teachers to order, structure and reflect on their experiences and thereby to help them to expand and/or deepen their repertoire.

For a mentor it is important to know how experiences are being processed and how they can lead to new flexible behaviour (see Figure 5.3). During teaching beginning teachers participate in a teaching-learning environment in a particular class (a series of events), they observe what happens and give meaning to these events − so far they are *experiencing*. Consequently, they store the events together with the given meaning in their cognitive scheme related to that particular class; it has become part of their classroom knowledge − they can put it into words. Now are we speaking of an *experience*. This experience is accompanied by either positive (success) or negative (failure) feelings. If no reflection takes place the teacher in

Figure 5.3 Learning from experience

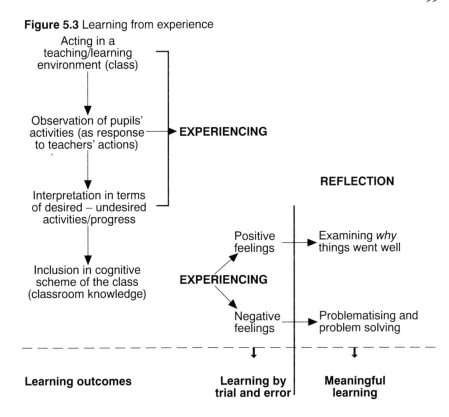

question will try to repeat events of success and to avoid those of failure. We say that a repertoire developed in this way is based on trial and error learning. It is inflexible, i.e. not applicable in other situations. To develop a flexible repertoire of actions one has to analyse (reflect on) both the experiences of success – why did it go well, and in what other situations is it usable – and failure – why did it go wrong and how to act more appropriately in comparable situations. The latter leads to a process of problematising – translating a (negative) experience into a problem which can be solved – and problem solving. In answering the 'why' question one has to confront or relate to the experience by means of existing, more general, research based knowledge of teachers' actions and other educational theory. In this respect we fully agree with Stones (1992, p. 13) as he defines 'theory' as 'bodies of principles that have explanatory power and the potential of guiding teacher action'. McIntyre (1993, p. 43) states that valuable theory for beginners has to lead to suggestions for practice. Processing experiences in this way will lead to the development of a flexible repertoire of actions and a solid professional knowledge base.[20]

The mentor's interpersonal skills base

In this section the various possibilities of mentor interventions in the context of mentor-protegée relationships and the related interpersonal skills will be discussed. We consider mentors as skilled helpers, i.e. a wide range of mentor activities have counselling like aspects. Essential in mentoring beginning teachers is the *supervisory conference*, i.e. structured discussions aimed at facilitating and supporting beginning teachers' professional learning processes. These conferences can have different formats: the *mentor-protegée conference* − most often a post-observation conference − or the *peer group conference* − a group of beginning teachers, assisted by a mentor, discuss their problems and examine together how these problems can be solved. The effectiveness of those conferences is for the greater part determined by the quality of the protegée-mentor relationship and in that context the nature of the mentor interventions. The basis for that relationship and the interventions is the nature of the protegée's needs for assistance. In this context the mentor-protegée relationship is very sensitive: How should a mentor act during conferences? In general, a mentor's approach of a particular protegée is − apart from his personal dispositions − mainly defined by his perception of the protegée's personal qualities, skills and the expected need for help. The nature of the mentor-protegée relationship and the related interventions is characterised by the extent of responsibility both players have with respect to changes in the protegée's repertoire of actions.[21] A classification of the various types of mentor-protegée relationships as it relates to the outcomes of mentor interventions looks as follows (see Table 5.1).

Table 1 Relation mentor approach intended outcome

Approach	Outcome
Non-directive (P)	Teacher self-plan
Collaborative (m,P)	Mutual plan
Directive advisory (M,p)	Mentor suggested plan
Directive control (M)	Mentor prescribed plan

Source: Glickman, 1990, p. 109.

Non-directive mentoring is based on the assumption that the protegée concerned knows best what changes he has to make and that he has the ability to think and act on his own. The mentor acts as an active prober and a mirror. Collaborative-mentoring is based on the principle that mentor and protegée are equal partners in the mentoring process. The mentor wishes to resolve the protegée's problems by sharing them. Apart from probing and mirroring, a mentor also actively participates in the problem solving process by proposing possible actions and/or solutions and then negotiating a solution that satisfies both the mentor and the protegée. With directive-advisory-mentoring the mentor acts as resource person: the mentor analyses the protegée's actions and identifies the problems, for which he subsequently provides various solutions. The protegée commits himself to using the offered solutions. Finally, there is directive-control-mentoring: this type of mentoring perceives the mentor to be the expert who more or less prescribes how the novice should act.

The nature of the mentor's interventions largely depends on the protegée's autonomy and self-concept. The more self-confident and knowledgeable a protegée is, the less effective directive mentoring will be. On the other hand, a protegée who lacks self-confidence may profit from more directive mentor actions. A well-trained mentor masters the whole scale of behaviours and is able to adapt his performance to his protegée's needs.

Whatever relationship may exist between mentors and protegées, conferencing — both peer conferences and mentor-protegée conferences — plays an important part in mentoring beginning teachers and, therefore, mentors need to have an elaborate repertoire of interpersonal skills. These skills coincide largely with the general discussion and communication skills, such as, listening, clarifying, encouraging, reflecting, directing, summarising, probing, negotiating, directing, and the like (Glickman, 1990, p. 105).

In this contribution we will only consider mentor-protegée conferences and in particular the post-observation conferences. As stated before, beginning teachers learn from inside, not from outside. 'Ownership' and 'commitment' are crucial conditions for the development of new or improved repertoire (Fullan, 1991), i.e. teachers have to see a need for change and to be convinced of the value of the intended change. This can be achieved only if mentors take their protegée's needs, abilities and beliefs about 'good teaching' serious. As a consequence, we prefer a non-directive approach of mentor-protegée conferences.

The conferencing procedure before us is non-directive in nature and a variant on existing procedures for the supervisory conferences as used in school practice during pre-service training or in clinical supervision. It consists of four parts: the *start*, the *core*, the *conclusion*, and the *evaluation*. Each part has its specific function which will be described below.

1. *The start of the conference*
   - *Letting off steam.* In case a protegée has just given a lesson and especially if he has experienced a lot of problems, he will be emotional and excited. By letting him tell his story he can release his emotions and tension. In this way he can distance himself from his experiences, which is likely to ensure a calm and structured conference.
   - *Making a conference agenda.* After the first reconnaissance, the discussion partners can mutually decide on the course of the

conference, what subjects should be dealt with, etcetera. It is most important to determine which experiences or issues the protegée wants to discuss and which he does not. In fact, if a protegée wishes to avoid discussion of a certain experience or issue, then it is no use placing it on the agenda. However, in some cases a little mild pressure can do no harm.

2. *The core of the conference*
   - In this phase of the conference, the *established subjects for discussion are dealt with one by one*. It is desirable to put the following questions for each item.
   - How did the beginning teacher experience it? (Recall)
   - What other information is available? These could be observations by the mentor, self-reporting (e.g. logbooks) by the beginning teacher, and/or reports by pupils, either with or without the assistance of a questionnaire.

By means of these reports a discussion can take place about what has actually happened (reflection); what went well, what did not and why (explanation)!
   - What could be handled in a different manner? What other means of action are available and would be effective in similar situations? Here not only the 'invention' of alternative performances is involved but also the question of how to acquire the necessary skills.
   - What concrete improvements/changes in the repertoire of actions are planned?

N.B. During the conference, items can be combined or dealt with in a different order. One should make sure, however, that all items are discussed.

3. *Conclusion of the conference.*
   It is a good idea to *repeat and record* a number of matters at the end of each conference, in particular for the mentor's report — a useful instrument for the mentor as well as the protegée in the evaluation of the learning process during the first year of service. The following points are of particular importance:
   - What has the protegée learned from the reflection on his experiences?
   - What will the protegée do the next time to improve his performance?
   - How will the improvement be checked? Will that be done by means of self-reporting, pupil questionnaires or observation by the mentor?

4. *Evaluation of the conference*
   Because both partners, i.e. mentor and protegée, are involved in a shared learning process, it is obvious that they must evaluate the conference. The evaluation has two functions:
   - First, to value the progress in the protegée's professional development (product).

● Second, to value the contribution of the conference to that learning process (process); i.e. aims of the conference, problem clarification and problem-solving procedures, discussion procedures, and outcomes.

The mentor's technical skills base

Before analysing the skills a mentor has to master, we will first analyse the various aspects of the mentor role. The setting of that role is like counselling: the aim of mentoring is to help beginning teachers to develop their own professional identity and to master the necessary knowledge and skills. Therefore a mentor can be seen as a 'skilled helper' (Egan, 1986). Apart from the counselling setting in which all activities take place, we distinguish four sub-roles for a mentor: observer, instructor, provider of feedback and finally evaluator (Turney *et al.*, 1982). To all sub-roles a set of skills is related. In the next section the various aspects of the mentor role are analysed and connected with the skills required to act as a mentor in an effective way.

Mentors in their role as counsellors

If we analyse the role of the mentor in his function as a counsellor, we can distinguish four aspects:

1. Creating an open and safe relationship between the beginner and himself, in which experiences, feelings, concerns and problems can be openly discussed: showing interest, listening, accepting.
2. Helping beginners to gain insight into the origins of the problems they experience (guided reflection) and to help them to find appropriate solutions for those problems: clarifying, inviting exploration, stimulating problem solving.
3. Stimulating beginners to develop a positive self-concept and a clear view on the profession: stimulating a positive self-concept, awareness of one's situation, guiding reorientation.
4. Helping beginners to develop strategies to deal with problematic and stressful events: recognising stress, coping with stress and emotions, problem solving.

Mentors in their role as observers

We strongly support the principle of classroom observation by mentors. In order to execute this part of his role properly a mentor has to master elementary skills related to observation, such as being able:

1. To define in negotiation with the beginning teachers what will be observed: to make a proper selection, to define the precise behaviour concerned.
2. To collect and record data: to create an observation scheme, to observe, to sort out and interpret the data.

Figure 5.4 Mentor roles

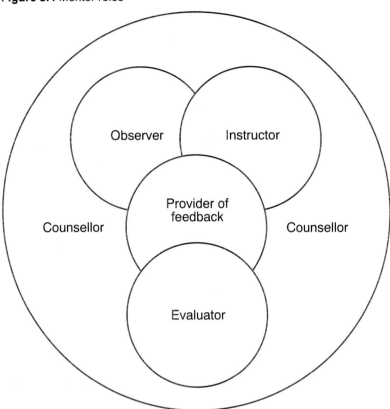

3. To analyse the data and the report: to make a draft analysis, to consider alternatives taking individual qualities and circumstances into account, making a report for feedback.

Mentors in their role as providers of feedback

Because not all feedback can be based on observation by the mentor, other methods such as recall-discussions and student questionnaires can be used to collect information. Most discussions on lessons, however, will be based only on the beginning teacher's own report. Therefore it is important for the mentor in the context of this role to develop skills relating to:

1. Discussions on lessons: recall-discussions, recognising problems, giving appropriate feedback.
2. Helping beginners to analyse their own behaviour: analysing teacher

behaviour, processing data with respect to the teacher's acting in the classroom, stimulating reflection and self-evaluation.
3. Thinking along with beginners about solutions for their problems: analysing teacher problems, advising about solutions.

Mentors in their role as instructors

Every beginner expects to receive that specific information from his mentor which he can use for solving the problems he experiences. The mentor should be aware, however, that expert solutions will not work with beginners because they neither have the necessary classroom knowledge nor the routines on which those solutions are based. Therefore it is important to offer:

1. Knowledge, ideas and examples that are related to the beginner's learning needs: identification of the learning needs, transformation of one's own ideas to the beginner's level, instruction skills.
2. Help in analysing the beginner's own ideas and teaching behaviour: questioning, prompting, confronting with the professional knowledge base.
3. Encouragement towards reflection and self-evaluation: mapping problems, analysing origins of the problems, offering strategies for problem solving.

Mentors in their role as evaluators

At the end of every discussion on lessons both the process and the product will be evaluated, i.e. the question will be raised whether the objectives have been met and whether the discussion as such was an appropriate means to arrive at those objectives. Apart from that, a summary of those evaluative reports is a good means to inform beginners about where they stand in their process of professional development. By the end of the year every mentor has to inform his protegées what he thinks of their professional abilities and perspective and to advise them whether to stop or to continue. This, in particular, has to be done very carefully. Therefore mentors need to master the following skills:

1. Communicating with beginners: explaining criteria and procedures of evaluation, creating a positive climate in which evaluation will be regarded as inducement for making further progress.
2. Collecting and interpreting evaluation data: sorting out evaluation data and considering their reliability, considering the influence of the environment, summarising the findings.
3. Assessing and reporting: giving an assessment based on the available data, writing the evaluation report, discussing the report with the teacher concerned.

106

Conclusion

In many European countries the need for improving the quality of teaching and for raising the status of the teaching profession has been increasingly discussed at the governmental level. However, to reach these goals time, budget, and energy have to be spent on programmes aimed at the professional development of the teaching force. That development, however, is not a bureaucracy-based effort − such as comes from the bureaucrat's naive belief that summative evaluation leads to improvement − but a professional activity, which could be put into motion and monitored by school management in their capacity as educational leaders. The care for professional development of teachers is an essential element in staff policy in schools, and in that context especially the care for beginning teachers is no less than a test-case for the professionality of those who develop the policy in question.

An effective way to model this care is to establish a mentor system in schools. A mentor system, however, needs resources, i.e. time, budget and facilities. We strongly plead for the creation of special positions for mentors, separate from those of the school management. The mentoring relationship is a very sensitive issue − it is based on mutual trust. Therefore a clear distinction has to be made between those who are involved in summative evaluation of the beginning teacher − i.e. school management, and those involved in formative evaluation − i.e. the mentor. Preferably, mentors should be given a status similar to school counsellors. However, as long as official bodies do not seem to be prepared to invest in the future teacher generation, the improvement of teaching and of the status of the teaching profession will not be realised. This issue is becoming urgent, in particular if we look at the trend in some European countries to replace initial teacher education by training on the job. At first sight this might seem effective because it seems to remove the theory-practice gap, but without a solid professional knowledge base for the teachers and without trained mentors to guide them this system will on the longer term not result in the improvement of teaching. On the contrary, it will produce inflexible teachers who are not able to adapt to innovations in the future and who are not real professionals.

Our view on teachers as self-directing professionals places teachers at the centre of the process of improving the quality of teaching. Teachers, individually as well as in groups, are responsible for analysing the needs of the school. They are able and willing to discuss, not only among themselves, but in open debate with the other legitimate and interested parties, possible solutions or developments and eventually to take decisions about what is to be done and to ensure its implementation. Teachers are expected to be capable of analysing their own actions, to identify pupils' needs, to react to them and to evaluate the outcome of their interventions (Vonk, 1991b, p. 165). From this perspective on the teacher's role we have tried to map out the basic knowledge and skills for mentors in this chapter, based on a review of relevant literature and on our own research into the professional development of beginning teachers, in order to help to develop effective mentor systems in schools.

Notes

1. See for a review of recent literature: Kagan (1992, pp. 150–64).
2. See for example the study of Ooms (1991). She reported about the drop-out of beginning teachers in the Netherlands during their first four years of service over the period 1980–90.
3. See: Tickle (1989, p. 105 et seq.).
4. E.g. the Oxford Internship model in the UK.
5. The post-modernist era contrasts sharply with the preceding 'modern' era – which was characterised by rationalism, universal laws and dominance of the scientific methodology for the production of new knowledge – in that the notion of legitimating universal values has collapsed, in questioning of the value of the scientific methodology for the production of knowledge outside the sciences, and in emphasising plurality instead of universality.
6. A *phase* is a rounded period in someone's career which is identifiable by characteristics specific to that period. The use of the term 'phase' evokes the notion of some general 'developmental sequence' that all teachers may go through. Attractive as this notion may be, also for purposes of planning in-service education and training (Huberman, 1993), career cycles of 'real' teachers do not follow easily predictable paths. Individual idiosyncrasies and environmental influences play an important role in shaping individual careers.
7. *Action* is defined as: a purposive change in the world of objects with which an individual is confronted.
8. Vonk and Schras (1987).
9. *Orientation* base consists of a conceptual framework related to a repertoire of actions and is based on a coherent whole of theoretical knowledge and practical experiences.
10. Levine (1989, p. 62), quotes Erikson: 'Generativity is primarily the interest in establishing and guiding the next generation of whatever in a given case may become the absorbing object of a parental kind of responsibility'.
11. The set of person-related factors is defined as those factors in personal life that influence one's professional functioning, such as individual disposition, life stage, crisis, family, leisure activities and participation in nonprofessional organisations.
12. The professional environment consists of several groups of persons with whom one is confronted while practicing the profession. These are colleagues, students, school administration, school board, local authorities and parents. Each group has its own expectations concerning the teacher's professional behaviour and each will try to influence his development.
13. See: Fukyama (1992, Ch. 13), where he analyses the philosophy of

Hegel, who identified the pursuit of recognition as the most important non-materialistic drive behind human behaviour.

14. For an overview of literature on 'teacher socialisation', see: Zeichner and Gore (1990).

15. In particular during the last decades we observe a shift in the pedagogical responsibility – of what used to be the hard core of family education – from parents to the school. In that respect teachers are being confronted with new facets to their professional activities. Beginning teachers experience this facet of their job as problematic, because they lack the necessary life experience to act adequately.

16. For a detailed overview of problems on this issue as reported by novices, see Vonk (1984a), pp. 110–12.

17. Important in the sense: related to the continuity of students' on-task performance, and of making progress (Brown and McIntyre, 1988).

18. Vonk (1984a, p. 117), describes the indicators that determine whether a beginning teacher has already passed the threshold to the profession or not.

19. We conceive learning as a process with more or less durable results, whereby new behaviour potential of a person arises or changes occur in that already present. Learning is directed towards changing the learner's repertoire of actions. We consider the learning process as a process in which that repertoire undergoes both quantitative and qualitative changes.

20. Gilroy (1989, pp. 104–9): discusses the concept of 'professional knowledge'.

21. Mentor responsibility high = M; mentor responsibility low = m; protegée responsibility high = P; protegée responsibility low = p.

CHAPTER 6

Selecting and Training the Teacher Trainers

John Dewar Wilson

Introduction

In 1987 the Standing Conference of European Ministers of Education recommended that 'a systematic review at national and European levels should be made of the recruitment and training of teacher trainers'. In Strasbourg, in March 1990, the Council for Cultural Co-operation (CDCC) of the Council of Europe organised an international seminar on 'The Selection and Professional Development of Trainers for Initial Teacher Training'. Twenty-three countries participated.

'Teachers are the yeast of society.' This observation by the Turkish delegate linked teacher education to the quality of teaching in schools. In '*Where the Buck Stops*' Turney and Wright (1990) argued that:

> The quality of teaching depends in large measure on the quality of the teachers; the quality of teachers depends in large measure upon the quality of their professional education; the quality of teacher education depends in large measure on the quality of those who provide it, namely the teacher educators. Thus to a considerable degree the 'buck stops' with the teacher educators.

But teacher educators are a neglected, often criticised and endangered species, particularly in the European context. In a questionnaire to Ministries of Education in member countries CDCC sought answers to specific questions on national policies on recruitment, permanent appointment and professional development of teacher educators. CDCC also commissioned Working Group (WG) 12 – the Professional Development of Teachers – of the Association for Teacher Education in Europe (ATEE) to provide a background paper for the seminar.

This chapter first addresses the question of the status and perceived quality of initial teacher education. Next it asks who are the teacher educators, where do they work and what is their clientele. It then considers the framework within which policy on recruitment and selection of teacher educators is managed, and describes practice in different countries within a linear model of the stages involved. Evidence is drawn from 14 country reports (Belgium (Flemish Community), Cyprus, Denmark, Finland, Greece, Iceland, Luxembourg, Netherlands, Norway, Portugal, Sweden, Turkey, United Kingdom and Yugoslavia), together with the case studies referred to above. The chapter makes no claim to be either comprehensive or definitive. It aims to illuminate some aspects of practice in some European countries from the perspective of institutional administrators and newly appointed teacher educators.

Status and perceived quality of initial teacher education

Professionals in the education service would almost unanimously argue for compulsory pre-service teacher education and training. At the same time what is currently offered does not always successfully impart new ways of acting to trainees. Over many years initial teacher education has been seen as a requirement for teaching in state-supported primary schools in Europe. Italy, however, is an exception in that no formal pre-service training in theory and pedagogy is required for any group of teachers.

Compulsory pre-service training for secondary teachers is more recent. Cyprus introduced it only in 1989 and 30 years after making it compulsory England, in 1990, introduced a 'licensed teacher scheme' which allows non-graduates with 'suitable' life experience (but no prior teacher education) to teach in secondary schools. Training on the job for new graduates is also now encouraged.

In Australia Turney and Wright (1990) reported that teacher educators in higher education had defensive, self-satisfied and often ill-founded views concerning the impact and effectiveness of their programmes. In the United States several reports linked performance of elementary and secondary schools to weak teacher education. Goodlad (1984), the National Commission for Excellence in Teacher Education (1985) and Magrath and Egbert (1987) have all argued for training of higher quality. In 1981 Rendle, a civil servant, noted of Scotland's teacher training institutions – the colleges of education:

> The colleges of education occupy a key position in the system; most teachers pass through their hands at least once; teaching practice in itself gives colleges direct links with the operational face of the system; and individually and collectively they should comprise a concentration of academic expertise in the matter of effectively transmitting

knowledge and experience. Yet the general impression that has come through is that, for whatever reasons, the colleges have not altogether fulfilled the promise which such a central position seems to offer, nor do they seem to have been able to adopt the progressive role which might be expected of them.

Strenuous attempts have been made to improve teacher education in Europe in recent years (Voorbach, 1992). Examples include tighter accountability criteria, lengthened and restructured courses, and attempts at better coordination to improve theory-practice relationships and to secure greater involvement of practising teachers.

In England a government publication – *The New Teacher in School* (DES, 1987) – reported only slight improvements in teacher quality, however, and government prescriptions for teacher education in that country have become progressively more specific about the performances that signify effective training More recently it has established a Training Agency to bring the supervision of teaching directly under government control.

Who are the initial teacher educators and trainers?

This section first refers to studies of teacher educators in different countries and describes their backgrounds. Then it describes the varied roles that they play within European systems. Finally, information is provided about teacher educators in the ATEE case studies.

Thorough reviews of research on teacher educators – at least in the United States – have been provided by Ryan (1975), Lanier and Little (1986) and Howey and Zimpher (1990). However, teacher educators remain an obscure group. A survey in New Zealand (Donn and Slyfield, 1988) found that over half the respondents (who comprised 87 per cent (418/482) of all teacher education staff) had been appointed within the previous two years, and one in five did not hold a permanent appointment. Turney and Wright (1990) characterise multicultural Australia's teacher educators as predominantly male, of British background, out of touch with contemporary practice in schools and close to retirement.

Wilson (1991), principal of a college of education in Scotland, claims that staffing accounts for 70 per cent of the budget in higher education, is a key factor in quality and yet is rarely discussed in the literature on recruitment and selection. He describes much variety of practice in the nine teacher education institutions (eight UK and one Dutch) whose management he interviewed.

Initial teacher educators in Europe may be differentiated by role and by institution. They include supervisors of practical teaching experience in schools, and staff who co-ordinate it there. They also include staff in higher education.

Practical teaching experience is gained in schools. In some systems (such as Austria and Finland) model or demonstration schools are attached to training institutions, but in most countries practice is obtained also or solely in typical schools. Supervision is normally by class teachers, but in Belgium (Flemish Community) inspectors may supervise and in Luxembourg educational advisers are appointed. Experiments (for example in England) to locate the entire pre-service experience in schools have meant that most aspects of professional knowledge have been gained from staff in such settings, and this has raised questions as to their qualifications for that job.

In most countries higher education institutions provide the theoretical studies believed to be required for teaching. These institutions may be denominational as well as non-denominational, or, as in Denmark, private but in receipt of state subsidy. Different categories of teacher may be trained in different institutions. In 1988 there were six institutions in Iceland providing initial teacher training, but the system has been reviewed. Prospective primary teachers are trained in higher institutes of education in Portugal and in a pedagogical academy in Cyprus. In Belgium (Flemish community) higher schools of education train teachers for primary schools and the first cycle of secondary education. Secondary teachers are generally recruited from students who are subject specialists. They may be trained in postgraduate courses in university, or, as in Cyprus, in a pedagogical institute. In some cases, however, they are trained concurrently alongside primary teachers and in the same institutions. In Greece a vocational and professional teacher training institute (SELETE) provides pedagogical training for engineers, economists and other professionals who wish to teach. There is a trend for teacher education institutions to merge with universities. In this chapter staff who work in higher education teacher education will be referred to as 'university level' teacher educators, although not all institutions have university status. Within the university there are various levels of staff appointment from director/professor to lecturer and tutor with different terms used in different countries.

Given the diversity of institutions and staff one problem facing all systems is how to promote cohesion within the team of teacher trainers, so that, for example, all speak a common language and share a common motivation to work together for the benefit of the trainee. This applies not only to university and field staff, but also within the university itself. In Belgium (Flemish Community) recruitment and staff development aim to ensure that the pedagogic specialist becomes familiar with research and the subject specialist familiar with issues of pedagogy.

Practitioners: the ATEE case studies

The background paper prepared for the seminar drew upon case studies from eight countries – Austria, England, Finland, Israel, Netherlands, Scotland, Wales and West Germany (Berlin). These were subsequently published in a special issue of the *European Journal of Teacher Education* (Wilson Ed., 1990).

Evidence was collected by interview from one senior administrator in one university level teacher education institution in each country, and from one person who had been recently appointed to a post in the same institution.

Thus both management and consumer perspectives were brought to bear on the process of recruitment, selection and induction. The interviewers were experienced teacher educators and interviewers. Each interview lasted about one hour. Drafts of interview reports were checked for accuracy with interviewees.

Senior administrators included a head of school (professor), deputy directors, heads of department, senior teacher educators, and a chief school inspector. They described institutional policy in general terms, and illustrated its operation in respect of a specific recent appointment.

Practice was illustrated by reference to the following appointments: teacher/tutor in an experimental school and university (Austria), lecturer in subject didactics (Finland), seminar leader (Berlin), subject tutor (Israel), history tutor (Netherlands), lecturer in nurse education (Wales), senior lecturer in design technology (England), and lecturer in primary education (Scotland).

Appointees

Appointees had been in post for different lengths of time. The Israeli and the Dutchman had worked in the university for three years; others for one year or less. In all but three cases – Austria, Netherlands and Wales – the appointees were different people from those referred to by the senior administrators. The following vignettes indicate their background.

The Austrian, a male with ten years teaching experience, had supervised student teachers, worked in teams producing textbooks, published several articles on methodology and contributed to in-service programmes. His new post involved him working for 75 per cent of the week in an experimental school, and 25 per cent as subject lecturer in the university.

The Finn, a female with 30 years' experience of secondary teaching in religion and psychology and one year of teaching in university, had a first degree in theology, a master's degree in psychology and education and was well advanced towards the licentiate degree. She was appointed as lecturer in the didactics of religion.

The Berlin appointee was a female of 40 who taught chemistry and physics and had held the position of Fachseminarleiter (head of pedagogic training group for these subjects) for one year.

The Israeli had a BSc, a teaching diploma and a masters degree and had been teaching biology for ten years. She had been tutor for four years.

In Netherlands the appointee taught history in a secondary school and supervised pre-service student teachers for the department. He also edited a professional journal. In 1985 the university 'leased' him from his school full time; between 1987 and 1988 he worked three days a week as a school teacher, and two days per week at the university; in 1989 he was again seconded full time as a tutor at university, an arrangement which was to end in August 1990, when a decision was required as to whether he should go back to his teaching post in school, or seek to extend his university contract.

The Welsh appointee was a qualified nurse tutor and midwife who had formerly taught in a school of nursing and who had been in post for one term in the further/nurse education section of the department of education.

In England the appointee, a male of 34, had three degrees (Bachelor of Education, Bachelor of Arts and a Master of Arts). He had taught for two years in primary, one term in secondary and five years as a peripatetic teacher of English as a foreign language in both primary and secondary schools. For 18 months prior to his appointment he had been an advisory teacher (on a temporary contract) in a multicultural centre. He was appointed to teach in the primary BEd programme.

The Scot was a male graduate in his mid-30s who, for the previous three and a half years, had been headteacher of a primary school in a deprived urban area. He was appointed to a 23-month temporary contract in mathematics and computing. He had contributed to in-service programmes run by the university and been an assessor on its program for selecting teacher education candidates.

Most appointees, consequently, were in mid to late thirties and starting in their first post as teacher educators. Most had followed a conventional route into teacher education, having taken qualifications in addition to their first degree and having acquired significant, successful experience as teachers, and as contributors, through writing and management, to the development of thinking and practice on education. Several were on short-term appointments, or in roles which combined classroom teaching with work in the university. Only the nurse could be said to be bringing a different perspective into training for teaching.

Recruitment, selection and induction of university teacher educators: a linear model

Appointments occur within a policy framework within an institution. They mark the culmination of a lengthy process comprising several stages. Figure 6.1 sets out nine stages in the total cycle. Stage 1 is the initial identification of a vacancy. Stage 9 is professional development subsequent to the granting of tenure. On the right hand side of the figure is the applicant's perspective on selection, which includes the decision in the first place to submit an application, to participate in the selection process, to take up an offered post, or to withdraw.

The linear model is based on a report of the Criteria of Teacher Selection Project (CATS) (Wilson *et al.*, 1985) which studied the practice of agencies such as the UK Civil Service Selection Board and Marks and Spencer plc which had evolved developed personnel systems.

Policy context

Country reports and interviews with administrators painted a uniform picture of the context affecting institutional policies on recruitment and selection. With the declining birthrate – except in Eire – and the consequent reduced demand for teachers, few teacher educators were

Figure 6.1 A linear model of the recruitment, selection and induction process

POLICY FRAMEWORK

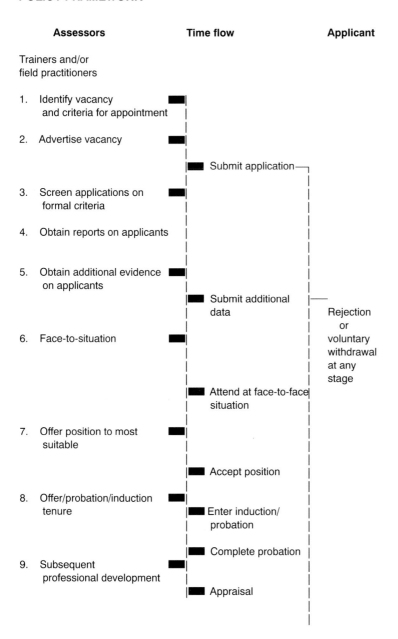

recruited in the 1980s, and there had been pressure to shed staff, many of whom were close to retirement. In Sweden 25 per cent of staff were expected to retire between 1990 and 1992. Being at the top of salary scales these staff were expensive. Their lack of recent school teaching experience meant that they were vulnerable to criticism of being out-of-touch, and in some cases there was a mismatch between their discipline qualifications and the demand for curriculum-related initial training courses. Where replacement staff could be justified short-term appointments offered the institution greater flexibility in responding to changing demands and reduced staffing costs. There was no shortage of suitable applicants for posts. Although recruited to teach on a particular pre- or in-service course the view in Scotland was that these staff were expected to contribute to all aspects of the work of the institution, including research and curriculum development.

Policy framework

Institutions differ in the framework within which selection policy is defined. In Belgium (Flemish Community) the 1970 Higher Education Act provides the framework. A university's independence is governed by its ordinance which is a legal document; in UK institutions have considerable apparent autonomy but there are accountability mechanisms. Some institutions have also evolved explicit internal policies which define the procedures to be employed; others have no set-down policy.

In Austria the process of appointing staff is defined by law. The principal identifies the need for new staff, and staff representatives endorse the proposal. A set of necessary and minimum qualifications is defined. But the Federal Ministry of Education must then approve the post.

In Denmark the Ministry of Education validates the qualifications of those selected by both private and public institutions before they are appointed.

In Finland, at least at the University of Helsinki, a Teacher Education Act governs the process of some appointments. Staff below lecturer level may be appointed by professors, subject to confirmation by the Faculty of Education. Decisions on lectureships are passed from Faculty to the Minor Council of the University, and then on to the Major Council, and from there to the University Chancellor. For professorial positions the Chancellor nominates to the President of the Republic. This process may extend over several years in some cases.

In Netherlands institutions have considerable freedom within the act of parliament but four conditions of appointment are specified: certification of proficiency for higher and vocational education, and of adequacy of preparation in educational theory and method, a certificate of 'good behaviour', and a medical certificate.

In Luxembourg senior lecturers and assistant lecturers are appointed by the Grand Duke, tutors by the Ministry of Education.

In Scotland an institutional policy statement may be developed. This describes the process for identifying vacancies, for preliminary screening and for subsequent short-listing. It outlines the stages in the selection process, the composition of panels for conducting face-to-face assessment, and the process for confirming appointments.

In Cyprus appointments to temporary posts are made by a five-member appointing body − the Education Service Commission (ESC). Applications are screened by a three-member Consultative Committee and a short list prepared. Applicants not short-listed may appeal to ESC. The final list of candidates is prepared and made known. ESC then selects the strongest. A further appeal to the Supreme Court is possible for candidates who are unsuccessful.

In former Yugoslavia selection in 1990 was by vote of the Teachers' Council. Once a decision to fill a vacancy is taken the Council of the institution sets up a screening committee to consider applications. The committee writes a summary report of the work of each candidate and indicates the arguments for the main candidate(s). The election then follows.

In Greece, too, staff are elected by faculty members of each department.

Stages in the process of recruitment, selection and induction

Identification of a vacancy

A vacancy may be identified for one of a number of reasons. A member of staff may resign due to retirement or promotion, a secondment to a new role may be authorised, or a new position may be created. The level of post − tutor, lecturer, associate professor, professor, or director − obviously affects deliberations on whether it should be filled, and when. A vacancy provides an opportunity for the institution to redefine an aspect of its functioning at a time when there are many pressures.

Decisions about filling a vacancy − or vacancies, as several departments may have staffing needs − invariably require institutional approval, for example by a staffing policy committee, chaired by the director, which keeps staffing under review and may consider priorities annually or as required. Representatives of staff are likely to be involved. The priority to be attached to filling particular vacancies may be debated at length. Where external funding is involved approval will be sought from the appropriate body. The decision to fill a vacancy is invariably justified in relation to the development plan of the department or institution and may involve a balance between academic, financial and resource priority considerations.

Wilson (1991) found that several institutions have created personnel offices and appointed personnel officers to assist in the management of staffing.

Recruitment process

Systems differ in the procedures that must be followed in advertising vacancies, and these may vary with the status of the post. For some posts, such as a tutor in Israel and in the Netherlands, there is no formal advertising, but simply a process whereby school staff are nominated by university staff with whom they liaise. In Cyprus advertising is by circular to all schools in January of each year. Advertising may be internal within the university, or more widely, within the national university system, in the first instance, with public advertisement only if no suitable applicant is identified. Where public advertising occurs there are differences both in terms of where posts are advertised, and in the nature of the advertisement. In Berlin and in Austria the Ministry of Education requires advertisement in a particular newspaper; in other systems the institution decides how widely it will advertise. In Finland it is stipulated that applications have to be lodged within 30 days of the advertisement.

Advertisements describe the post and supplementary notes may indicate the range of duties staff will carry out, salary and conditions of service. An explicit job description or person specification is unusual. It is of course open to applicants to find out more about the position by visiting the institution, and seeking information about the reason for the vacancy and their perceived suitability for it. The Austrian and the Israeli appointees both discussed their application with university staff prior to lodging it.

Formal criteria for selection

Formal criteria can be both legal or statutory requirements. Specific requirements reflect the nature of the post. For example, personal characteristics may be an important deciding factor, and perceived compatibility with an already functioning team.

One statutory requirement in all systems is a degree or diploma in post-secondary education, with an expectation of studies beyond the initial qualification. Relevant successful professional experience as a teacher is also almost a universal requirement, though in Galicia in Spain, for example, someone aiming to become a professor in theory of learning could proceed from undergraduate studies to the PhD, and from there into university teaching, without necessarily obtaining experience as a teacher in a school. In Portugal success in examinations is the basis for selection as a trainer of primary teachers.

In Austria a teacher educator for subject matter methodology must have:

● a teaching certificate for that subject;
● at least four years of teaching experience in a compulsory school and an outstanding assessment as a teacher;
● a series (approximately four) of publications in the field.

In Belgium (Flemish Community) the 1970 Higher Education Act stipulates that candidates must have (i) a degree complemented with 'agregation' (i.e. the teaching diploma), or, with technical subjects, a certificate of aptitude for teaching and (ii) evidence of relevant experience, either by having worked for six years in higher education or by having held, for a minimum of three years, a definitive full-time appointment in a secondary school.

In Finland, regulations specify that professors and assistant professors require a doctoral degree, 'scientific merit', and good teaching ability.

In Berlin the list of personal qualities includes 'ability to tolerate and solve social conflicts, ability to tolerate frustrations, ability to present clear arguments which convince others, and ability to guide and counsel young teachers and Fachseminarleiter'.

In Scotland all candidates are required to be registered, or to be eligible for registration, as a trained teacher with the national professional body, the General Teaching Council for Scotland. It has been argued that this 'closed shop' denies the training system people with relevant expertise in psychology, sociology, management and computing because they have not themselves taken a qualification as a teacher. The introduction of credentialling courses for those who aspire to roles in initial teacher education (Buchberger, 1989) may also be viewed in some quarters as restrictive.

Screening reduces the applicant pool to those who satisfy the formal criteria. The criteria specifically relating to the appointment may not be decided until later in the process, and these may not be made known to the applicant.

Obtaining reports on applicants

Applicants may be invited to nominate persons to whom reference as to suitability may be made in confidence. In some situations management will obtain reports on all applicants prior to deciding rank order on suitability; in others (for example Wales) applicants will be rank ordered and reports obtained only on those whom it is intended to interview. Reports may also be obtained from staff who know the applicant but may not have been nominated.

Where there is no formal application process, as in the Netherlands and Israel, no written references may be sought.

Obtaining additional evidence on applicants

Additional evidence may be sought on applicants. In Berlin applicants for seminarleiter are observed at work in school by a chief school inspector whose report is forwarded to the appointing committee.

In Finland two 'experts' are appointed by the education faculty to examine the research record, postgraduate activities and publications of lecturer applicants who meet the formal criteria. Research relevant to teacher education is preferred to experience, since it is believed that this leads to broader views of how to teach and to more flexible patterns of teaching. Each is also required to give a public lecture and performance is evaluated on a three-point scale viz: A excellent, B very good, C good. Reports are fed back to the relevant committee.

The face-to-face situation

The standard employment-type interview of a panel of three or four persons to one applicant is only one of the possible range of face-to-face situations in a selection process. The distinctive feature of the interview is the opportunity it provides for those interviewing to interact with the applicant, and to explore relevant factors such as previous experience.

Rank ordering on the basis of application form data supplemented by written reports and other evidence is one basis on which the decision is made as to which applicants are to be called for interview. Interviewees may be invited to make an informal visit to the institution prior to the interview. Interview procedures may comprise more than one stage, involve several participants, and take a variety of forms.

In Scotland a one-stage process occurs for lecturer appointments. Interviews last for 40 minutes. The panel comprises five staff and typically includes the head of the institution, and deputy, the head of the unit in which the successful applicant will work, a senior member of staff of a related unit, and a local professional, such as a headteacher. Gender representation is also considered. The panel members have access to all the documentation supplied by the applicant, and in a pre-meeting decide on lines of questioning, and who will be responsible for each. Four or five applicants may be interviewed, and each rated on a five-point scale on a number of dimensions believed to be relevant to the post. At the end of the interview an overall score is calculated, the specific grades serving as a guide to overall suitability rather than being summed. Applicants for senior management posts take part in a two-stage process, the first being a group discussion, the second an individual interview.

In England there may be a three- or four-stage process for lectureship appointments. In the ATEE case study applicants first heard a talk from a senior administrator. Then, individually, they went with a tutor and three students to a seminar class. There followed an interview with the leader of the course. Lunch was taken with other applicants and with staff from the department. At this point some applicants learned that their application had been unsuccessful; the remaining applicants had a panel interview.

In other systems other kinds of evidence on suitability are taken into account. In Berlin each applicant analyses a videotape of some instructional sequences prior to a panel interview. All the evidence is then forwarded to those who take the actual decision to appoint. In Finland no interview is held, recommendations begin made on the basis of academic and research record and observed teaching performance.

Wilson (1991) reported that training for interviews was not provided in any of the institutions he studied.

Offering the post

Decision-makers may be professional teacher educators, administrators or representatives of political interest groups; they may be those who collect evidence on the quality of the applicants directly, or those who receive it at second hand. In some cases a decision has to be confirmed by a higher authority. Outcome decisions may be communicated to applicants immediately after the face-to-face process or some time later.

In Berlin chief inspectors collect the evidence, but the decision as to who is to be offered the post is made by a group of four – two chief school inspectors, the chief of administration and the landesschulrat (director of education). In Finland, professionals rank applicants, while faculty canvasses staff views and recommends to the chancellor who nominates to the post. In Austria nominees of political parties are the decision-makers; professionals have only a consultative role. In Scotland, Wales and England the interview panel – management in the institution – decides, though in England departmental staff have a say.

Decision-making involves weighing up and judging the meaning of all the available evidence, and coming to a view as to who should be offered a post. Where formal requirements are met value judgements about the weight to be attached to specific criteria may influence the final decision. These criteria may never be explicit. For example, only in some cases is teaching quality defined in terms of skills in non-directive approaches. In Finland the debate is about which applicant's research is most pertinent to teacher education; in England it is the balance between academic and research qualifications, teaching and other kinds of professional experience; in Scotland there is a premium on 'innovative flair and analytical capacity'. The committee will seek consensus, but may make a decision by vote.

Probation, induction and tenure

Conditions relating to appointments vary by country and by level of post. In Denmark and Sweden practically all appointments are tenured. In Netherlands, Iceland and Berlin tenure comes one year after appointment. The Israeli was tenured after three years' probation, and subsequent to a visit to her class by a senior professor. In Greece tenure is automatic for professors, associate professors and staff of SELETE. Turkey has a similar arrangement. Lecturers and assistant professors are not eligible for tenure but may have renewable fixed term appointments. In Cyprus all positions below that of Director of the Pedagogical Institute are temporary and filled on an annual basis, though contracts may be renewed, and in 1987–88 one in three staff had four years of continuous service. In former Yugoslavia posts were for three or six years, depending upon rank.

In UK there has been a trend away from permanent appointments to short-term contracts. The latter provide management with the opportunity to evaluate the suitability of the appointee, and constitute a kind of probationary system since contracts may be extended for those who are suitable and if the need for the position remains. In Scotland in 1989 between 10 and 15 per cent of staff held temporary posts.

The probation system operated by the Welsh institution was a 'mentor' scheme whereby a senior colleague acted as an adviser to a new appointee.

At the end of the one- or two-year period there would be a formal reporting stage on the new colleague's performance. In practice mentors were not appointed, though senior staff did write reports on probationers, without their being informed of the fact.

Induction is the process whereby staff new to a role are helped to adjust to its demands. Induction may be formal or informal and may comprise taught courses, planned activities and informal help (Gartside *et al.*, 1988). Formal induction refers to the creation of structures through which the individual is systematically introduced to the demands of the role, given support in coming to terms with it, and feedback on effectiveness. Informal advice and support given incidentally by colleagues is something experienced by most new employees. Wilson (1991) found consensus amongst administrators that new staff needed information about the administration of the institution, learning and teaching approaches, and school-based activity, including supervision of school experience.

Formal induction features in some countries. In England it may be offered both by the local administrative authority and by the university. Induction by the former is aimed at staff entering both further and higher education. Consequently it is very general in nature, focussing on university facilities, administrative procedures, and relationships with students. Specific teacher education issues may not be addressed. Since most induction was offered only at the start of the academic year, the appointee, who took up his post in mid-year, missed much that might have been relevant. Timetabling constraints also limited attendance at what was available. Where induction included meetings with senior managers and appointment of 'mentors' or personal advisers, practical constraints limited their effectiveness. One mentor had only half an hour per week timetabled for this work, and his trainee complained that he was never there to give advice when needed. No attempt was made systematically to monitor performance during induction.

In Netherlands the appointee was offered a two-day training course on issues related to student teachers. The theoretical aspects of this were favourably appraised although the appointee felt that he already knew most of the things discussed from his experience as a supervisor.

Most induction is informal. In Austria it is the responsibility of the head of department who has to introduce the syllabus of teacher education, and the curriculum of the college. All new staff members receive a handbook where the concept of teacher education is formulated and the specific tasks of the particular component of the teacher education programme are interpreted. Staff are also attached to teams who are developing the curriculum for particular programmes.

Appointees expressed a wish for more formal induction. The Berlin and Austrian appointees wanted courses prior to appointment; the Scot, who felt he had gone from 'Chief to Indian', wanted senior staff to explain procedures. Although his university had documented policy statements they had not been issued to him. The Welsh appointee commented that 'teacher trainers have no overall policy or strategies for staff retraining and development in the field'. The Israeli tutor devised her own induction programme through visiting classes of more experienced teachers.

Subsequent professional development

Professional development can mean acquiring a wider range of responses to professional tasks. Many appointees saw service in the university as itself a principal means to their professional development because it facilitated their attendance at seminars and workshops, and allowed them to engage in activities such as research, course development and writing. The appointee in the Netherlands remarked: 'I did not want to "fall asleep" as a teacher.'

Staff development is not a well-developed concept for teacher educators. But countries differ. In Norway each college offers courses in the professional development of practice. In Cyprus grants are available from Government for study at foreign institutions. Turkey has invested heavily in the upgrading of formal qualifications and foreign language proficiency. In Finland the Teacher Education Act gives lecturers (and the principals of the practice schools) a right and an obligation to take one term of study leave every seven years. In UK staff development policy lies with the institution. But in England, Wales and Northern Ireland the requirement to meet criteria of the Council for the Accreditation of Teacher Education (CATE) – e.g. in relation to recency of classroom teaching experience – means that available funds are often channelled in specific directions. CATE's replacement by the Training Agency may change this policy.

Many staff enhance their formal qualifications while in teacher education. The New Zealand survey found that just under half of respondents gained additional academic or professional qualifications subsequent to their first appointment. But there are relatively few structured in-service opportunities specifically for teacher educators.

Montero and Vez (1989) reported a three-phase course for teacher trainers of English language teaching and the pedagogy of language in Galicia, Spain. The course was piloted in 1988–89 with 30 participants. Phase One was residential and provided information on principles and practice of English language teaching; Phase Two was project based in the participants' work place; Phase Three was again residential when final reports were submitted and discussed. Boud (1988) has provided a report in the Australian context.

Recruitment, selection and induction of school-level teacher educators

Trainee teachers often claim that placement in schools to practise teaching is the most valued aspect of their training. In the UK 60 per cent of the one-year pre-service postgraduate programme must be school-based and some can be totally so. The quality of this experience is clearly dependent upon two factors: first, the extent to which objectives for the placement are known and agreed by all the parties involved, and, second, staff in the receiving institution being able to maximise the potential of the placement.

The categories of teacher educator at school level were mentioned earlier. The organisation of school experience is a contentious issue with 'normal' or 'model' schools being phased out, or now only supplementing provision in conventional schools. It has been argued that their staff should have only short-term appointments.

In UK it is a requirement that state schools accept trainee teachers but now universities must pay schools for this service. Supervisory teachers are generally – but not in all cases – experienced teachers who have the status and salary of 'merit' teachers, on account of their pedagogic skills. There are formal criteria for such appointments, such as length of service, and evidence of skill as a teacher, but selection is not based on demonstrated competence in the classroom. In Greece teachers are paid to supervise students and offered in-service training as an additional incentive to participate. Induction is provided in Flemish Belgium where school teacher trainers meet with college-based counterparts who assist them to define content and methods of training and the principles of assessment.

Schools (and teachers) differ in their responsiveness to the opportunity to supervise students. In Sweden an attempt is being made to place students with ordinary schools which wish to develop their practice, and which see benefits from partnership with teacher training institutions. Staff in higher education institutions, equally, differ in their willingness to become involved in supervision of students in schools. In the past in Scotland only staff in pedagogic departments were allowed to observe lessons by students on teaching practice in schools; now course teams drawn from both the theory and pedagogic departments have responsibility for all aspects of student development, including assessment of performance on teaching practice. However, there is little orientation for either university or school staff, although the issues are frequently discussed and there is no lack of literature on clinical supervision and available resource materials (e.g. Turney *et al.*, 1982). In a study of practice in Scotland Elder (1988) concluded that 'despite the acknowledged centrality of this element there appears to be only a very vague notion as to what should happen on school experience and why'. University status also poses new dilemmas for staff who doubt the efficacy of school visits, which are expensive of time which, some would argue, is better devoted to research.

Conclusion

Throughout Europe teacher educators recruited in the 1960s and 1970s are now nearing retirement. Despite criticism initial teacher education seems likely to continue, although increasingly on a school-based, internship model. There will be jobs in teacher education in the 1990s. An increasing number will be at school level in pre-service supervision and training, mentoring, and in-service, for example through follow-up to appraisal. Policy in higher education institutions is to recruit staff on short-term contracts. Those appointed are likely to be experienced teachers who have successfully supervised trainees, have acquired formal academic qualifications beyond the minimal, and have a demonstrated interest in pedagogical issues. Where these institutions are faculties of universities research experience is already important, and that is the trend for all.

Being in what they perceived to be a 'buyers' market' it is not surprising that administrators expressed satisfaction with current patterns of recruitment and selection; only in regard to induction was there a sense that more might be done. While not always fully understanding the reasons for their success those appointed welcomed the informal professional development opportunities offered through their new role, but also requested fuller induction.

It is curious that training for the teacher educator role is not seen as an intrinsic part of the appointment process at any level. It might be thought self-evident that educating and training teachers is a different job from teaching school age students. This holds for supervision at classroom level, and designing and managing training in higher education. What is not clear is the nature of the knowledge and skills required for these different roles, or the means to acquire them. The criteria currently employed − experience plus academic qualifications − are clearly felt by appointees themselves to be insufficient. The emphasis on 'experience' and informal learning as the principal means to learning the roles of the teacher trainer, indeed, in some respects undermines the whole basis of teacher education as a professional activity. The restricted field from which managers recruit trainers would indicate little prospect of radical change from within teacher education in the immediate future.

Induction would help experienced teacher educators define and clarify the body of professional knowledge about curriculum, evaluation, teaching, learning and assessment that should, but does not yet, consciously underpin all pre-service training of the next generation of teachers. It could also promote dialogue and shared language between trainers. Induction could also be evaluated for its helpfulness to new appointees in the short term and for its longer term effects on the quality of training itself. This will remain the critical issue.

The 'buck stops' in short, not so much with the teacher educators, many of whom are struggling to come to terms with the complexities of a short term appointment, as with those who have appointed them and who have the responsibility to create the conditions for effectively doing the job.

Acknowledgments

This chapter is in part based on case studies collected in 1989 by Peter Bannink, The Netherlands; Friedriech Buchberger, Austria; Peter Gaude, Germany; Paul Hellgren, Finland; Pinchas Tamir, Israel; Angela Thomas, Wales; John Wilson, Scotland; and Tony Wilson, England.

PART THREE

Teacher Education in Europe:
Issues and Trends

CHAPTER 7

Teacher Education and Training for Teachers of Human Rights

Monique Prindezis and Daniel Premont

The Centre International de Formation à l'Enseignement des Droits de l'Homme et de la Paix CIFEDHOP

The work of CIFEDHOP in the field of training for the teaching of human rights and peace is by definition interdisciplinary. Three distinctive disciplines, at least, are involved: pedagogy, law (and more specifically international law on human rights) and peace research. Ideological tensions have tended to keep these three domains separate and only recently have the main protagonists, teachers and law practitioners learned how to communicate and co-operate closely on the training of teachers, children and adults in the field of human rights and peace.

To our knowledge the CIFEDHOP is unique. In the majority of countries this sort of training exists only in embryo and specifically designed national programme are more or less non-existent. However, with the lessening of political and ideological objections an increasingly large number of teachers, ministries of education, training institutions, as well as non-governmental organisations involved in human rights, and trade unions, are becoming interested. This chapter gives in outline a list of some of the CIFEDHOP activities which are aimed at encouraging research and study as well as initiatives and innovations, publications including audio visual material, and the dissemination of new pedagogical methods. CIFEDHOP ensures that all these are accessible to teachers who then adapt them to the local, national, sub-regional, regional or, even if this were possible, universal context, as appropriate.

Introduction

Few countries have integrated the teaching of human rights and peace *per se*, in the education provided in schools or for adults. Yet, as early as on 10 December 1948, the General Assembly of the United Nations, in adopting the Universal Declaration of Human Rights, had urged countries to ensure that the full text of the Declaration be 'distributed, publicised, read and discussed especially in schools and other educational establishments'.

Until the late 1960s such integration was difficult:

(a) Because of the 'cold war'; the study of human rights on the one hand and research on peace was politicised and used as if it were an ideological instrument of the cold war: the American/Western European/Christian/Liberal interpretation of human rights (the champions of civil and political rights) or Socialist (the champions of economic, social and cultural rights) and the Soviet/Eastern European/Atheist/Marxist's view of peace. The governments of the so-called 'Third World' countries sided with one or the other of these tendencies or counted the blows in a North-South war, endeavouring to reject human rights and peace concepts as if they were merchandise exported from the North and therefore poorly adapted to the southern climate. They, given the competing demands of economic development, give such concepts a low priority.

(b) Because the integration of human rights education, in an already overloaded curriculum, was difficult to pursue. 'Human rights' stem from humanist values and from lived experience, yet historically, semantically and logically they belong first and foremost to the discipline of law, human rights can not be proclaimed without reference to law (the Universal Declaration of human rights was first adopted as an instrument of international public law); human rights are recognised and guaranteed at a national level through the constitution, the laws, the rules, court verdicts.

Once the American/West European countries had in the 1960s given independence to the majority of the countries which they had dominated, the international context changed. In the early 1970s, those newly developing states who had been able to use their entitlement to autodetermination became increasingly familiar with the procedures set in place to implement human rights inside the different international organisations.

The two ideological blocs in the North worked hard, particularly within the United Nations and UNESCO, to reach common ground on the majority of human rights and on the importance of disarmament to secure peace. It is in such a context that in 1973, the United Nations Commission on Human Rights asked that UNESCO should facilitate education for human rights, particularly in higher education. A year later, the General conference of UNESCO was to adopt the 'recommendation on education for international understanding, co-operation and peace and education connected with human rights and fundamental liberties'. This gave teachers some pedagogical directions but more significantly recommended that countries should implement certain recommendations through legislation or, depending on the country's constitutional set up, the production of reports on the progress made in the initial training of teachers, teaching methods and resources, the research and experimentation as well as international co-operation. In 1976, the international treaty on economic, social and cultural rights in which article 13 declares that education is there to reinforce human rights, became operative. In 1978, UNESCO organised in Vienna an international congress on the teaching of human rights in order to celebrate the thirtieth anniversary of the Universal Declaration and to adopt proposals to develop the teaching of human rights at all levels. Furthermore in 1978, the Committee of Ministers of the Council of Europe was to adopt resolution (78) 41 in which all member state governments were asked to implement any measure deemed to be appropriate to their own educational context to ensure that the teaching of human rights is given adequate attention in initial and in-service training provision at all levels.

In 1985, it was UNESCO who adopted recommendation (85) 7 concerning teaching and training provision for human rights in schools. This recommendation provides some practical suggestions concerning the curriculum, aptitudes and knowledge to acquire, the school climate and the training of teachers. In 1987, UNESCO organised in Malta a second international congress to review progress and start new initiatives and in 1989, the United Nations Convention on children's rights recognised that one of the aims of schooling must be to ensure that children grow to respect man and fundamental liberties ... prepare the child for a responsible role in a free society, in a spirit of understanding, peace, tolerance, equality between sexes and friendship between all the people and ethnic national and religious groups as well as with his own people. More recently the African convention on co-operation and security in Europe have also become active towards this objective and invited other involved states to follow suit.

Once political and ideological difficulties were overcome, progress could be made towards introducing law into the curriculum. Some education ministries used the new declarations of rights as a lever to ensure that the population at large became familiar with the issues through the teaching of such things as, for example, the federal and provincial Charts of Canada; others used existing related disciplines such as civic education in France, or morals in Belgium and Luxembourg. In some countries, initiatives arose through the national commissions on human rights (Australia, Togo), national commissions set up by UNESCO (Guinea) through political parties (the socialist party in France), through non-governmental organisations (the world organisation for school as a peace instrument in Geneva, and subsequently in a number of other countries).

CIFEDHOP aims to promote the teaching and education concerning human rights and peace in primary and secondary ordinary or professional schools and in the education of adults and the in-service training of

132

teachers. Most significantly this occurred through the organisation of training sessions towards:

- teachers who belong to different disciplines;
- teachers of specific subjects (civic education, history, etc);
- educational civil servants, research institutes and centres.

for pedagogical documentation, inter-governmental organisations, and associations involved in the teaching of human rights and peace.

Every year CIFEDHOP organises an international session of training open to teachers from all disciplines, from all levels and from all countries. These sessions now have Spanish, French and English sections.

CIFEDHOP endeavours to respond to education ministries' requests for training support. Following a first African training session, CIFEDHOP obtained a consultative statute in relation to the African commission on human rights and people, whose headquarters are in Banji in Gambia, and it has received the prize given by the French national consultative commission for human rights, during celebrations organised as part of the bicentenary of the French revolution, in 1989. This prize was used for the publication of a collection of documents of the first African session which has since been disseminated through the schools of Guinea and in a number of French-speaking countries. A collection of the documents of the second session has also been published.

In 1991, the Portuguese government invited CIFEDHOP and the Centre for Human Rights of the United Nations to organise in Lisbon a training workshop for civil servants working in the Ministries of Education, Justice and Foreign Affairs concerned with Portuguese speaking countries. In April 1992, the French National Union of Teachers invited the CIFEDHOP to organise a workshop in Notre Dame du Pre, in the Savoie.

The Centre offers teachers, researchers, PhD and MA or degree students, and to probationary teachers, a support structure which includes a specialist library and a media library, study facilities and even guidance and research supervision. The CIFEDHOP stimulates and co-ordinates research initiatives on the design of pedagogical material for local, national, regional and international contexts. The Centre has for some time been conducting a review of the terminology of human rights and produced an introduction to the issue entitled 'Terminology and concepts referring to the rights of men, women and children' which appeared in 1992 in English, Spanish, French and Portuguese. Its aim is to clarify the concepts and to ensure a better understanding of the judicial terms which apply to human rights.

L'ecole instrument du paix

The world association pour l'ecole instrument de paix (EIP), created by Jacques Muhlethaler, has since 1967 been developing a programme of activities in schools to ensure that the provision of education for human rights and peace is recognised.

In order to push the frontiers of exclusion and to participate actively in the elements of progress which contribute to the well being of the world population, the EIP, as an international non-governmental organisation encourages the take-up of human rights and peace education into account in the design of educational activities.

In this context, the work of the EIP since its creation has been aimed at developing attitudes, aptitudes and increasing knowledge in order to promote respect for fundamental rights and freedoms and as a consequence to promote non-violent solutions to conflicts.

In the 1980s, the EIP developed in-service training programmes on the teaching of human rights and peace aimed at primary, secondary and further education teachers. It aimed to create familiarity with international and national texts which related to human rights on the one hand, and to their implementation on the other. Once exposed to such teaching, children should be able to refer to the principles outlined in the Universal Declaration of human rights in their daily conduct, in their command of a language and a vocabulary appropriate to circumstances, in their thinking and decision making processes.

The EIP realised that the promotion of this type of teaching and education required that it should work with teachers. With national workshops on human rights and peace. In view of the success of this enterprise, the EIP proposed in 1984 the creation of an international centre for the teaching of human rights and peace, with responsibility for the organisation of training workshops. This Centre was inaugurated in 1987.

Activities

In order to achieve its objectives, the EIP is an international non-governmental organisation with a consultative status in relation to UNESCO and the Council of Europe.

The EIP attempts to ensure that human rights and peace are given due consideration in national educational systems, particularly in the areas of teacher pre-service and in-service training.

In the field of pedagogical research, the EIP initiates and evaluates educational developments which are appropriate to human rights and peace, for example:

- pedagogies aimed at raising awareness and values, teaching through projects, collaborative teaching, and so forth;
- transfer of values, resistance to change, psychological associations and their impact on human rights education;
- equality of opportunities in education; ending of any discrimination in school textbooks, moral and citizenship education, education for democracy, including simulations in human rights and peace education.

The EIP has a teachers centre which is available to teachers and educators who wish to develop human rights and peace education programmes. It also collaborates with other organisations where material which is relevant to its objectives is produced and allows the use of its logo on educational projects which share its objectives. It also intervenes in educational and training institutions which request support and offers initiation or training modules in response to specific requests for various professional sectors: health, communications, work places etc.

The EIP is responsible for training the trainers responsible for the promulgation of its objectives, for the dissemination of knowledge of international and national instruments of human rights.

In order to disseminate international instruments which relate to human rights, the EIP has published:

(a) An abridged version of the Universal Declaration for human rights.

In 1978, the EIP invited teachers and university researchers to translate the Universal Declaration for human rights into a language simple enough to be accessible for children and people who are unfamiliar with judicial language. This simplified version is available in English, Spanish, Roumanian, Hindu, Russian, Urdu and Thai.

(b) A collection of drawings and cartoons and a record based on the Universal Declaration for human rights.

Draw me a human right is an album of drawings and cartoons for which 53 Algerian, Belgian, Spanish, Italian, French and Swiss artists have produced illustrations on the Universal Declaration, on international treaties which concern human rights, on the Geneva Convention and other international documents. This initiative has been reinforced by a recording, 'Freedom, 33 ... for human rights', in which 11 Canadian, French and Swiss artists have produced a song based on the Declaration.

(c) Friendship exercise book: the cover on the rights of children.

To promote the rights of children, the EIP has produced book covers illustrated with the Declaration for Human Rights and article 29 of the Convention which assumes that educational objectives include the respect for the rights of children. Because of the well-established arrangements for international school to school and pupil to pupil correspondence, this initiative has allowed teachers to introduce pupils to the rights of children and to contribute to the implementation of the Convention in their country. The pedagogic aims of this communication is:

- to lead to an increase in awareness and respect of others;
- to instil in the pupils involved an interest for their culture and for the traditional positive values of their countries;
- to lead them to a civic and humanitarian commitment towards a better understanding of their country, of the problems it faces and of its successes;
- to encourage teachers from a school establishment to collaborate on themes which address the issue of children's rights.

(d) A bulletin on school and peace.

The EIP publishes an information Bulletin for its members, intergovernmental and non-governmental organisations, education ministries and the national UNESCO commissions describe their plans and projects to ensure the promotion of human rights. Initiatives described by teachers who have worked on these themes are also published.

(e) National representation.

The activities of the EIP are taken up in some 20 countries and subsequently adapted to the development and the culture of each country. There is a concentration on the creation of national organisations which are responsible for informing public opinion on human rights issues in order to integrate them to school programmes. They also disseminate the most recent publications on the theme of human rights in education produced by intergovernmental and non-governmental organisations and create activities aimed at informing school pupils.

English, Spanish, French and Portuguese versions of these documents are available. The aim is to clarify the concepts and to ensure a better understanding of the judicial terms which apply to human rights.

CHAPTER 8

The Media Education Revolution and Teacher Education

Len Masterman

The 1980s was a decade of spectacular development for media education in Europe. The motor which drove that development, in a period generally characterised by educational retrenchment and conservatism, was the determination of many media teachers to ensure that an era of unprecedented expansion and technological development in the media would be matched by a commensurate expansion in the critical consciousness of students and pupils. Of central importance in shaping the thinking of European media teachers was an extensive programme of conferences, courses and publications organised by the Council of Europe throughout the 1980s.[1] Space does not permit a nation-by-nation account of specific developments in member countries of the Council of Europe, though these are available elsewhere (Council of Europe, 1989). Instead my intention is to outline some of the main lines of development in what has been an exciting period for the media education movement, and to suggest some guidelines for future action, particularly in the field of teacher education.

Why media education? From protection to empowerment

Answers to the question 'Why study the media?' changed perceptibly over the past decade. Up to the early 1980s a good deal of media teaching was still largely paternalistic and 'inoculatory'. It had its origins in a deep-seated distrust of the media themselves, which were often viewed as agents of cultural decline and seducers of the innocent. In particular, it arose out of a concern that children were watching too much television and that much of what they were watching was mind-numbingly trivial and perhaps even dangerous. Media education was seen as a counter-balance to these tendencies. If the media were something akin to infectious diseases then media education, it was thought, was necessary as a kind of inoculation. It is worth stressing that this view of the media, although now routinely rejected by most media teachers, still has a lively general currency even amongst educators.

The earliest answer to the question 'Why study the media?' then, was 'In order to protect both our children and the continuity of our cultural values from the worst excesses of the media.' There were two principal variations on this kind of approach to media education. Some argued that the development of discrimination, fine judgement and taste depended upon pupils grasping the basic differences between the timeless values of authentic culture as embodied in the traditional arts (in which teachers were themselves initiated) and the essentially anti-cultural values of a largely commercial mass-media. This was the earliest version of media education in which popular forms were introduced into the classroom only to be put smartly in their place as teachers demonstrated the effortless superiority of literature to films, television and advertisements.

A second variation was more sympathetic to the media. It argued that the popular media were themselves capable of producing authentic works of art, and that the function of media education should be to encourage pupils to discriminate not *against* the media but *within* them, sorting out the good films, newspapers and television programmes from the bad. This, the 'Popular Arts' movement, represented a decided step forward, and at its best, as exemplified in the film studies movement, mobilised an energy and a genuine enthusiasm for the engagement with popular forms that was always going to yield more positive results in the classroom than the knee-jerking rejection of more traditional approaches. Yet the Popular Arts movement was still essentially protectionist. In spite of its name the movement generally sought to undermine the genuinely *popular* tastes of pupils in favour of the more 'serious' media preferences of their teachers.

By the early 1980s there was a discernible and radical movement away from 'discrimination' and 'appreciation' as the key objectives of media education towards much more *investigative* approaches to understanding the media. This development broke with two time-honoured educational traditions. First of all it pushed the whole question of aesthetic and moral values – the whole question of precisely how good or bad a film or television programme was – away from the centrally dominant position it had always held within media education. And secondly it severely undermined the hierarchical role of the teacher as the accredited expert and purveyor of approved knowledge within the classroom. The teacher was no longer the arbiter of taste, but a partner or co-investigator in what was now a much more open-ended process. (S)he was something akin, perhaps, to a senior colleague rather than the sole repository of knowledge and wisdom.

What lay at the heart of this major transformation and re-conceptualisation of media education? The answer is simple. Media teaching was in

138

trouble. The old certainties were proving conspicuously unsuccessful in laying the foundation for workable classroom practice. Indeed they were a major part of the problem. This was because:

(a) Media education was still an essentially negative exercise. It was unable either to command the enthusiasm of its students or to sustain the early energies of its teachers because it worked against the grain of popular tastes. It remained an essentially 'improving' exercise which had little discernible impact upon the vast majority of students who continued, obstinately, to assert their right to enjoy what they, rather than what their teachers, liked in the media.

(b) There were no widely agreed standards or criteria available for evaluating the media. The teacher as arbiter of media standards and tastes was thus a deeply unconvincing figure whose 'authority' was ultimately quite spurious, and whose confidence in his/her own judgement was without any real foundation. When it came down to it nobody knew precisely what good news reporting or bad documentary was. At the heart of the subject lay a theoretical vacuum.

(c) Added to the problem of deciding what precisely constituted good or bad advertisements, news, or sports coverage were doubts about the appropriateness of applying aesthetic criteria at all to a wide range of media output. It seemed to be important, too, for pupils to understand something of the nature of media institutions, the routine working practices of media professionals and the ways in which the media operated as consciousness industries. Much more was at stake here than the evaluation of media texts. What pupils needed to grasp, if they were to begin to make sense of the media, was the wider context within which media products were being produced, circulated and consumed.

This movement away from appreciation towards understanding did not completely dispose of the 'value question' however. The question 'Precisely how good or bad is this newspaper or TV programme?' was, in some circumstances, still a question worth asking. What it did make impossible was any transcendental, transcultural, transhistoric notion of value. The value question had become, unquestionably, a *transitive* one (value for whom? Value according to what criteria of thought and judgement? Value for what strategic purposes?). Opened out here was the possibility that value was not such much a quality of the text itself, but of its usefulness or relevance to particular sets of readers. In the classroom it would no longer be good enough to subordinate pupils to the dominance of the text or of the teacher. Pupils' own responses had to be taken, perhaps for the first time, very seriously indeed.

The movement from appreciation to understanding, then, involved a transformation in the role of the pupil from being a passive recipient of already formulated textual meanings to an active maker of meanings. It heralded, too, a new agenda for media education away from narrowly aesthetic questions towards more 'technical' and 'scientific' ones: How and in whose interests do the media operate? How are they organised? How do they produce meaning? What precisely is their ideological effectiveness? How do they represent 'reality'? How are these representations read and valued by different audiences? The development of a critically informed intelligence in relation to the media now became the key objective rather than the nurturing of a finely honed aesthetic judgement.

Finally, in the past two or three years, that notion of developing an informed understanding of the media has itself undergone a further evolution. It is now clear that successful media education involves an empowerment of learners essential to the creation and sustaining of an active democracy and of a public which is not easily manipulable but whose opinion *counts* on media issues because it is critically informed and capable of making its own independent judgements. At a time when the management and manufacture of information by governments and vested interest groups has grown apace it is now the *liberating* potentialities of media education which perhaps provide its chief rationale. Without retreating into mechanistic and pessimistic mass-society theories (in which the so-called 'masses' are seen as easily manipulated by the state or trans-national capital via the agencies of the mass-media) it is nevertheless true that we live in an age of universal public relations, an age of misinformation and disinformation, an age in which politics is increasingly converging with advertising, and in which images appear to have more substance than issues and arguments. It is an age, in short, in which the engineering of public consent across a wide range of issues is very big business.

In these circumstances it is not difficult in most European cultures to see the media less as bastions of free expression than as weapons used in the service of powerful interest groups. This has given rise, even in advanced democracies, to new kinds of poverty and new kinds of inequality: between those who have easy access to the media and those who do not; between those whose world-views, receive coherent expression within existing media, and those whose do not; between those with the power to define, and those who are always only defined; between those who can speak about the world as they know and understand it, and those whose experiences are inevitably framed and interpreted for them by others; between, in short, the media-rich and the media-poor.

Media education is one of the few weapons any society possesses for challenging these inequalities in knowledge and power, and for closing the gap between those in whose interests media information is produced and disseminated, and those who simply consume it 'innocently' as news or entertainment. Media education can empower its learners and greatly strengthen the democratic structures of the society which it serves by challenging the 'naturalness' of media images, by foregrounding questions of representation and examining the democratic structure of broadcasting institutions and raising questions of human rights in relation to communication.

The movements, sketched out above, from a *protectionist* through an *investigative* to an *empowerment* rationale for media education have been accompanied by further important transformations in the concept of media education itself.

The concept of media education: from school subject to lifelong process

In the early 1980s perhaps the most significant question facing media educators was 'Is it possible to teach about the media in a coherent and disciplined way?' This remains an important question, and an attempt will be made to answer it in the next section of this chapter. But by the early 1990s the terms of the major debates had moved on. Today it is important to see media education as a *lifelong process*. Interest in and attachment to the media begins, for most children, well before they attend school and continues throughout their adult lives. A media education which fails to recognise the implications of this will fall short of its fullest potentiality. High student motivation, for example, must now become rather more than a desirable spin-off from effective teaching. It must become a primary objective. If media education is not an enjoyable and fulfilling, as well as instructive experience, then pupils will have no encouragement to continue learning about the media after they have passed beyond the gates of the school.

Seeing media education as being, inevitably, a lifelong process has other important effects. It changes classroom objectives in fundamental ways. Media education becomes an education for the future as well as the present. The whole *point* about media education is that it should develop in children enough self-confidence and critical maturity for them to be able and willing to apply critical judgements to TV programmes and newspaper articles which they will encounter *in the future*. The acid test of the success of any media education programme lies in the extent to which pupils are critical in their own use and understanding of the media when the teacher is not there. The primary objective of lifelong media education is not simply critical awareness and understanding but *critical autonomy*.

The importance of this objective has profound implications for course content, teaching methodology and methods of evaluation. It is no longer good enough for pupils to process or reproduce ideas or information supplied to them by their teacher (as they do in most other lessons). Nor is it adequate for teachers to encourage pupils to develop their own critical insights in the classroom (though this is certainly important). The really important and challenging task for the media teacher is to produce in pupils both the *ability* and the *willingness* to want to go on doing this for the rest of their lives.

In the classroom this means, as I have already suggested, that high pupil motivation becomes an important priority. It also means that it is essential to teach for transfer. That is, it is always going to be necessary for teachers to move their pupils beyond an understanding of this or that particular issue or text towards an understanding of those *general principles* which will have relevance to the analysis of similar issues or texts. Evaluation will not be of what pupils *know* but of how they *apply* what they know and, often, how they respond in situations where they *do not know the answer*. It is worth emphasising how seldom we expect this of school pupils in our teaching of most subjects.

What should be taught? From fragmentation to coherence

To be convinced of the need for media education is one thing. To develop a successful media education practice is quite another. It is unfortunately true that much of what passed for media education in the past was fragmented and chaotically divergent, depending as it often did, on the enthusiasms and interests of individual teachers. In the past decade, however, widespread agrement has been reached on ways of studying and teaching about the media and the adherents of media education would now claim that their educational practice is every bit as systematic and intellectually rigorous as that of more traditional and established subjects. It now makes sense to speak of a coherent international media education *movement*. How has this development occurred?

The major epistimological problem facing media teachers can be simply stated. It is this. How is it possible to make any kind of conceptual sense of a field which covers such a diversity of forms, practices and products? The very object of study itself, 'the media', turns out to be, on examination, little more than a convenient catch-all category into which many very different forms of communication can be bundled, rather than a clearly defined field. And each medium itself serves a multiplicity of functions. It was for many years far from clear how even a single medium like television (which serves the functions of cinema, newspaper, magazine, sports arena, theatre and music-hall all rolled into one) could be studied in a disciplined and rigorous way, let alone *all* of the other media and their complex inter-relationships.

Up until the early 1980s the most common 'solution' to this problem had really been no solution at all. It was that the 'obvious' starting point for thinking about the media lay in the uniqueness (or 'specificity') of each medium. The subject was deemed to consist of the aggregated sum of these discrete parts. So, a one year course on the media might typically consist of a term on film, half a term on television, half a term on newspapers, a few weeks on advertising, a little time on pop music and so on. The problem here was not simply that the subject was being fragmented at the level of content. It was that different kinds of principles, concepts and modes of enquiry were being brought into play in studying in the next term by the study of TV news, which in turn might be followed by work on the techniques of persuasion used in advertising or images of women in women's magazines. But what gave coherence to these very different topics? A particular mode of enquiry? The examination of important cross-media concepts? Or what?

Answers to these questions emerged slowly as media teachers began to meet and discuss their work throughout the 1980s. Continuities and correspondences began to emerge out of the most diverse range of practices and contexts, so that it is now possible to map out some of the ways in which the media can be studied in a more disciplined way. It has to be said, too, that the answers which emerged were influenced by the growing recognition of teachers (many of whom had had in the past a particular commitment to film studies) that if their work were to be firmly grounded in the actual media experiences of their pupils, and if they were to begin the task of responding to the significant ideological issues raised by the media, then television should play a much more dominant role in their thinking and practice than it had ever done in the past.

It is now possible, then, to say that media education has a first principle. It is a principle from which all else follows. It is a principle which particularly illuminates the nature of television but which also has a surprising degree of potency across all media. I am speaking of the principle of *non-transparency*. It insists that the media are rather more than simple 'windows on the world' or 'mirrors' which reflect external reality in a way which needs no further explanation. It insists that TV, newspapers, films, radio and advertisements are actively *produced*. They are involved, that is, in a process of *constructing* or *representing* reality rather than simply transmitting or reflecting it.

The crucial distinction which is drawn, then, by all media teachers and students is that between images and their referents, between representations and reality, between (to use the structuralist jargon) the signifier and the signified. And this has given rise in turn to a characteristic discourse in which media teachers and their students talk incessantly not about 'women' or 'sport' or 'poverty' or 'prisons' or 'Africa', but about *representations* of these things. The central unifying concept of representation indeed has become, in English, a kind of professional pun: the media do not present 'reality', the re-present it.

The principle of non-transparency, then, insists that the media are the product of human agency. The media *mediate*. They are not, oppressively, the reflections of a reality which we must *accept*. They are, liberatingly, representational or symbolic systems which we must read, understand and act upon.

If media products are constructions then a number of other areas immediately suggest themselves for further investigation:

(a) *The origins and sources of media representations.* Who owns, controls, produces and influences the images that we see? Why are the media as they are? This whole area has always been, by common consent, one of the most difficult aspects of the media to teach. It continues to be so. However there have been a number of interesting developments in this field since the early 1980s:

    (i) There is now a much more sophisticated understanding by media researchers and educators of the rather intricate web of often conflicting interests and pressures at play within the media. In the past, what used to be thought of as questions of 'ownership and control' led all too frequently to a simplistic model of the media within which texts could be briskly 'explained' in terms of the power and control exercised either by 'the capitalist system' or by the influence of a few wealthy and powerful individuals within it. Without denying for a moment the powerful influence exerted within the media by individual owners (concentration of ownership, rightly, continues to be a matter of concern in many European countries) or by transnational media conglomerates, teachers of media are now just as concerned to unravel the precise influence upon the media of a complex network of inter-related determinants such as advertisers, the government and the state, the legal constraints surrounding the media, a wide range of economic determinants, audiences, sources, the routine working practices and professional ideologies of media workers, the role of media unions, the part played by self-regulation within the media, and so on. Media teachers are now less likely than ever before to pass on to their students a monolithic view of the media as ideological apparatuses transmitting their messages to a largely passive audience. Rather, they are likely to promote a view of the media as a *site for struggle* between contending (albeit unequal) interests, a struggle within which both teachers and students can themselves play a positive, if minor role.

(ii) The second major development in teaching about this area has been teachers' growing recognition that it is probably counter-productive to attempt to deposit large amounts of information upon students about the nature of media institutions. It is a practice which is likely to de-motivate students, and to discourage real learning. It is far more important for students of any age to know where to find and how to use information which they may need about the media than simply to commit to memory or regurgitate information which will quickly be out of date. Today's media classroom is also a media information resource centre which pupils are trained to find their way around not just for their present but also for their future needs.

(b) The second area for investigation within media education is *media rhetoric* – the techniques used by the media to construct meaning, to produce their effects. On the whole this is now very familiar territory for media teachers. It covers such things as visual and sound editing, the role of commentary, the inevitably selective nature of sounds and images, the use of set-ups, the structure of narratives and so on.

What is involved here is a reversal of the process through which a medium selects and edits material into a polished, continuous and seamless flow. It involves the *deconstruction* of media texts by breaking through their surface to reveal the rhetorical techniques through which meanings are produced. It is yet another important step in moving from subordination to a text to critical liberation from it. And it is an important element both in the analysis of media images, and in practical media work in which pupils can try out the effects of particular rhetorical techniques for themselves.

(c) The third area of investigation in media education is that of *ideology*. To a large degree the ideological power of the media resides in the ability of those who control and work in them to pass off what are inevitably selective and partial representations as true, rational, authentic and necessary. Not constructions but simply part of the way things are. It is media education's staunch refusal of the naturalness of the image that makes it an essential democratic tool, one of the few counterbalances we have as ordinary citizens against the ideological power of those who have easy access to the media.

Media teachers' interest in ideology signals a belief that communication issues and questions of value are inextricably intertwined. It is characteristic of media education that it moves from the apparently trivial – the game show, the soap opera, the appearance of the newsreader – towards a consideration of the often large and significant ideas which underpin them – into a consideration, for instance, of gender stereotyping, or of what counts as knowledge, or of the relative importance attached to competition and co-operation, or the equating of honesty and 'truth' with class-based codes of dress or tones of voice.

Ultimately what are being explored here are questions of power. Whose interests are being served by these images and ideas? Out of what sets of material interests and conditions do they spring? Who has easy access to the media and who does not? These are questions which are inevitably going to be raised when the media are read as representational systems. The work which students do on the origins and sources of media representations (see (a) above) invariably reveals that the answers to these questions are rather more complicated than students at first imagined.

(d) *Audience.* Work on media audiences has come a long way in the past decade. Indeed audiences have been much neglected by media educators in the past, being regarded as more or less passive receivers of meanings determined elsewhere. Of predominant importance within media education has been the text. That was where, it was felt, meaning resided. Recent audience research has changed all of this. It has demonstrated that extent to which meaning is not so much *inherent* within a text as produced by the *interaction* of reader (or viewer) and text. Audiences, that is, are not slack-jawed and glassy-eyed morons soaking up everything which the media produces. They are, rather, active and ceaseless producers of meaning. Television or newspapers may *offer* to their audiences a range and diversity of positions from which to view and understand the world. But these positions are then worked upon by audiences. They're often disputed, argued with, integrated, modified or ignored, and generally subjected to complex processes of negotiation, acceptance or rejection. Audiences are responsible for making meaning, as they integrate (or decide not to integrate) media information into their own ways of making sense of the world.

The implications of this research for media education are important. For children are meaning-makers too. In the past media teachers have, perhaps, paid too much attention to the text's immanent meanings, and too little to what the child was bringing to the text. Whereas in the past media teachers tended to seek *consensual* and relatively *homogenous* responses from their pupils, now they are much more likely to welcome *diversity*, encouraging students to negotiate their own meanings, argue back with the media on their own terms, and make sense of the media's values in terms of their own.

How should media education be taught? From discussion to dialogue

The teacher-student relationship, according to the great Brazilian educator, Paulo Friere, generally possesses a fundamentally *narrative* character. In the teaching of most subjects the teacher, the possessor of legitimised knowledge, transmits to pupils appropriate packages of information, attitudes and judgements which are, in their turn, given back by the pupils to their teachers for evaluation. The teacher narrates. The pupils listen passively and, at the appropriate time, regurgitate. In the process of being narrated the contents of education become lifeless, the teacher speaking about reality as though it were 'motionless, static, compartmentalised and predictable'. Education, Friere (1972) pronounced, 'is suffering from narration sickness'.

Traditionally, teaching methodology within media education has taken the form of what may be called *disguised narrative* in which the real agenda of the teacher has been hidden from the pupils. This manipulative form of teaching was the logical outcome of the paternalistic objectives of early media education which sought the subtle improvement and development of pupils' media tastes. Central to this methodology was the class discussion, a liberal form in which pupils were offered the illusion of discursive freedom within a situation tightly controlled by the teacher.

As media education matured and developed, so did teaching styles appropriate to it. Simulations, practical audio and video work, sequencing exercises, prediction activities, code-breaking games and a whole battery of techniques for encouraging effective group learning became, by the mid-1980s, part of the armoury of most media teachers. They were techniques which encouraged pupils to take on much more responsibility for their own learning. They were appropriate to the objective of encouraging the critical autonomy of pupils since this could only be accomplished by gradually loosening pupils' dependency upon teachers and nurturing confidence in their own ideas and judgements.

But it was not simply the changing objectives of media education which encouraged an evolution away from discussion (in which teacher-pupil hierarchies were perpetuated in disguised form) towards *dialogue* which offered the promise of resolution of some of the contradictions between teachers and learners. This movement was encouraged by the nature of the media themselves. For the media *equalised* teachers and pupils. Both were equally and equal objects of the media's address. Furthermore, the media tended to communicate *laterally*, rather than hierarchically. They spoke *across*, rather than down to their audiences, addressing them, for the most part, in familiar and homely terms. Contrary to popular belief, the media did not encourage passivity. Teaching, because of its predominantly hierarchical mode, did that far more effectively. What the media encouraged, given the right circumstances, were *reflection and dialogue*. Why was this?

Simply, the introduction of media images into the classroom offered, to both teachers and pupils alike, objects for critical reflection. The simple act of projecting an image on to a screen possessed, almost magically, the potential to transform the teacher-pupil relationship because it introduced a third element into the classroom, one which was just as familiar to pupils as it was to teachers and one which could be investigated on equal terms, and from different perspectives by them both. It opened up the potentiality for genuine dialogue.

Traditional narrative teaching had never done this. There it was the *teacher* and the subject with which he/she was identified which were the principal objects of pupils' attention. And that attention had to be paid not simply to the content of the teachers' narratives but also to the idiosyncracies of the teachers themselves, their moods, whims and preferred ways of working. This was a situation which greatly discouraged mature reflection and critical questioning because both represented direct threats either to the personal authority of teachers or to the knowledge with which their status was associated.

Media education ultimately offered a way out of this impasse. It offered new dialogic ways of working upon material which was not closely associated with the teacher. It provided a forum within which teachers and students could continually learn from one another as co-investigators and co-participants. And it offered a new epistimology in which knowledge was not an oppressive, inert body of facts and ideas narrated by teachers to pupils, but was actively created by both through a process of dialogue and reflection.

Practical work: from cultural reproduction to critical practice

As I have suggested, media education is essentially active and participatory. It is about doing things. And most media programmes have allowed students as many opportunities as possible to communicate their own ideas through the production of their own newspapers, radio and TV programmes, films, photographs and photomontages, and advertising posters and campaigns.

Practical activity does not, in itself, constitute media education, however. In the early 1980s many media educators fell into what I will call *the technicist trap*: the belief that media education could be reduced to a series of purely technical operations, and that through their involvement in practical projects, students would *automatically* acquire critical abilities. Much of this early work was in fact a form of cultural reproduction, as students attempted to emulate professional media practices rather than to subject them to critical scrutiny. Far from de-mystifying the media, this kind of work all too often increased media mystification when students compared their own tentative efforts with the polished products of media professionals. This was a practice which naturalised rather the deconstructed media codes and conventions.

In the 1990s, it is now much clearer that:

(a) the link between practical work and analytical activities needs to be consciously forged by media teachers. It must be worked for. It cannot be assumed;

(b) practical work is not an end in itself, but a necessary means to developing a critical understanding of the media. If students are to understand the nature of media texts as constructions it is of great importance for them to have first-hand experience of the construction process from the inside;

(c) re-affirming the primacy of cultural criticism over cultural reproduction has led to a fundamental re-assessment of priorities for practical work. Many media teachers would now argue that the most significant forms of practical activity may not necessarily be those highly publicised (and often time-consuming) projects which call for the use of elaborate and sophisticated equipment. They may be very simple activities, doggedly low-tech, and within the reach of every teacher in every classroom: manipulating still images, writing commentaries, editing news stories, experimenting with interviewing techniques and the like. Some practical work may call for the use of more sophisticated equipment, but even here most media teachers are now more concerned to encourage students to experiment with alternatives, and to break or play around with dominant codes and conventions, than to slavishly reproduce mainstream media forms.

Cultural reproduction, then, is a poor aim for media education. It is uncritical. It enslaves rather than liberates. It freezes the impulses towards action and change. It naturalises current conventions, and thus encourages conformity and deference. Media education, on the other hand, in raising questions about how media texts are constructed (and might be constructed differently) and in its insistence upon the nature of media texts as the products of specific human choices, aims to encourage not only practical criticism but a genuinely critical practice.

Media education in the future

So much for the past and the present. What of the future? In what ways will media education have to change and develop through the 1990s? Let me suggest two related points for future growth:

(1) First of all I think we will need to wake up to the full implications of the marketing revolution which has been taking place throughout the 1980s. The growth and expansion of commercially based media during that time has produced a situation in which advertising can no longer be seen as something which takes place between programmes on television, or in the spaces around the editorial material in the press. Rather, the whole of the media has now been opened up, not simply to advertising but to a whole range of marketing techniques such as product placement, public relations, sponsorship, plugs for films and records, advertisements, news management, and the creation of disinformation in a way which makes the old distinctions between advertising and editorial material almost obsolete.

Similarly it's simply not possible for anyone to be media literate today if he or she doesn't understand that the primary function of commercial media is the segmentation and packaging of *audiences* for sale to advertisers. Up until now media education has been based upon a premise of the most astonishing naivety: that is that the primary function of the media has been the production of information or entertainment. What we have principally studied in media education have been *texts*: television programmes, newspaper stories, and magazine articles for example. But these are not the chief products of the media. They are what Dallas Smythe has called *the free lunch*: the means by which the real product of the media, from which its profits are derived − *the audience product* − is summoned into existence.

What I'm suggesting here is not simply that we improve our teaching about advertising and marketing as *a topic*. Rather, a critical understanding of the basic techniques and tenets of marketing will need to be brought to bear upon the study of all media texts and institutions and will have as central a place in the analysis of today's media as such concepts as authorship had within films studies in the 1960s, and representation and ideology had in the 1980s.

(2) The second area of concern is really the obverse of the first. For the growth of commercial media has been accompanied by the increasing impoverishment of public service and pluralistic media. The spaces in which we, as members of society, can communicate with one another without governmental or commercial interference are begin closed down dramatically. In Britain, for example the great media debate of the 1990s has concerned the future of the BBC, and whether indeed it has a future as a cheap and universally available high-quality public service paid for by an annual licence-fee.

As media teachers I think that we are going to have to develop an explicit commitment to the principles of open and universal access to information, and to preserving the independence, from undue commercial influence or government interference, of at least some information producers. As teachers working within public educational systems I believe that we do have a *de facto* commitment to the maintenance and defence of public information systems, and that we have to find ways of expressing this not in terms of an uncritical partisanship or on the basis of a narrow anti-commercialism, but rather as an open and generous allegiance to democratic values. And that entails, as always, putting all of the arguments to our students but leaving them with the responsibility for making their own choices.

Very large issues are at stake in struggles over the future configuration of the media industries. Should information be regarded only as a commodity or does it have a social value? Is it preferable to produce information which meets general social needs or information which makes a profit? Is access to information a right, or should it be restricted to those who can pay? Is information only an extension of property rights or does it lie in the public domain? It is scarcely an exaggeration to say that the future shape of all European cultures lies in the ways in which they answer these questions.

The existence of an informed and articulate public opinion on these issues will be an important − perhaps *the* important − influence on how these issues are settled. It is our important task as media teachers in the 1990s and beyond to help create that informed public. For that is one of the slender threads upon which the future of media freedom in all countries hangs.

Teacher education in media education

There has been a lively growth of national and international INSET provision in media education across Europe throughout the past decade. Involvement in initial teacher training, by contrast, has been distinctly patchy. Yet the issues affecting this area are clear enough.

Most obviously, initial training courses cannot assume, as 'method' training in traditional subjects has, a high level of student competence in the subject itself. Most students have no formal qualifications in this field, so that training courses have to possess a dual focus. They must aim to educate students about the media at their own level of sophistication. And, of course, they must explore pedagogic issues at both theoretical and practical levels.

Whilst this is a more formidable task than that facing teacher-trainers in more traditional subjects, it nevertheless has its advantages. It isn't simply that student motivation tends to be high, because the field is one of distinct interest and relevance to them. More importantly, the process of becoming critically autonomous themselves enables students to understand the hollowness of the educational processes which many of them, as recent graduates, have just completed. Having to formulate their own ideas and opinions frequently comes as a distinct shock to many students. It is something which few of them have had to do before. Even students with good degrees in literature or the social sciences confess to having achieved success largely through the manipulation and regurgitation of other people's ideas. Yet the process of sorting out their own ideas is one whose importance they can immediately recognise. And they can see the point of school students being encouraged to do the same thing as early as possible.

At this point, the second major issue in teacher-training in media education has to be acknowledged. Some degree (sometimes a high degree) of student insecurity may be endemic to the whole process. The worry of working in a new field is compounded by the risks involved in having to articulate one's own ideas without the supportive props of an established cultural tradition or the opinions of a range of experts. Add to this the brevity of the training course itself (at Nottingham I see my students for only seven three-hour sessions before they embark upon teaching practice), all of the perfectly normal anxieties surrounding teaching practice, and the frequently inflated expectations which schools can have of students who have at least *some* training in media studies, and you have all of the ingredients for a deep-seated sense of unease within the group as teaching practice comes ever closer.

Facing up to, and talking through such insecurities is of obvious importance. The fact that they are a normal and predictable response to a challenging situation and that many other students have been through all of this before and come out of it successfully can assuage any incipient tendency to panic. Though there are obvious drawbacks to setting such short-term goals, my own priority as teaching practice approaches, has been to ensure that students possess a survival kit of basic competencies and resources. Such competencies are theoretical as well as practical. All students will need to have a clear idea of what they are trying to achieve and why. That is, they will have had to engage with most of the theoretical debates outlined in this chapter, and to have reached their own settlement of them. They ought not to be too ambitious in planning their own teaching programmes. It is much better for students to be realistic about what can be done in a relatively short period of time, and to set themselves limited and achievable objectives. Most secondary school students, for example, still do no possess the rudiments of media literacy. They tend to lack practice in discussing and analysing media images, so anything which students can do to develop a familiarity with the language, concepts and techniques of media analysis will generally represent a distinct step forward. 'Image analysis' is frequently thought of as the earliest stage of media literacy. In fact images themselves are complex amalgams of visual, verbal and aural signs, and there is much to be said for giving school students practice in encoding and decoding the meanings of gestures, facial expressions, clothing, objects, sets and settings, sounds, commentaries and all of the other strands of meaning evident in the 'simple' image.

There are now a multitude of resources available for teaching about these and many other aspects of media literacy (Masterman, 1980, 1990) and it is invaluable to exhibit these for student perusal in the weeks before teaching practice, and to have them available for student use in schools. Indeed with the publication of the magnificent guide to *Media Literacy* produced by teachers in Ontario in 1990 there is now a wealth of down-to-earth and highly practical ideas for classroom work in virtually all aspects of media education.

In spite of their initial insecurities, students invariably report back positively on their early experiences of media teaching. Commonly they report higher pupil motivation, greater content relevance and higher standards of work than in more traditional subject-teaching. Frequently they become, because of their experiences, life-long converts to the cause of media education.

As in teacher-training courses in all subjects, it is the rich and multifarious experiences of teaching practice which provide the basic material for the 'post-practice' element of media education courses. At Nottingham, for example, individual students take responsibility for teaching most of the remaining seven sessions based upon their own teaching and the work produced by their pupils. Typically other sessions might be led by former students who are now working in schools, so that the group can gain a realistic sense of the kind of work and responsibilities which might be taken on in the early years of teaching. Additionally, I try to bring the group up-to-date with national examination syllabuses in media studies, as well as with the statutory obligations, and (non-statutory) possibilities for teaching about the media within the UK's National Curriculum.

Finally, at Nottingham I assess students by giving them an examination in which they are asked to write critically on two 'unseen' television extracts. Students are expected to respond at their own critical level, and to describe some of the ways in which they might use the extracts in the classroom. Whilst there is, originally, some student resistance to the idea of a formal examination, the point of the exercise is actually to transform the notion of 'examination' from a regurgitative process, involving much revision and memory-work to one in which students have an opportunity to *apply* the aptitudes they possess in a new situation. It is an empowering process, since students discover, often for the first time, that they can indeed make a great deal of sense of a text they have never encountered before. Ultimately it gives them confidence in themselves as critically autonomous adult learners. And the confidence to encourage similar aptitudes (and to develop similar ways of evaluating them) in their own pupils.

Notes

1. Council of Europe conferences and publications in media education include: Gambiez, C. (1981) 'The use of the media at school to prepare youngsters for life', Strasbourg: CDCC; Corset, P. (1982) report of the Symposium on 'The secondary school and the mass media', Grenoble, France, 29 June – 3 July 1981, Strasbourg: CDCC; Masterman, L. report of European Teachers' Seminar on 'Mass media education', Kristiansand, Norway, 8 – 14 August 1983 (DECS/EGT (83) 82); Report of the 26th Council of Europe Teachers' Seminar on 'Young people and advertising: the role and the responsibility of the school', Donaueschingen, Federal Republic of Germany, 19 – 24 November 1984 (DECS/EGT (84) 7); Robert

Gerbex, report of the Colloquy on 'The Press in School', organised by the Council of Europe and the *Association régions, presse, enseignement, jeunesse* (ARPEJ), Strasbourg, 20–22 March 1985 (DECS/EGT (86) 7); Report of the 33rd Council of Europe Teachers' Seminar on 'Mass media education in primary schools', Donaueschingen, Federal Republic of Germany, 6–10 October 1986 (DECS/EGT (86) 73); European Teachers' Seminar on 'Mass media education in the secondary school', Messilä, Finland, 10–14 August 1987; Seminar organised by the European Association for Education in Audiovisual Media (AEEMA) in association with the Council of Europe. Bad Marienberg, FRG, October 1990; New Directions in Media Education. Conference organised by Council of Europe, UNESCO and the British Film Institute, Toulouse, July 1990.

CHAPTER 9

Teacher Education for Technology Education

M. J. De Vries

Technology education: a subject in development

Understanding the key issues in contemporary technology teacher education
is not possible without an insight into the nature of the changes that take
place in technology education as a school subject itself. Most problems that
technology teacher educators face are the result of the fact that technology
education is a subject that is going through fundamental transitions now.
This not only holds for the European situation, but worldwide. In this
chapter we will illustrate the issues we describe by European examples,
because the publication it is part of, deals with European teacher education
specifically. It is, however, not difficult to find examples from other
countries that are quite similar to the European situation. In fact, the variety
of approaches to technology education that can be found in Europe is so
wide, that most approaches outside Europe have equivalents in Europe. All
the possible approaches in technology education together form a spectrum
that can be described by mentioning some of the most striking 'wavelengths'
in this spectrum. Most programmes are combinations of 'wavelengths'.
Nevertheless, the wavelengths described here can serve as indications of the
kind of programmes that can be found. No programme for example is exactly
'green', but several are 'greenish'. The approaches are (De Vries, 1993a):

- a craft-oriented approach, in which teaching how to handle tools and
  materials by making predesigned workpieces is the main content;
- a production-oriented approach, in which preparation for contributing to industrial production is the main aim;

- an applied-science approach, that sets all technology in the context of science learning;
- a high-tech approach, that teaches how to deal with advanced technological products;
- a technological-concepts approach, that teaches major technological theoretical concepts, e.g. the systems concept, and is rather analytical in nature;
- a design approach, in which the process of designing new products forms the heart;
- a key competency approach, in which the learning of competencies like co-operation, creativity and innovative thinking are central;
- an STS (science, technology, society) approach, that teaches primarily science-technology and technology-society relationships.

In most Western European countries the origin of contemporary technology education is some type of craft-oriented approach. The changes that the subject goes through nowadays have to do with the struggle to overcome the limitations of such an approach and the search for new, rich combinations with other approaches. For the Eastern European countries the transitions are from the industrial production oriented approach and in most cases the future is unclear (see e.g. Uzdzicki, 1992). A systematic analysis of these Eastern European approaches has never been made. Jenkins suggests this should be a first issue in a research programme with respect to technology teacher education (Jenkins, 1992, p. 461).

These changes have as a consequence that teachers need in-service training to update their knowledge and skills in the field. It also means that existing preservice training programmes need to be changed in order to bring them in accordance with the new directions that technology education takes. This, of course, is a process of mutual influence: changes in technology education curricula in schools change because of new ideas in technology teacher education programmes and vice versa.

The personal background of the (future) technology teachers

Some of the problems in technology education that influence technology teacher education, have to do with the fact that the concept of technology is problematic. Time and again the problem of defining what is meant by 'technology' is discussed at international conference (Mottier, *et al.*, 1993). Not only those who are involved in the development of technology education struggle with this problem, but also for the pupils there is often a lack of understanding of the nature of technology. The pupils' attitude towards technology and their concept of it has been and still is studied in the context of the international PATT forum (the work of PATT comprises both attitude research studies and a series of conferences to discuss those studies as well as developments in technology education in general) (Mottier, *et al.*, 1992). For this research a set of characteristics of technology has been defined that serves as a benchmark to investigate which characteristics are present and which are absent in the pupils' concept of technology. These characteristics are:

- technology as a human activity, in which human needs, norms and values play a vital role;
- technology as a process of designing, making and using new products and processes;
- in technology as the 'raw materials' which are matter, energy and information;
- in the development of these products and processes where there is an interaction with science;
- present when technological developments interact with society.

It appears that pupils are quite one-sided in their concept of technology: they see it much more as a set of products than as a process that leads to products. This holds for girls more strongly than for boys and has been shown to relate to their lower interest in technology (de Klerk Wolters, *et al.*, 1990). This lack of interest probably also contributes to the fact that so few women opt for a career in teaching technology. Special courses are organised in teacher training programmes to attract more women into technology teaching (Man in't Veld, 1992 describes an example of such a course). Mottier (1989) describes other intervention methods, like media campaigns and student bonuses. Female enrolment in technology teaching is important, because it provides role models for girls in technology. Other arguments are: provide a larger pool from which science and technological leadership can develop, provide more career options in technically based jobs and professions for more students, develop a base of scientific and technological literacy for the general population (Selby, 1989, p. 338).

The pupils also tend to think primarily of advanced technologies. Another bias is the minimal recognition of bio-related technologies as being technological in nature. Studies into potential technology teachers have revealed the same sort of biases. Although the future teachers were better aware of the process aspect of technology (although not fully; see Whitehead, 1992, p. 204), they had the same preferences towards advanced technologies and electrical and mechanical technologies above older technologies and bio-related technologies (De Vries, 1992).

No doubt one of the factors here is the often non-science background of the future teachers. They were often educated in the craft and/or art area where science hardly plays a role (see e.g. Poole and Shepard, 1992). The science-technology relationship, which is one of the characteristics of technology (De Vries, 1992), is often absent in their concept of technology. This kind of research shows some of the challenges that technology teachers face: to teach technology as it takes place today, meanwhile avoiding the pitfall of enhancing the one-sided concept of technology as being advanced technologies only, and teaching technology in such a way that it shows the process aspect so clearly that it will raise the girls' interest too. To a certain extent it helps technology teachers by taking the pupils' interests as a starting point for teaching technology (Blandow and Ungewiss, 1990).

156

In order to teach technology education in such a way that it helps pupils to acquire a more balanced and complete concept of technology, the same set of characteristics that was mentioned earlier can be used as a benchmark again (De Vries, 1990).

Preparing teachers for working in a subject without tradition

In a number of countries the changes from a craft-oriented type of technology education to a broader type of technology education are so fundamental, that one can speak of a subject without tradition. This places the teacher in a peculiar position: he or she has to build up the subject almost from nothing. In the Netherlands for example, the teacher that leaves the teacher education programme and finds a job at a school, where technology education in the new mode has not yet been taught, will have to start by making decisions on things that in other subjects are present already. These include the following matters:

1. creating the classroom for technology education. Often a classroom that so far had been used for a different school subject has to be rebuilt into a technology education laboratory. The new teacher in fact needs a lot of knowledge about the construction of the curriculum for the classroom, etc;
2. deciding on the curriculum. General attainment targets should be transformed into a well-structured and teachable curriculum. This can only be done when the new teacher has skills in curriculum development. In other subjects the curriculum has already been determined in the tradition of the subject. In the case of technology education the teacher has to make decisions on concrete objectives, the structure of the curriculum (systematic or thematic), teaching methods, evaluation methods;
3. choosing course material. In countries, where technology education is completely new (like the Netherlands), the number of courses, published by commercial publishers, is rather low. On the one hand this makes the choice easy, but on the other hand, there is a great chance that the few courses that are available do not match the requirements of the teacher or do not fit in his or her teaching style. In fact the new teacher needs skills in writing his or her own course material.
4. choosing and buying equipment and tools. The new teacher has to be able to work with a rather small budget to acquire all the equipment and tools that are necessary to realise the curriculum he or she designed.
5. developing assessment tools. This is an issue that does not yet get the attention it deserves. The development of good test materials for evaluation project work in particular is a problem that requires special abilities from the teachers. This also holds for the evaluation of pupils' attitudes towards technology. For this purpose a special instrument for teachers has been developed: the Technology Attitude Scale (TAS) (de Klerk Wolters, 1989, p. 296).

6. gaining support from colleagues, the school board, pupils and parents, and industry (Dyrenfurth, 1989). New technology teachers are faced with the fact that the status of the subject that preceded technology education (some type of craft education) generally had a low status. School boards are hesitant to put a lot of effort and funds into such a subject (Grot, 1990, p. 250). Colleagues are not inclined to show a great deal of interest in co-operation. Pupils and parents tend to think of the subject as not relevant for future training and careers. Industries have only just begun to show interest in working with technology teachers (in particular in the UK there are several successful initiatives; see e.g. Shield, 1991). In fact the teacher needs to market his own subject by showing its potential.

The teacher education programme in fact has to prepare him or her for all those tasks. This is quite a burden on the programme, as all the more usual components, like learning the subject matter and teaching methods also are part of that programme. These high demands conflict with the fact, that in some countries, the teacher education programme for technology education is only a part-time programme (e.g. three half days per week) during three or four years. In such cases teachers to a large extent have to rely on experiences they had outside the teacher education programme, such as mechanical hobbies or previous jobs.

The components of technology teacher education

A survey of technology teacher education programmes has shown that the major components − as in most other subjects as well − are: techno-logical/engineering subjects, professional/educational subjects, industrial experience, classroom teaching experience (De Vries, 1989). Each of these components have their problems that are caused by the fact that technology education is a subject in development and change.

Technological concepts in technology teacher education

When technology education was still in its craft-dominated phase, there was no need to look for technological concepts. Pupils only needed practical skills to make workpieces and the education of teachers for this subject contained the same type of skills. But now the general feeling is that technology education should not only have a psychomotor, but also a cognitive component. This means that learning technological concepts will be part of the curriculum both for pupils and in the training of teachers. The problem here, however, is that technology education, unlike other subjects such as physics, mathematics, languages, geography, etc, has no academic equivalent from which it draws its knowledge base. There are traditional engineering faculties, that focus on concepts and principles, that are specific for one type of technology, for example electrical or mechanical engineering. Concepts that are broader and can be used in the whole field

158

of technology, and are characteristic of the way technologists approach the problems that are given to them, are few and not well developed yet. Probably the best known is the systems concept. Although this concept was not born in engineering, but in science (Von Bertalanffy was a biologist), its use is widespread throughout the field of technology. An example of a principle than can be used in all areas of technology is the so-called functions triangle, that points out the interrelatedness of the function of a product, its form and materials and the treatments that are needed to bring the materials into the right forms. Designers have to take into account these relationships when (re-)designing products.

But the avalability of this type of concepts and principles is still very rare. The academic interest to develop such concepts and principles is increasing and the philosophy and methodology of technology is a growing field of research in universities. But it will still take some time before these concepts and principles are well established and meanwhile the developers of technology teacher education programmes will have to do their own development work in this respect. It often involves the need to develop both a school subject and an academic discipline at the same time. And even mere agreement on technology being a discipline of its own right and a body of knowledge that is unique and different from all other disciplines, has not been reached yet.

Apart from the more general concepts and principles technology teachers need to know a number of concepts and principles that are more specific for one engineering discipline. A selection of concepts and principles from electrical, mechanical, construction, chemical and biological engineering should be made that together gives a balanced survey of the various engineering fields.

Educational studies in technology education

A second component of a technology teacher education programme, that is faced with the fact that technology education is going through drastic changes concerns educational/professional aspects. These aspects deal with the following questions:

- what do I need to teach to the pupils in my subject (what knowledge and skills are relevant to them, what is 'teachable'),
- what are the personal characteristics of my pupils (with respect to e.g. their social background, level of intelligence, interests, preconcepts about the subject),
- how do I teach my subject in such a way that I reach my educational goals (in terms of knowledge, skills, attitudes, conceptualisation of the subject)?

The problem here is the lack of a sound research base for answering these questions. The area of educational research with respect to the subject technology (in German 'Fachdidaktik') is still underdeveloped. The contrast with a subject like physics becomes very clear when one looks at all the work that has already been done to find out pupils preconcepts in e.g. electricity, mechanics, optics and the ways in which these concepts can be reconstructed in the pupils' minds by means of a curriculum that allows for confronting 'natural' concepts of pupils with results of experiments. For technology education the solution is still quite different. We do not know much about the pupils' 'natural' understanding of for example the systems concept. Here we still have a long way to go. But the interest for such research is increasing. This can be concluded from e.g. the French initiative to start a research centre LIREST (Laboratoire Interuniversitair de Recherche sur l'Education Scientifique et Technologique) in Cachan, that will conduct educational research in technology education, focused on the pupils' thinking, and is related to the training of technology teachers at the Ecole Normal Superieur de Cachan near Paris.

For the time being we have to give preliminary answers to these questions in our technology teacher education programmes. Results of studies like PATT attitude studies can be used to give the programmes a certain empirical validation.

Industrial experience as a part of technology teacher education programmes

In most programmes for the education of technology teachers we find a component in which the future teachers work in industry, or at least make a number of visits to industries. For a technology teacher it is necessary to be well acquainted with the way technology functions in today's industrial reality. Especially in the industrial production-oriented approach, which was found in the Eastern European countries before the dramatic political changes took place there, this component was seen as one of the most important ones. But in the Western European countries it was and is also seen as a necessary component in the training of technology teachers. In some cases, technology teachers or technology teacher trainers have an industrial background. This, however, is rather exceptional, because in most European countries, engineers are paid much better in industry than in education.

Relationships between technology education and industries are increasing, thanks to the fact that technology education moved away from the craft-oriented approach. Industries were not interested in this approach because it can never be advanced enough to teach the pupils to work with the new equipment that can be found in industries. In some countries, like the Netherlands, contacts between industrial corporations and schools are still scarce, especially in general education. In teacher education these contacts are stimulated and hopefully this will lead to more contacts (pupils and teachers visiting industrial sites and industrialists coming to schools to tell about their work). Direct contacts between pupils, teachers and industrialists is necessary to give the pupils a realistic insight into the possibilities of a future career in industry. And as technological developments in industry by politicians often are seen as the 'motor' of economy, industrial experience is a crucial component of technology teacher education.

Classroom experience

It is a natural component in every teacher education programme to provide opportunities to get practical experience in teaching the subject for which the future teacher is trained. This also holds for technology teacher training programmes. Again there is a problem here, that is related to the changes that take place in the school curricula. Even when at the level of teacher training ideas, concepts and methods for technology education have been established, there is a lack of schools in which these ideas, concepts and methods can be seen to function in classroom practice. Most schools are either in confusion about the future approach for technology education or still resistant to changes. It is hard for technology teacher trainers to find good examples of school situations that future teachers can use as models – to be adapted to their own personal teaching style of course – for their own future teaching practice.

Of course there are other ways of categorising the various parts of the programme. Banks (1992) mentions three strands: the skills, issues and reflection strands. More detailed descriptions of programmes can be found in Kiss *et al.*, (1990) for Hungary, Blandow (1989) for Erfurt, Germany, Peters, Verhoeven and De Vries (1989) for the Pedagogical Technological College in the Netherlands, Grodzka-Borowska and Szydlowski (1989) for Poland, Booth (1989) for Wolverhampton, UK, Page (1989) for the South Bank Polytechnic in the UK and Morrison (1988) for Glasgow, Scotland.

Trends in technology education that influence technology teacher education

Recent international debates about technology education have shown that some common trends can be identified that operate in several (European) countries. In most cases these trends are driven by the teacher training institutes, in other cases they come from the teachers that already teach technology education. The first major trend in technology education is the search for an integration of the process aspects of technology (in particular the design process), with the concepts and principles that form the knowledge base for technology. In the past these two aspects have often been separated. In respect of the design approach that could be seen in the UK for example, a complaint of engineers was that it was too poor in its use of technological concepts and principles and thus lead to too shallow and simplistic solutions of design problems. On the other hand, in Germany, at the level of teacher training, very sophisticated analysis of technological systems were taught without a clear relationship to the way these systems had been and are developed. The awareness is growing that these two – the process and the content – need to be combined into one approach in which the pupils learn to integrate strategic knowledge (how to tackle a design problem) and domain – specific knowledge (engineering concepts and principles). In fact it is highly questionable whether process knowledge can exist apart from domain-specific knowledge (McCormick,

1993, p. 313). Is there anything such as 'general problem solving skills', that is not directly related to specific technological areas and problems? For some time we have taken the answer 'yes' to this question as the obvious right answer, but recent research has shown that we still have difficulties in identifying and developing such general process skills. This should make us suspicious about their existence. Therefore any trend that is focused on combining process knowledge and domain-specific knowledge should be regarded as more promising.

The issue of how to make this combination in practice in the education of future technology teachers is still being studied. Already now it is clear that this trend will stimulate contacts between technology education and other subjects. Some people go as far as to say that technology is cross-disciplinary in nature and therefore should be taught in a cross-curricular mode. The danger of this is that the nature of technology will become unclear. Besides that it seems that one subject after another now claims to be cross-disciplinary, so that the entire curriculum would consist of cross-curricular activities (such claims are made by e.g. environmental education, information technology, peace and health education). In primary education that would be a good way of helping young children to explore the reality in which they live. In secondary education, a different approach would be more suitable, namely to have projects in technology education, that are focused on technological design and problem solving, and that are enriched by inputs from other subjects, while at the same time keeping the various subjects separated in the timetable and thus allowing subject teachers to help the pupils find a structure that in reality is provided by the various disciplines. In the training of technology teachers for primary education this raises a special problem. Here traditionally there is not much attention for science and the teacher trainers seldom have a background in physics, chemistry or biology. This makes it very difficult to integrate scientific knowledge with the technological process in the education of future primary technology teachers.

Challenges for the further development of technology teacher programmes that are related to this trend are the issue of how to train future teachers to guide pupils in their project work in such a way that on the one hand it gives them directions and structures their use of scientific and technological concepts and principles, and on the other hand does not frustrate their creative thinking. The programme in Erfurt, Germany, is an interesting effort to realise such a combination of strategic (innovative thinking) skills and subject content (Lutherdt, 1990). The assessment of such project work is another issue that still needs careful consideration. A promising approach is described by Kimbell *et al.*, (1991). He shows how design projects can be assessed in a holistic way. Other concerns in assessment are the search for co-ownership of the assessment by the pupils. We should not only ask for their input/interests when determining the content of the programme but also when assessing their work.

A second trend in technology education, and the training of technology teachers, is the integration of environmental issues into the technology education curriculum. Here too the issue of cross-disciplinarity should be mentioned: dealing with environmental issues in technology projects requires knowledge from different areas: economy to find the balance between environmental and economic restraints, law to study the development of new regulations that require more environmentally friendly solutions to design problems, science (physics, chemistry and biology) to know the natural properties of materials and processes, etc (De Vries, 1993b).

Both the theoretical functions for integrating environmental issues in technology education and strategies for practice are still being developed (Giordan and Souchon for example provide some interesting practical examples for teachers). It is evident, however, that this will be an important trend for the coming years, as environmental concern is growing rapidly in society.

Post-educational support for technology teachers

So far this chapter may have given the impression that the situation in technology education is only problematic for prospective teachers. But this would be a distorted impression. In the past years a lot of experience has been gained in countries, where the transition from craft to technology education has already been made a number of years ago. Here the UK should be mentioned as a special case, because of the tradition in craft, design and technology (CDT) that certainly has provided a number of good examples to build on when introducing technology education (or rather: design and technology, as the subject is called in the UK). At the level of teacher training the Open University published a very useful set of materials for teacher education that covered many aspects that have been mentioned here (McCormick *et al.*, 1987; a new set was just about to be published when this chapter was written). At the same time it should be mentioned that recent debates about the outcomes of design and technology so far showed that even in the UK there are problems with teachers not being able to realise the attainment targets because of lack of experience in this new subject (DFE and Welsh Office 1992, p. 10).

These problems reveal the need to help teachers after they have left the teacher training programme. In some countries a support system has been set up that provides services to technology teachers to assist them in realising the curriculum: in the choices they have to make about the classroom, the equipment and tools, the curriculum, the course material. Some examples of such support systems for technology teachers are:

- the advisory work through Local Education Authorities (LEAs) in the UK (Harvey, 1988) and the Technological and Vocational Education Initiative (TVEI), that provided funds for projects in schools in that country;
- the Oxford Schools' Science and Technology Centre (Fisher, 1989). This centre is a place where teachers can come to look for literature, video tapes, to meet other teachers and discuss common problems, to take short in-service courses, to inspect course material, to learn to work with specific tools and equipment;

- the networking of schools by the Christian Brothers Marino Service in Ireland, based on concepts of Heywood (Steffens, 1992);
- the three Dutch pedagogical centres. They organise meetings where teachers can meet publishers that present their course material, meetings where teachers are instructed about specific problems related to the introduction of technology education as a new subject in the school, they do advisory work for individual schools that need help for the introduction of technology education.

Similar support systems can be found in other countries as well. In several cases these support systems are more closely related to universities and colleges than in the examples mentioned above. The organisation of short in-service courses by universities and colleges can also be seen as a support for technology teachers. The need for such courses is particularly urgent when there is no formal pre-service technology teacher training. This is the case in the Dutch-speaking part of Belgium (Flanders), where the subject 'Technologische Opvoeding' is taught by teachers of other subjects that have only taken some in-service courses. This is certainly not seen as an ideal situation, but was caused by the limitations in financial resources. Here a group of teachers and inspectors was established to develop course material that could be used by teachers with little experience in technology and help them to carry out problem-solving projects in the classroom. This initiative has been quite instrumental in the introduction of the subject in Flanders by its very practical approach.

International co-operation

The unification of Europe also has its effects on the development of the subject technology education. EU programmes like ERASMUS and TEMPUS have been used by several institutions to realise international exchange of ideas and development of curricula in international collaboration between teacher educators. International PATT-conferences have been organised since 1986. In 1992 in Weimar, Germany, the World Council of Associations for Technology Education (WOCATE) was established to serve as a network for technology teacher associations. Both PATT and WOCATE are not limited to Europe, but have a worldwide focus. At European level, the Europaische Gesellschaft fuer Technische Bildung (EGTB) functions as a network between national organisations within (Western) Europe. National associations, like the Design and Technology Association (DATA) in the UK, the Vereniging van Techniek Docenten (VeDoTech) in the Netherlands, just to mention two such associations, stimulate participation of people from other countries in their annual conferences. These initiatives have enabled many contacts between teachers and teacher educators, that disseminate good examples of technology education and technology teacher education practice internationally. They also stimulate international research in the field of technology education for which there is a great need. Although the situation in each specific country is different from other countries, there is a general feeling that international contacts are helpful, especially in a situation where the whole subject is in change and development. As stated before, it would be incorrect to describe the situation in technology teacher education as problematic entirely. In all European countries good, innovative examples of classroom and teacher education practice can be found. But often these good examples remain hidden and are not used as models for others. International contacts stimulate the presentation of such examples so that they can be adapted to the specific needs of other situations and thus serve as a resource for further developments.

CHAPTER 10

Teachers and Mobility

Francine Vaniscotte

The Europe of 1993 created the momentum for a free flow of goods, people and ideas. The institutionalisation of this change has so far only had an effect on the 12 member states: the Community, however, will be expanding and what has been established between the 12 member states, shortly to increase to 19 countries (EEC and soon EFTA countries) must be considered to be a first step, with implications for other states involved in the construction of an open Europe.

Free flow and mobility are ancient European traditions and there is a long history of cross European travel. Today's positive approach to cultural and study trips is based on a similar tradition. The past has often, however, invoked invasion and destruction as much as dialogue and discovery. Nonetheless, whether it is seen as the last hope in the face of economic and political tyrannies, or because it is a step towards others, *mobility* remains at the heart of the concept of freedom. It is in this spirit that the entire educational community is being asked to promote and develop a principle of *mobility*.

There are no real precedents on which to base the development of teacher mobility. Soon after the end of the war pairings, twinnings and exchanges began gradually to increase. It has to be acknowledged, however, that for teachers mobility, more often than not, meant words, and rhetoric rather than to the daily reality of the school's classroom and of the pedagogical experience. Many teachers, however, do see mobility as a real issue for the future; they know that they will be expected to be involved at some level and some know that this mobility will lead to a radical reshaping of school life and of the teaching profession. These changes, however, are still barely perceived in certain countries. Everyone merely hopes that Europe, the

166

cradle of democracy, will know how to cope intelligently with the pluralist imperative.[1]

The concept of mobility is developing in a context which has two characteristics:

- a long-standing crisis in the teaching profession and in the training for this profession;
- a search for models and values in the teaching profession.

Against such a background, concepts of mobility must define both the pedagogical sphere and the implications for developing a European dimension in education. It has to be developed carefully and purposefully knowing that the objective is an important one. The educational community must represent its approach to mobility in an action plan and in new, perhaps innovatory, scenarios.

Teacher mobility and the experience of the teaching profession

It is now generally accepted that the teaching force is affected by a deep crisis and that there is an increasingly large gap between the responsibilities of teachers and their working conditions. There are many problems associated with the profession. They mesh into one another and constitute a complex pattern which it is difficult to disentangle.

A profession which must resolve serious difficulties is unlikely to be open to innovation. In such a difficult climate it is necessary to establish how to introduce in to the life of the school the new cultural emphasis that is a key attribute to the concept of mobility. Mobility is undoubtedly a way of thinking, an ability to consider change, an interest in other countries and other cultures. It can, of course, occur through exchanges and journeys; but it is first and foremost an ability to adapt, to welcome, to imagine the benefits of travel, and this is why mobility is a training issue. The first step towards mobility is in the mind and the first initiative to take in the training of teachers is to instil in future teachers the openness which will ensure that they are aware of and make use of the opportunities for mobility provided within their communities. The attraction of international mobility for long or short periods will then become a natural development. The building of Europe will be achieved faster if mobility is not seen to be the exception but an internalised cultural attitude.

Teaching conditions and mobility

A fundamental aspect of the crisis facing the teaching profession is decline in status, a phenomenon which can be attributed to the democratisation of education. In order to cope with a new constituency of pupils, it has been necessary to recruit large numbers of teachers. This in turn has led to an increasingly female recruitment pattern and as a consequence a lowering of the professional and social status of teachers. As a solution to the democratisation of education and to the failure of some pupils, compensatory pedagogies have been developed and new posts created which are not timetabled (counsellors and guidance posts are examples that come to mind). Such posts have required new training programmes and represent a human and technical support for teachers. They had also led to a loss of normative practices and an increase in the stratification of the teaching force. Whilst they may have succeeded in responding to the expectations of an heterogeneous public they have not succeeded in resolving the malaise of the teaching profession.

As a consequence, public opinion is generally critical of teachers and dissatisfied with their work. In turn teachers are demoralised about the future. Although educational systems vary a great deal from one country to another − most noticeably in the ideologies and historical traditions on which they rest − this discontent can be observed almost everywhere most particularly through society's, parents' and industry's unmet requirements (Vaniscotte, 1992).

Because they have to respond to important immediate social pressures, teachers do not always give serious consideration to the concept of internal or international mobility. Teachers on the whole only have scant knowledge and experience of the worlds of commerce and industry, agriculture or administration and do not generally relate comfortably to other areas of society. They are often public servants whose career advancement does not depend on the need to move, who left school to go to school, and who therefore fail to see the significance of the concept of mobility.

This is why internal mobility really does appear to be a practical tool to help resolve the stratification which bears so heavily on the career of teachers.[2] Internal mobility is intended to refer to horizontal movements between schools, vertical or horizontal mobility between educational functions, and also mobility between school and industry. All these could give teachers the knowledge which might allow them to triumph over social pressures and to master competently the diverse tasks given to them.

A less differentiated teaching profession and one less limited by specialisation would, as a consequence, be more flexible. It would be more adaptable and as a consequence be in a better position to answer social demands. This internal mobility is not, however, as accessible as it might appear. The teaching profession has strong rules, rigid school structure, and teachers do not feel empowered to exploit the opportunities for mobility that exist.

If the simple concept of internal mobility meets with obstacles, international mobility has to face unimaginable obstructions. In a context in which educational systems all differ, the formulation of a common interpretation of international mobility is a complex affair. It is important, however, to clarify this issue if the objective is to prepare teachers and pupils for a mobility concept responsive to the needs of society and satisfying parental expectations whilst contributing to the democratic process in education. The commitment of teachers to an active approach to mobility would furthermore constitute a step towards a reassessment of teacher status. In restating their professionalism in such a way teachers would contribute to an improvement of their social standing.

Teaching quality and teacher mobility

Another feature of the crisis which has shaken the teaching profession is reflected in the debate concerning the quality of teaching. In Western countries the democratisation process is well established in the primary and middle school sectors. It is also a declared objective for the majority of the EC states, and teachers must be prepared for it. It is simply not sufficient to change the structures of secondary provision to develop quality whilst suppressing inequalities. The conflicting debate between excellence and equality of opportunity, the tensions between the retention of quality and the development of improved quality have led to the peculiar situation we currently face: namely acute difficultly in identifying the determining factors which affect the quality of education. This problem is compounded by the difficulty we have in identifying precisely those factors which lead to the failure of certain children in educational systems and in finding the remedy. Such a difficulty brings into question the training structures. (Vaniscotte, 1989a, p. 263).

Whilst the concept of teachers' work differs from country to country, one aspect is shared: teacher training is based on the role as currently defined rather than some future role. Little attention is given to the elaboration of progressive building blocks in initial training and professional development. There is no *dynamic* between these two processes. Initial training is often badly suited to the needs of the new teacher and certainly does not provide the means of facing the tensions between excellence and quality. This explains why despite all we know about the difficulties teachers face early in their career, there are no real strategies to enter the profession progressively. There are many difficulties, therefore, in providing a structure for in-service training.

The idea that initial education and training and future professional development might be one and the same thing requires some qualification. There is very little empirical evidence about the link between different strategies and effective innovation in schools. Do, for example, open and innovatory modes of initial and in-service training and education create teachers in post who are open to change and development? (Vaniscotte, 1989b). It is now generally accepted that you cannot seek to transmit major values and behaviours through training alone. Training which has too little structure or is too innovatory, training which is too academic and remote from the school reality create insecurity. Teachers then return to familiar and even childhood memories of how the teacher role might be conceived.

Against this background the idea of inter-institutional mobility during the initial training period is slowly becoming more common and accepted. There is, for example, in a number of training institutions and schools, a change in the profile of this work. Staff are being appointed to take on an international relations role, not just to *managing mobility* but also to contribute in a leadership role to the development of innovatory strategies of international and European relations within the curriculum. This premise, however, relies on the ready availability of information, a common understanding of systems and precise definitions of the ways in which issues are approached in other countries.

Greater teacher mobility during initial and in-service experience must be accompanied by a clear understanding of what is meant by quality and equality in different countries. You cannot mention international mobility without seeking some way of *validating* the knowledge acquired through the experience. To be significant this must go beyond increased mutual trust to examine what constitutes a consensus about professional development, and where differences exist how they can be perceived as enriching rather than undermining the international community.

Teacher mobility and professionals

During the 1960s, in an earlier period of educational research and enquiry, there was the search, to use the anglo-saxon concept, for a new professionalism freed from the narrowness of vocationalism. In fact the ideas were seen in juxtaposition. Today, professionalism embraces vocationalism emphasising the acquisition of knowledge, skills and experience as well as career related issues. Professionalism also has further meanings:

- a personal responsibility for intellectual development;
- a scientific activity, devoid of routine and which is non-repetitive;
- lengthy and consistent training.

These are the three reasons for which in the majority of countries training has come nearer universities.

It is also, however:

- a practice which is closer to an art than a scientific theory;
- a way of joining a group which has cohesion and a powerful structure.

These two issues in themselves justify the location of training in specific institutes or university departments.

Finally, it is:

- the exercise of an altruistic activity of benefit to society as a whole (Lemosse, 1989).

It also brings together a whole series of personal qualities besides the acquisition of professional competency and it integrates the transmission of traditional teaching values within a given society.

There is only scant data on the way in which training can shape future professional identity. This is perhaps one of the reasons why countries hesitate between an academic reappraisal of training with a preponderant role given to the university and a psycho-pedagogic reappraisal which would locate training into institutions which have direct access to the workplace, even within universities. There is a clear tendency to opt for the university option for teacher training. It is worth perhaps questioning, however, whether in becoming more scientific, training will become immediately a more fertile ground for mobility. A certain intellectualisation of training might certainly bring about an increase in openness, but it could also create, at least in the first instance, a situation in which increasingly narrower specialisations, stratifications and reliance on a circle of initiated people prevail.

Mobility of the educational community and teacher professionalism

The turning point represented by Maastricht is essential not only for the countries of the European community but also for the totality of Europe. The introduction of Education in the Treaty of Union articles 126 and 127) illustrates the acknowledgement of the need to introduce a European dimension in the training of teachers and in education. This will involve establishing a conceptual basis to the European dimension which recognises *cultural memory* and the values so enshrined. There needs, however, to be space within that framework to allow individuals and groups to benefit from the new perspectives brought about through mobility.

Past experience, the work of organisations such as OFAJ (the Franco-German office for youth), different projects and scholarships available through the Council of Europe, study visits, pilot projects through the European community, and weightier proposals, still allow a reappraisal of two essential aspects of mobility: long- and short-term international mobility.

Long-term mobility currently faces a large number of obstacles to which only long-term solutions can be applied. Harmonising the working conditions of teachers, taking into account the number of years taught abroad, and the terms offered on return, are issues being addressed currently. It is obvious that the free flow of people will not resolve the question of pensions, or terms of social protection; but it will bring a certain urgency to the need to recognise public service qualifications. Whilst all these problems could be solved, there will remain a need to investigate, offer and demand, in order to avoid a two-tier Europe based on differences in the linguistic and pedagogical climate. For these reasons, a long-term mobility plan generalised to the teaching profession is unlikely and there remain doubts that a European job market for teachers can be established in the near future.

Short-term mobility, therefore − a week or a school year − is the most likely area for development. Given the current climate, the concept of six months or a year's mobility is more appropriate to teachers and students of languages or students of new technological developments. Study visits and stays of a minimum duration of three months can, of course, take on board improvements in linguistic performance, but they increasingly also provide the means by which communications and dialogue centred on the European dimension occur. Mobility programmes which emphasise the European dimension will in themselves promote expectations that such programmes become integrated into the evolving concept of professionalism.

For a long time, because activities concerning mobility were aimed first and foremost at linguistic objectives, the impact was most obvious in countries whose language was popular: the United Kingdom, France and Germany. And for the same reason exchanges were bilateral. One of the consequences of this is that today certain countries have a broad experience of mobility whilst others are only beginning to discover the process. Taking account of the European dimension in education and training in the Resolution of the Council of the European Communities, dated 24 May 1988, Recommendation 1111 of the 22 September 1989 by the Parliamentary Assembly of the Council of Europe, registers some fundamental statements on the importance of promoting the European dimension in the curriculum. The two concepts of European dimension and mobility are thus defined and thought through in parallel.

The European dimension and mobility

The European dimension thus becomes a new frame of reference for teachers: a frame which has to become legitimate. One of the ways in which this can be achieved is to define fields of subjects and classroom action for the new frame of reference. Various national and international plans are beginning to lead to a culture of mobility hitherto absent in the educational and training systems. These build on the notions of partnership and networking.

These two ideas form the basis of a new concept of mobility and pre-suppose a training institution (or a school) as support. A common project developed by different institutions allows different partnerships to be constructed. A joint project can ensure that a whole range of staff become aware of the European dimension. It is not necessary to train everyone, but it is important to distinguish physical and intellectual aspects of mobility. This is in marked contrast to the classical idea of exchanges. In the new designs physical mobility is the means by which a more important goal is reached: the entire institution contributes to a European project.

Against such a background, the European dimension cannot be limited to a bilateral partnership; it has to become multilateral and provide the appropriate climate which goes beyond the privileged framework of exchanges which are, for example, represented by the exclusively linguistic links between France, England and Germany. A multilateral partnership builds around a project of pluralist disciplinarity thereby ensuring that the European dimension really occurs within every discipline. The progressive extension of multilateral and interdisciplinary partnerships ensures the development of mobility and of both short-term and long-term exchanges.

Notions of networking and partnership help define a culture of mobility which incorporate institutional projects as reflected in cultural exchanges led by the Council of Europe.[3] These appear to support a new didactic structure that takes into account the interrelationship of teachers with the European dimension.

Teacher mobility and the search for values

To teach is to transmit knowledge and the values attached to this knowledge: values which alter over a period of time and around which teachers can build professional identity. It is this cultural memory which, whilst reinterpreting regularly its history, permits the placing of new frames of reference. This continuous reinterpretation of the past should be subject to a critical analysis inscribed in the educational objectives of every teacher training institution and every university; such an analysis would permit schools to go beyond national interests but it still would not be sufficient. In any case, school systems can no longer ensure the reproduction of culture. They must ensure that more than this reproduction occurs and that they promote the cause of cultural autonomy going beyond national interests.

Following in the footsteps of the debate on the quality of teaching and without ignoring it, the last few years have seen the search for values for the teaching profession. Some of these values may appear to have been acquired and to be common to all the systems of Western Europe. They are values which are at the roots of Western democracies: human rights, freedom, solidarity, tolerance, acknowledgement of others and of their culture; although they may be imperfectly applied, these values represent an acquired capital, and their questioning in some countries, however important they may be, could not be considered as questioning a consensus.

The fact that the teaching profession is in Europe a profession which is organised is also an acquired value. However imperfect and worthy of criticism, the training of teachers is there and the vast majority of children are taught by teachers whose competence is recognised. Respect for democratic principles, for regional and national identities, the organisation of the teaching profession and of the training of teachers, can be assumed to have acquired value in the educational systems of Western Europe.

Besides such acquired values, others appear in embyro. They are part of the new aspirations of the educational world: the quest for Europe and the desire to create a pluri-ethnic, pluri-cultural and pluri-lingual Europe, based on mobility and with good interpersonal relationships as a prerequisite.

Today, European teachers cannot be thought of as national servants; they have to be considered as a European resource and it follows that the European dimension must be given a place in the educational and training systems: this presupposes that a proportion of the National Curriculum is abandoned in order to put in place a culture of mobility permitting meetings, European-type projects and exchanges. This evolution, sought by many teachers, leads to difficult questions of choice since it requires a different way of looking at the timetable and the curriculum and might lead to a modification of national legislation. This difficult evolution is unavoidable since, as long as the European dimension is ignored in the programmes of teacher training the culture of mobility will not be defined in the sort of pedagogical terms discussed above.[4]

The institutionalisation of the concept of mobility is already occurring. The next phase will require a speedy reassessment before proceeding to a generalised mode of operation. It is crucial to prepare teachers to such radical changes, and it is far from certain that the present training model is appropriate to the future shape of mobility. Training continues to rely on an implicit model which combines the scholastic medieval tradition, Renaissance humanist values, 18th-century rationalist thinking, the influence of 19th-century psycho-pedagogical theories and the more recent psycho-cognitive interpretations. It is worth questioning whether such a succession of principles, often poorly assimilated, can simplify the movement of a population which is bound to become increasingly multi-cultural, multi-ethnic and pluralistic: a society in which the first task a teacher must accomplish is to promote a pattern of living which is both free and responsible and based on the right to differ and the acquisition of autonomy. It would be difficult to implement mobility without questioning models of teacher training.

The ambition to build Europe and to increase mobility cannot be fulfilled without the acquisition of a language, the indispensable communicating tool. If an ordinary linguistic exchange is not sufficient to create the true European integration it would be a grave mistake to underestimate the importance of language in the mobility of teachers. The work of the Council of Europe on the Seuil thresholds and the publications focusing on the learning of communication as well as the LINGUA community programme are key factors in the development of mobility. European integration must change radically the teaching of languages in educational systems. The mobility of teachers can only become a reality if a quantum leap is made in both the learning and the practice of foreign languages. One aim is to ensure that teachers acquire the competence and mental agility to teach their subject in a minimum of two languages. To this extent the attention to language is a value which will ensure that teachers become privileged initiators of a new way of thinking European and will permit long-term mobility.

In recent years thinking has evolved and migrations have increased, factors which have led to a heterogeneous European society in which ethnic, cultural and linguistic pluralism are embryonic values, values which are accepted whilst they preserve the individual within a recognised plurality. If this acceptance is to be successful there needs to be no 'stratification', no hierarchy; 'there needs to be an assurance that individual differences will not be interpreted as inadequacies or inferiorities'.[5] In such circumstances the mobility of the entire European community could become a new element in a new frame of reference.

Teacher mobility

A contrasting situation

The situation varies from country to country and comparisons are difficult to make. In a country such as Luxembourg all the educational institutions are expected to work in partnership. They all organise teacher and pupil exchanges and teachers are trained in universities abroad. Mobility is the daily reality as is the use of three common languages: Luxembourg, German and French languages to which a good command of English can be added. Conversely Eastern European countries and those whose language is less widespread do not have the same pattern of organised mobility and have a very scant history of exchanges. Germany, however, is currently involved in twinnings and programmes of mobility with Eastern and Central European countries, and more particularly with Poland.

In some countries there are in place structures to help and support teacher and pupil exchanges (France, Germany and Great Britain); in other countries, Greece for example, mobility may be given occasional encouragement but there is practically no support structure.

Scandinavian countries on the other hand, as part of the programme 'North plus' have been organising teacher and student exchanges. They have an agreement within this scheme which covers the period 1989–1993, to allocate 1,200 bursaries a year. Bursaries for exchanges lasting from two weeks to two months are also offered to young people aged 16 to 19 as part of the programme 'Junior North plus'.

Because of these disparities it is difficult to draw a map of the programmes of mobility within the European Community. Teachers whose country belongs to the Council of Europe have access to bursaries to support stays abroad with as a consequence an increase in the awareness of innovation and mobility in the training of teachers. European Community members can have the benefit of specific programmes such as Teacher Exchanges, ARION, LINGUA, PETRA). Countries which belong to AELE, as well as those of Central and Eastern Europe can also benefit from programmes such as ERASMUS in the former and TEMPUS in the latter.

In-service training: teacher exchanges

The 12 countries of the European community currently benefit from a programme of teacher exchanges. The European Parliament has since 1989 earmarked a budget for bilateral reciprocal exchanges of 400 teachers from member countries.

This programme was created through the Resolution of the Council of Ministers meeting of 24 May 1988 which agreed to promote the reinforcement of the European dimension in education on the strength of Article 6: *the promotion of measures aimed at encouraging contacts between pupils and teachers coming from different countries* and Article 14 *measures to encourage the co-operation and exchange of views between national interests with a view to encourage exchanges of teachers and pupils.*[6]

This important statement was made in a context in which the mobility of teachers participating in exchanges could be seen to give strength to a programme which affects all educational institutions and leads to an increase in co-operation. Such teacher exchanges are seen as an element of in-service training and the starting point for institutions followed by the creation of networks and inter-school associations. Thus the stated aims of the programme are to ensure that institutions initiate exchanges and integrate them to their development plans and to programmes of co-operation with other institutions. Projects have to be inter-disciplinary, aimed at all teachers of 10 to 18 years olds, open to teachers of any subject. However, generalist teachers are given priority because teachers in technical and professional institutions can have access to PETRA II. Foreign language teachers can obtain bursaries as part of their initial training and for their in-service training within the LINGUA initiative.

The management of this programme is decentralised. This means that member states have a structure which is responsible for the administration of exchanges and the collaboration with the structures of other member states and the Commission. Institutions participating in the exchange there-fore receive the full support of the authorities. Exchanges last three or four weeks and can occur simultaneously or in sequence. Teachers do not have to teach the same subject but they generally belong to the same discipline.

This project is mentioned specifically because of its pedagogical emphasis involving a team of teachers. The inter-disciplinary dimension, requiring the involvement of a number of teachers leads to the opening of the institution and to a psychological or intellectual mobility for all, through the physical mobility of a few: teachers and then pupils. Teachers who are thus engaged in a pedagogical project with a European dimension can become aware of the need to integrate to schools the inter-cultural reality of Europe. The reality of Europe alters their teaching and the perception of the educational reality and the different pedagogy of other countries leads to a questioning of the pedagogical certainties.

The exchange of teachers which at the onset was a bilateral arrangement has progressively evolved. Preparation or evaluation seminars held in 1991 and 1992 have led to an evolution of exchanges towards, on the one hand, a stronger co-operation between establishments, and on the other a broadening of multilateral partnerships and networks. This project may therefore lead to an evolution of thinking and possibilities for the mobility of teachers.[7]

Whilst the subject of a parliamentary initiative, and managed by national structures, this project meets a number of problems: the rigidity of programmes and school legislation, the difficulties of cover, the school calendar, the varying level of motivation within school institutions remain obstacles to overcome. The heads of establishments and inspectors can also benefit from short programmes (a week long study visit to another country on a theme) under the auspices of the Arion programme.

Initial training

Teacher mobility during initial training is promoted through the community programme ERASMUS, but this programme does not yet respond in a satisfactory way to the requirements of the training of teachers. This is the reason why the European Community has encouraged:

- on the one hand, the constitution within ERASMUS of a network called NEROPED. This network involves 120 universities each involved in the training of teachers. This group of universities encourages students study visits abroad and ensures that they receive a broadly similar academic training whilst there;
- on the other hand, the network named RIF which involves 150 institutions and universities responsible for initial and in-service training, gathered in 15 thematic sub-networks. The common objective is the introduction of the European dimension in the initial training of teachers. To achieve this the trainers employed by institutions which are part of RIF meet twice a year and prepare projects: training modules on Europe, construction of didactic material, mobility projects. A mobility of four to six weeks initiated in 1991 – 92 for approximately 100 trainee teachers has been supported by ERASMUS. It centres on a particular aspect of initial training: professional training.

Mobility in the ERASMUS context generally seeks to supplement academic training. Whilst concentrating on the professional training, the RIF programme introduces an innovation: a group of students from different nationalities visiting classes and schools in another country and whilst there teaching part-time. Meeting other pedagogical practices as an integral part of their curriculum is the first step towards a European-type training aimed at encouraging long-term mobility.

Pupil mobility: some perspectives

It is impossible to mention teacher mobility without referring to the mobility of pupils: the makers of a future Europe. In this context the situation is as diverse as in the case of teachers. In some countries, exchanges are an integral part of the educational tradition; in others they hardly exist. National authorities sometimes only barely encourage exchanges and to date the European Economic Community has no power with regards to education except in so far as it concerns professional training. This is the reason why pupils of technical and professional establishments and young workers can be supported through specific programmes. The ratification of the Treaty of Union should facilitate the implementation of a community action in favour of the mobility of pupils and a pilot programme involving 40 school partnerships has already started.

With similar objectives: multilateral interdisciplinary, teacher exchanges projects could form the basis of a larger programme which might allow the creation of mobility for the entire educational community.

Conclusion

This chapter has attempted to show the tight relationship between the European dimension and training and the present and future mobility of teachers. The European dimension needs to be thought through and integrated with a global perspective. It represents the ideal of a society based on respect for cultural diversity. This ideal presupposes that there can be an international response to every problem even if the responses are different; it requires that determined changes be made to certain aspects of the curriculum, the content and method of teaching. For mobility to become a cultural habit it is necessary to integrate it to initial training, to careers and to the work of teachers. This requires setting up research projects to help create these new ideas and this new awareness.

To achieve the integration of the desired objectives of 'Europe', 'mobility', 'mastery of languages' requires us to come out of the current paradoxical situation where everyone relies on its country to perpetrate knowledge, experience, specificity, and the cultural patrimony whilst Europe relies on its teachers to go beyond the national frame of reference and create European values or even European citizens. The training of teachers remains the first lever in the change and the force behind the move to integrate the European dimension to education. This training which currently barely goes beyond the intention to build an identity which goes a little further than national interests must in the future create a culture of mobility. It must constitute a field of epistemological reference which will give legitimity to the European dimension conceived as an ideal of society which integrates everyone's free and natural mobility within an open and global solidarity.

Notes

1. Acts of the International Conference on the Teaching Profession. Noordwikjershout, Netherlands, 5–7 October 1993.
2. *Ibid.*
3. *Ibid.*
4. *Ibid.*, Rapporteur's Report.
5. See meetings of the Council of Europe Network on school links and exchanges.
6. European Union (1991) Guide to Teacher Exchanges in the European Community. Brussels.
7. European Union, *op. cit.*

PART FOUR

Research on Teacher Education

CHAPTER 11

Teacher Training in Europe: A Research Agenda

Maurice Galton

Introduction

The Council of Europe's Project No. 8, *Innovation in the Primary School* (DECS/EGT (87) 23) made a number of recommendations, one of which was that the Council should devote more attention to the issues concerning the training of teachers. There were several reasons for this recommendation but the principal one derived from what project members saw as a major barrier to the successful innovation in schools. In most European countries a sharp distinction existed between the academic content which teachers were required to master in order to cover the range of subjects in the primary curriculum and the acquisition of the practical skills necessary to pass on this knowledge to their pupils. Often these practical skills were acquired through an extended apprenticeship. This separation of university education from training to teach meant that little effort was made to integrate the academic parts of the course with the practicum. Each successive generation of teachers therefore acquired, through this apprenticeship, the habits and methods of their predecessors, thus producing a strong element of 'conservatism' into the profession.

In any school-based innovation process, particularly given Project No. 8 report's main recommendation that innovation should operate by means of what Vandenberghe (1988) defined as '*backward mapping*', it was not good enough to change only the practice of experienced teachers. This is because while changes are taking place there is, at the same time, another generation of practitioners who are learning to operate the same practices which the innovation is designed to eliminate. Accordingly members of Project No. 8 considered that the reform of teacher education at this initial training (IT) stage was equally important as in-service training (INSET). Since in the past IT had received little attention from member states the authors of Project No. 8's final report argued that the Council should give the topic greater prominence in future deliberations.

The Council has been unable to meet this recommendation completely in part because it was already committed to carrying out a parallel study to Project No. 8 on secondary education where it has been argued (Bourdoncle, 1990) that the situation across Europe is in greatest need of reform. The Council did, however, commission a survey of the different approaches to the organisation of initial training in member states (Neave, 1987) which was the subject of discussion at the Ministerial Conference held in Finland. More recently other international organisations, for example the Organisation for Economic and Cultural Development (OECD, 1990) has put teacher training high on its agenda (CERI, 1990).

The urgency of the matter has increased, given the ratification of the single European Act and its implementation by the end of 1992. Not only does increased teacher mobility require that issues of training and qualifications should be examined in the search for common European standards but the development of these standards needs to emerge through a firm research base. In the past the disparity between systems of teacher education in different countries has meant that such research as there has been tended to be idiosyncratic in its conception depending as it did on funds from national governments, each of which had its own priorities at any given time. Now, however, with the pressures resulting from the 1992 European Act these wide variations are no longer so apparent and common areas of research interest are beginning to emerge.

This greater degree of cohesion is clearly illustrated by the proceedings from a conference on Teacher Education in Europe which was held in September 1990 at the Jordon Hill College in Glasgow (Bone and McCall, 1990). In their summary report of the conference Bone and McCall identify a number of important themes where research has either already begun or where new developments are urgently required.

Previous research

In the past the major focus of research has been concerned with aspects of curriculum, particularly the nature of the content of programmes of initial teacher training. During the last decade, as Project No. 8 confirmed, the knowledge base required of the primary school teacher has expanded considerably to include not only additional subject areas, such as computing, science and technology but also trends such as the integration of the handicapped into main stream education have required teachers to become familiar with ways of teaching such subjects to pupils with a range of ability including those with special educational needs. At the same time concern to provide equal opportunities with respect to pupils from different ethnic backgrounds, including migrant groups within different European countries and also with respect to differentiation between male and female pupils have come in for increasing attention. Given the limited time available for schooling it has been necessary, as a result of this expansion in the knowledge base, to find ways of linking the different subject areas through cross-curriculum themes including that of European awareness (Bell, 1991). Other studies concerning cross-curricular issues include those from Germany dealing with the world of work (Dahncke, 1989) and gender (Schmidinger, 1988).

A second research area concerns the structure and organisation of teacher training. Here the emphasis varies according to the established pattern in different countries but there is particular concern about training at secondary level where it is still the practice in a large proportion of member states for university graduates to have immediate entry into teaching without any further training other than a period of observation followed by a short apprenticeship. One aspect of the debate therefore concerns the need to increase and improve this training and whether it should be concentrated immediately after graduation, as in the United Kingdom with its one-year PGCE (Postgraduate Certificate in Education) course or whether continuity of training should be achieved by a programme of regular in-service education such as that which operates in Spain (Montesinos, 1990).

Another theme concerns the need for teachers to work closely with parents, given the fact that rising standards of education in all member states has meant parents have become more articulate and demand a greater say in the educational provision for their children (Macbeth, 1990). Previous studies have shown that little attention has been given to this aspect of the teacher's role and that parental dissatisfaction has been a powerful influence in government reforms of teaching during the last decade, for example Bastiani (1988) in the United Kingdom and (Walthert et al., 1989) in Switzerland. Such reforms have raised questions about the need to establish firm standards within the teaching profession so that part of the new reaearch agenda has concerned itself with attempts to establish a set of minimum competencies which all teachers should acquire before beginning their career in the classroom (Cameron-Jones and O'Mara, 1990).

This leads on to the third area of study concerned with the didactics of teacher training involving the different roles of the classroom teacher and the college tutor and attempts to identify the nature of the learning which student teachers gain from working alongside more experienced colleagues in the classroom (Brown et al., 1988). Much of this recent work emphasises the need for teachers to reflect on their own practice in order to articulate their own 'craft' theories of teaching. This has been a very important theme within the United Kingdom (Pollard and Tann, 1987) and in Finland (Aljonen, 1990).

Historical background

In the immediate post-war period leading into the 1960s research in teacher education largely concentrated on matters of selection and on the attitudinal changes which took place among intending teachers both during their training and during their first year of full-time teaching (McIntyre and Morrison, 1967). Usually in these studies, where, for example, selection criteria were later correlated with teaching success, a student teacher's classroom performance was generally judged by means of a rating scale. The source for many of these scales was the work of Ryan (1975) in the United States. These correlations were generally low but the quality of the measuring instruments made it difficult to draw firm conclusions since it was difficult to know whether the explanation lay in the inconsistencies of the interviewers or in the unreliability of the rating scales.

Attitudinal studies provided more consistent results. At the time the most favoured instrument was the Minnesota Teacher Attitude Inventory (MTAI) with its main scales of liberalism, conservatism and dogmatism. Typically during the training course students became more liberal in their attitudes with respect to issues such as classroom discipline, child-centred approaches to learning and integration of subject matter. Once these students had entered full-time teaching, however, their views became more conservative and much closer to their more experienced colleagues. At the time, the explanation of these findings seemed straightforward, namely, that once absorbed into the school and classroom 'milieu' the theoretical stance required of the student during training was found impractical and these new teachers turned increasingly for advice from other staff in their school. Such findings contributed to the polarisation of theory and practice with the result that during the 1970s the amount of time devoted to studying the educational disciplines was considerably reduced (Alexander, 1984). In their place educational 'issues' courses were created covering problematic aspects of current schooling such as 'mixed ability teaching', 'gender education' and 'assessment'. On the new courses knowledge derived from the separate educational disciplines was integrated around these common themes and illustrated, wherever possible, by examples of classroom practice.

In retrospect there is a need to question the wisdom of these changes. Studies which explored the validity of attitude inventories such as the MTAI have been largely ignored. In these latter studies students were asked to fill in the attitude questionnaire to produce a result which ensured they would be classified either as liberal or conservative in their attitudes to teaching and to children. The bulk of respondents had no difficulty in selecting answers to items which ensured that they would be classified in the predicted manner. From this result stems an alternative hypothesis, namely that students filled in the attitude questionnaire in a manner which indicated support for liberal attitudes, not because they believed in such ideas but because they judged it accorded with the 'educational orthodoxy' of the college in which they were training. In responding in this manner they hoped tutors would regard them in a favourable light and this would ensure more favourable ratings for both their academic and practical course work. This explanation contradicts the view that recruits into the teaching profession are subject to 'cycles of fashion' so that each generation adheres to the latest educational orthodoxy within the training institution. Instead it would seem that within the general teaching profession, including beginning teachers, there is a strong strand of conservatism and traditionalism which initially opposes any attempt to change or innovate at school or classroom level. Such a view, if accepted, requires a different approach to training since essentially it recognises a common pattern of teacher development in which each stage of that process needs to be matched by appropriate forms of support. Such models, for example, have been proposed by Galton *et al.* (1992) and view any change or development in teachers as a three stage process involving *initiation, consolidation and re-orientation.*

Galton's model is not unlike that developed by Hall *et al.* (1975) in the United States. At the initiation stage, the main concerns of the teacher or student are personal involving what Doyle and Ponder (1977) call the 'practicality ethic'. At this stage the demands placed upon the teacher, for example, the time needed to engage in training or the disruption to the present classroom organisation, are set against what are perceived to be the benefits of these changes. Only if the benefits are seen to outweigh these personal costs does the teacher agree to participate, willingly in the innovation. At the *consolidation* stage, teachers set out to implement the innovation in the manner prescribed to the best of their ability. This stage is very task orientated and is mainly concerned with 'getting things right according to instructions'. Only at the *re-orientation* stage, once a strong commitment to the innovation has been established, are teachers able to engage effectively in what has come to be termed 'action research'. This stage is characterised by concern for the pupils and as a result teachers are eager to take on the 'ownership' of the innovation within their own classroom with the aim of modifying the innovation in ways they feel will improve the quality of pupil learning. During the 1970s, 'action research' was widely adopted within Europe as the main way of changing teachers' practice regardless of the stage in their development the participants had reached (Brinke, 1990).

The notion of the teacher as a researcher with the classroom the equivalent of the scientists' laboratory was originally developed by Stenhouse (1975). In the United Kingdom this approach was embodied in the IT – INSET projects funded by the Department of Education and Science over the period 1980–87. The premise on which the approach was based derived from the findings of the earlier attitude studies cited earlier which saw the student teacher gradually absorb the conservative belief and therefore practices of their experienced colleagues while at the same time, at the instigation of government policy, considerable money and manpower were expended in these experienced teachers to adopt less traditional ways. The IT – INSET approach sought to conduct both the initial training and the in-service training in one and the same classroom through an 'action research' approach based upon continuous curriculum review (Ashton *et al.*, 1989, Ashton, 1990). In each classroom a group of students, the class teacher (and the university) or the college tutor formed a research team to investigate a particular aspect of classroom practice. Research questions could range from matters of subject content or classroom organisation such as 'How should we introduce the topic of fractions to seven year olds?' or 'How can resources be organised so that children can use them independently of the teacher and therefore increase the amount of time available for instruction?' to matters of didactic such as 'What is the best way to maximise the learning in small group situations?' The group would take turns to do the teaching, the observing and the recording and each teaching session would then be the subject of later discussion in which attempts would be made to link the practice to theory. At the height of the programme nearly two-thirds of the training institutions in England were taking part. The evaluation, however, proved inconclusive partly because although the basis of the curriculum review required the team in each classroom to ask the question 'What did the children learn from the experience to indicate that student teachers trained in this way were more effective?' Data collected largely consisted of the perceptions of the participating teachers, students and tutors who, having invested a considerable amount of time and effort on the project might, in terms of Doyle and Ponder's (1977) practicality ethic have been expected to have supported statements to the effect that it had improved their performance and understanding. The case studies carried out as part of this evaluation did demonstrate a number of shortcomings particularly as regards to theory practice links. By and large the tutors level of theoretical knowledge was often limited since they had gained their positions largely on their previous reputations as good practitioners rather than for any contribution to educational theory. As a result, the post-teaching discussions tended to become little more than general discussions where 'commonsense' suggestions were made and where often the lack of recent and relevant experience by the college tutor put him or her at a disadvantage. Where tutors did attempt to insert theoretical explanations these were often provided in ways which led to rejection by the classroom teacher. Only in a limited number of cases did the notion of partnership between the classroom teacher, the student and the tutor operate successfully. For the most part the power relationships inherent in this situation predominated so that often the students perceived themselves to be little more than helpers rather than active participants in the 'action research'. Nevertheless the influence of the IT – INSET approach has continued so that in a recent survey of training institutions over 8 per cent responded that their approach to training was based upon the notion of 'reflective teaching' prescribed by Pollard and Tann (1987) where the notion of the reflective practitioner corresponds closely to the model of practice developed by Ashton in the IT – INSET studies.

Almost as a reaction to these classroom-based approaches to training government policy in the United Kingdom has moved rapidly in the opposite direction. The setting up of a Council for Accreditation of Teacher Education (CATE) has sought to lay down requirements for entry into the profession, the breadth and the balance of the curriculum and the nature of the school experience. Such demands have been backed up by inspections of each course by teams of Her Majesty's Inspectors thus introducing a measure of accountability since accreditation is only granted subject to satisfactory inspection. In spite of these controls many of the perceived current ills within the educational service mostly ascribed by politicians and the media to falling standards of literacy and numeracy, have led to new proposals whereby the responsibility for the bulk of training is to be given to schools who for the first time will be paid for these duties. Government sources argue that the present system is too prone to the influence of unrepresentative theorists within the teacher-training establishment in spite of the evidence cited earlier of the essential conservative and traditional nature of teachers. Alternative routes are being developed, notably that of the school-based programme which would allow the introduction of an apprenticeship model for graduates and mature candidates who have at least five years experience of work. In some ways, therefore, the wheel has come full circle in that at the beginning of the 20th century universities who were mostly very reluctant to engage in the training of teachers (Patrick, 1990) are, nearly one hundred years later, finding themselves gradually playing a *decreasing role* in the enterprise. As Sir William Taylor, the first Chairperson of CATE has observed, these trends within the education system can be found elsewhere. Most recently in France with the creation of the IEUNs (Taylor, 1990). Everywhere intermediate bodies standing between central government and the university, such as the Higher Education Funding Council in the United Kingdom, the Regional Academies in France and the National Board of Education in Sweden have, according to Taylor (1990) lost ground.

Research methods

In Europe, as elsewhere, much of the 1980s was characterised by extended debates about the advantages of using quantitative as opposed to qualitative methodologies in social science research. Whatever the outcome in different member states, depending largely on the initial balance between the different methodologies, it can be said that everywhere, over the decade, the use of qualitative methods involving case studies and ethnography gained ground. This is clearly demonstrated in the case of teacher training conclusions reached at the 5th European Conference of Directors of Educational Research Institutions held in Liechtenstein in October 1988 on the theme of effectiveness of in-service education and training of teachers (CDCC, 1988; DECS/RECH80). According to the Final Report 'The importance of qualitative methods was repeatedly emphasised to be achieved by ethnographic approaches, non-standardised interviews and case studies.' It would be true to state that both in the United States and, to a lesser extent, the United Kingdom, there is less polarisation between advocates of different methodologies where, in more recent work on teacher training, it has been recognised that the nature of problems encountered is often best served by a combination of different methods. Part of the reason for this lies in the advances made within the field of quantitative methods where in both countries there has existed since the early 1970s a strong tradition in the use of systematic observation (interaction analysis) for the study of teaching (Croll, 1986; Anderson and Burn, 1989). In most other European states, with the exception of Scandinavia, quantitative methods still largely relied on the use of large-scale questionnaires and rating scales, as demonstrated by the reports of research in Bone and McCall (1990). The limitations of such approaches, particularly when seeking information from teachers about their classroom practice, is well documented because of the phenomenon which Galton (1989) has described as 'the perception gap in teaching' whereby because teacher decision-making behaviour operates at what the psychologist Allport defined as the expressive rather than the coping level, there is often a gap between what teachers perceive themselves to be doing and what an external observer might record. In certain cases systematic observation has the advantage of ethnographic methods and it allows a wider sample of behaviour to be examined. Whatever the final conclusions drawn with respect to different methodologies the debate has tended to distract researchers' attention away from any serious study of the processes of teacher eduation. Thus the largest study of Postgraduate Initial Teacher Education ever undertaken in the United Kingdom in the early eighties, commonly known as the SPITE Project (The Structure and Processes of Initial Teacher Education within the universities of England and Wales) merely gathered questionnaire information supported by interviews (Bernbaum et al., 1985). While such studies replicated in other countries can help policymakers with respect to strategic decisions about the organisation of initial teacher training they can have little to say at the tactical level to determine, in particular, the processes of change which the novice teacher experiences in the first few years of training. Yet as can be seen from the earlier discussion important questions of innovation need to be based on some understanding of this transition process which seems to produce an overwhelmingly conservative profession. Such longitudinal studies, based upon observation of practice, are lacking. Indeed one of the criticisms of educational research on teaching is that, generally, those who are actually responsible for the training and therefore might be considered in the best position to carry out this kind of research, have shown very little interest in such studies (Galton, 1989).

Such studies are, however, beginning to find a place in educational research within the United States. For example, Borko et al. (1992), in the United States have studied the first attempts of mathematics students to teach their subject. They make use of the distinction developed by Shulman (1986, 1987), who argues that as teachers grow in subject knowledge they improve their subject content pedagogy, particularly those aspects to do with diagnosing pupils' learning difficulties. He calls for studies of teachers' professional development.

Such studies are, however, beginning to find a place in research on teachers' professional development. In one case study, Borko *et al.* (1992) describe how one student, a mathematics graduate, fails to teach pupils how to divide fractions. While acknowledging this task itself is very difficult other than providing rule and practice example, Borko *et al.* concentrate on the fact that the subject knowledge which this student gained as a mathematics graduate did not enable her to teach effectively. Their explanation will receive sympathetic consideration from many of those calling for reform of the teacher education system within Europe for they argue that the failure lies in the nature of the university teaching where the course tutors largely taught topics that were of interest to them and not what was relevant to the needs of the student. In this particular case the student's course was largely concerned with rote learning numerous computational techniques and did not treat such topics at higher levels of abstraction encouraging pupils to develop proofs for the algorithms. In particular, the course studied did not address the rational number topics which were central to the middle school American mathematics curriculum which the student was required to teach. The mathematics graduate by having a higher proportion of subject knowledge and less time dealing with subject pedagogy in the training college actually received less help towards the teaching task than non-mathematics graduates.

Borko *et al.* (1992) go further and follow the students during their method courses. The course itself emphasised the importance of what they term conceptual rather than procedural knowledge. The latter concerns mastery of specific skills and knowledge of procedures whereas conceptual knowledge deals with the underlying structures of the subject. In mathematics this would be the relationship in connection with ideas that explain and give meaning to mathematical procedures. Teaching division of fractions for conceptual knowledge would be exemplified in the use of concrete and semi-concrete models such as using rods, in drawings and other apparatus and in the discussion of the links between different ideas. In summary, therefore, procedural knowledge would enable a pupil to do calculations but conceptual knowledge would help the pupil to understand the procedures being used to obtain the correct answers. Using the same student as before, although a mathematics graduate, the researchers demonstrate that there is little conceptual understanding, partly for the reasons given earlier that the undergraduate course concentrated in particular on procedures. More importantly, however, they discussed the reasons why, when both the method tutor and the classroom teacher with whom the student was placed, both emphasised the importance of conceptual knowledge in mathematics the student, nevertheless, was still at the end of her course unable to teach in a way that met this objective. Borko *et al.* (1992) report that the pressures on course time meant that the method tutor tended to work through presentation and demonstration rather than providing the students with practical workshop experiences. The students, therefore, came to see the tutor's effort to provide conceptual knowledge rather as a set of routines similar to those they had received when on the university mathematics course when the emphasis was on procedural knowledge. For example, the tutor often used the same kinds of procedures to elicit understanding, favouring the use of rods, folding paper or colouring in squares. Students, therefore, saw these three routines as a technique to be tried whenever a new problem was started rather than examining which of these three techniques was the most appropriate for a specific task.

At the school level, the major constraint against teaching for conceptual knowledge according to Borko *et al.* (1992) was the demands of the local school board which placed the emphasis on standardised testing as a diagnostic measure to identify weak student performance and to provide remedial help. The formal evaluation system tended to drive the teachers into teaching for tests and therefore largely for procedural rather than conceptual knowledge. Similar occurrences were found in other schools where headteachers while largely expounding the value of conceptual development in mathematics nevertheless emphasised testing for diagnostic purposes. This is not unlike a similar finding reported by Alexander (1991) to the effect that the more the headteacher taught and theorised about teaching methods the less likely practice was to relate to these ideas.

In summary, therefore, the major obstacle to students developing ways of teaching that did more than require children to learn routines was the fact that the school mentors themselves largely ignored such teaching although they stated that it was an important aim. While, therefore, the mentors in schools paid lip service to the goal of teaching for conceptual understanding they were themselves held accountable only for the procedural knowledge which was demonstrated when the children passed the test. In this way the students never had opportunities to see more experienced teachers practice in the skills they themselves believed in and were trying to develop.

Future directions in research

The kind of study described above provides examples of the kinds of research which are now required as a matter of urgency within the European context. For example, the work of Borko and her colleagues suggests the need for very close monitoring of the kinds of changes which have resulted in the reform of the French educational system and the creation of Les Institutes Universitaires des Formation des Maitres (IUFM) which seeks to reduce the influence of the university subject specialist and to give greater prominence to pedagogy in the training of all teachers both at the primary and secondary phase. Other similar concerns are evident in the changes proposed within the Spanish education system. At the other extreme are countries such as the United Kingdom where over the last few years the emphasis, at the primary phase, has been to increase the proportion of time given over to mastery of the subject with correspondingly less time for pedagogical considerations which are thought to be best acquired through longer exposure to classrooms with the support of mentors. Indeed the

United Kingdom with its current emphasis within the National Curriculum upon assessment and standardisation has all the ingredients which in the training conditions described by Borko *et al.* (1992) has provided new entrants to the provision who lack competence to teach their subject in ways which enable children to learn effectively. The weakness of Borko and Eisenhart's research is that Shulman's distinction between subject knowledge and subject knowledge pedagogy is treated relatively unproblematically. Nettle *et al.* (1990) have reviewed some 18 research articles where the concept of pedagogic content knowledge has been used and has found considerable variation in the way the term has been conceptualised. In particular there seems to be a confusion about pedagogy which is specific to the subject and that which might be more generalisable, as, for example, with effective classroom management or such direct teaching approaches as use of techniques for improving higher order questioning. The links between different types of pedagogy and the relative importance and emphasis to be given at the initial stages of training to these different aspects is a matter requiring urgent attention. Closely associated with such research is that related to studies of teachers' theories and belief systems based upon the collection of teachers' narrative accounts (Cortazzi, 1990). Recent reviews of this research (Kagan, 1990; Lampart and Clark, 1990) both stress the need to develop linkages between the various constructs identified through these narrative analyses. At the moment because they tend to be highly specific the constructs themselves are at a very low level of generality and there is a need to establish more general principles which underlie teacher descriptions of classroom teaching and learning and to relate these principles to specific teaching behaviours and outcomes in order to estimate their significance.

The third part of the research agenda concerns the notions of teacher development which were discussed earlier in connection with different models of training. In the United States, a considerable amount of attention has been devoted to the study of differences between novice and expert teachers (Berliner, 1992).

Berliner sets out of number of reasons for giving priority to this research. First, because knowledge gained through such can have practical benefits in helping novices to gain greater confidence. Second, it is important, given the public criticism which exists of teachers, to demonstrate that there are some teachers who can de identified and who represent an unusual level of competence in the same way that experts do in other professions. Third, the information about such expertise may help policymakers who seek to draw up arrangements for merit pay and for alternative certification programmes and fourth, the study of expert teaching in itself makes the point that the activity is very sophisticated and complex, taking years to learn. This in turn may lead to greater appreciation of these skills by the public.

The findings from these studies are generally in agreement that expertise is context specific. Teachers who therefore gained expertise in teaching older pupils in the primary school will not necessarily be expert when taking children in the reception class. Consequently in any training they will

will need to go through the processes of initiation, consolidation and re-orientation referred to earlier although in the case of experts they may be able to pass through each stage more rapidly than someone who was deemed to be less competent. More importantly experts are much more flexible in their approach than novices tending to ignore information previously acquired in school records in favour of judging each pupil in the particular context in which they find them. All experts have a well-established series of routines for dealing with standard activities such as introducing lessons. This in turn, Berliner argues, frees expert teachers from clutter so they can concentrate on responding to opportunities for stimulating higher order thinking and adjusting to specific social situations in the classroom. Novices in particular seem unable to decode social situations so that they do what they were asked to do rather than attempt to initiate change to maximise the learning opportunities in any given situation. Experts also tend to be opportunistic in their problem solving whereas in contrast novice teachers were often unable to maintain the direction of a lesson when faced with pupil questions and became side-tracked as a result of these exchanges. The major reason for this is that experts represent problems quantitively different from novices. In a number of studies dealing with pupils' performance in mathematics and science, experts were consistently able to make more inferences about students' learning problems from the results of testing. This was not a only because they had had more experience of dealing with these student errors but they were also able to engage more constructively in what might be called critical feedback in which mistakes on the activity were used as a learning experience rather than simply as an opportunity to correct wrong results. Inexperienced teachers simply corrected work. Overall expert teachers have a much greater capacity to make sense of the total classroom rather than novices who tend to look at specific events when viewing video tapes of other teachers teaching. The point which emerges is that expert teachers are not simply examples of more effective instructors in comparison with novices or beginning teachers. They do not simply do more of the same thing and do it better. The evidence suggests that they actually operate and think in different ways in promoting more effective classrooms. They become, unlike beginning teachers, more student-orientated with a strong sense of obligation towards pupils. As a result they concentrate on providing a strong positive motivational system in the classroom and a belief in their own efficacy and in the students' abilities to learn provided they create the right classroom climate. Linked closely to this view is that until teachers move away from the more limited conceptions and more specific orientations associated with beginning teaching, it may be inappropriate to attempt to develop programmes of training in which the Schön notion of reflective teaching (Pollard and Tann, 1987) incorporating Schön's (1987) vision of the reflective practitioner. This is because beginning teachers lack sufficiently holistic views of events taking place in the classroom. Instead, more appropriate forms of training may revolve around in the sense used by Schwab (1971). In this approach, rather than developing theories and beliefs through action the novice is required to use existing theories in order to study and reflect on classroom events he/she observes. The use of specific teaching models in the manner suggested by Joyce and Weil (1980) in conjunction with a coaching approach (Joyce and Showers, 1983) may also be appropriate.

The research, however, also has implications for in-service training although the detailed discussion of this topic is beyond the scope of the present chapter. If, as the research suggests, differences which exist between novice and expert teachers are such that they demand different methods of training and, if as Berliner (1992) argues, by definition is only acquired by a few then there is a question of appropriate forms of training for the many teachers who are characterised as coming somewhere between the novice and expert stages. Berliner advocates a programme based upon a five-stage model of teacher development based upon a model of skill acquisition developed by Dreyfus consisting of novice, advanced beginner, competent, proficient and expert stage. The most detailed attempt to make use of this model in a training context has been attempted by Benner (1984) in the training of clincial nurses and she concludes that very distinct methods of training are needed for each stage arguing, for example, that at the fourth stage, the proficient stage, where the student begins to perceive situations in holistic terms, which are guided by a set of beliefs and principles, then problem-solving approaches based upon case studies are the most appropriate ways of bringing about improved performance. So far the model has not been tried in an educational context. Neither is it very clear how the stages which each teacher has reached can be identified empirically in order to create appropriate groups for study. Indeed even the novice/ expert research is marred in this respect in that many studies tend to equate expertise with experience and not to judge on performance using a set of agreed criteria. More recent reviews, offering alternative paradigms of professional growth of teachers, have been carried out by Kagan (1992) who observes that 'despite four decades of empirical research, researchers appear to know remarkably little about the evolution of teaching skills' and Grossman (1992). Kagan's review in particular raises wider issues in relation to teacher development and in particular the historical links between the students' own experiences as a pupil and the manner in which they conceptualise their own role as a teacher both initially and as a result of different approaches to training.

Currently then the organisation and development of programmes of training teachers is in a considerable state of flux across all of Europe. While some countries are attempting to lessen the influence of subject expertise and reduce the academic content of training courses, others are seeking to remedy what they see as a defect in their training systems by giving greater emphasis to the acquisition of more and more subject expertise. Amongst those responsible for the training in didactics and teaching methods, a conviction is emerging that this is just done in schools with practising teachers acting as mentors. Theory when introduced should come about as part of a collaborative process within an 'action research' approach. But the research on the processes of training teachers, both that concerned with subject knowledge and with the nature of professional growth and the most effective methods of training to bring this about all challenge aspects of these policies as either taking an over simplistic view of the training process or, still worse, seeking under the guise of change to introduce new systems which can produce qualified teachers at less cost than currently operating. The context in which schooling takes place in the United States is vastly different from that in most European countries and even within Europe the variations between member states are considerable. It would therefore be dangerous to transpose the results now emerging from American studies to a European context without replicating some of the more important findings. This is the challenge for European researchers into teacher education over the next decade.

Bibliography

Advisory Conciliation and Abitration Service (ACAS) (1986) Teachers Dispute ACAS Independent Panel: Report of the Appraisal Training Working Group. London: ACAS.

Alexander, R. (1984) Innovation and continuity in the Initial Teacher Education Curriculum. In Alexander, R., Craft, M. and Lynch, J. (eds) *Change in Teacher Education*. London: Holt, Rinehart and Winston.

Alexander, R. (1991) *Primary Education in Leeds*. University of Leeds.

Alarcao, I., Tavares, J. and Maia, M.C. (1992) Teacher Education Development in the 90s in Portugal. In: *European Journal of Teacher Education*, 15, pp. 191–6.

Anderson, L. and Burns, R. (1989) Research in Classrooms. Oxford: Pergamon Press.

Andersson, K. and Michaelsson, P.E. (1992) Teacher Education in Sweden. In Buchberger, F., 1992a, pp. 307–27.

Archer, E.G. and Peck, B.T. (1992) *The Teaching Profession in Europe*. Glasgow: Jordonhill College of Education Publications.

Arh, J. (1992) *The Development of Education in the Republic of Slovenia 1900–1992*. Ljubljana.

Ashton, P., Henderson, E. and Peacock, A. (1989) *Teacher Education Through Classroom Evaluation: Principles and Practice of IT-INSET*. London: Routledge.

Ashton, P.T. (1990) Editorial. In: *Journal of Teacher Education,* 41, 2, p. 2.

Askling, B. and Jedeskog, G. (1993) *The Teacher Education Programme in Sweden*. Paris: OECD/CERI.

Association for Teacher Education in Europe (ATEE) (1989) *The Selection and Professional Development of Trainers for Initial Teacher Training. Case Studies*. Strasbourg: Council of Europe: Council for Cultural Cooperation. CC-TE (89) 22.

Attanasio, A. (1993) Teacher Training in Italy. In: Karagoezoglu, G. (1993) pp. 83–9.

Badertscher, H. (1993) Handbuch zur Grunausbildung der Lenrerinnen und Lehrer in der Schweiz Strukturen, Bedingungen, Unterrichtsberechtigungen. EDK. Bern.

Baker, C., Muschamp, P. and Dracup, D. Z. (1993) *Teacher Quality. English Case Study*. Paris: OECD/CERI.

Ball, S. (1981) *Beachside Comprehensive*. Cambridge: Cambridge University Press.

Banks, F. (1992) The Development of New Courses to Support Teacher Training of Design and Technology Teachers. In: Blandow, D. and Dyrenfurth, M. (eds) *Technological Literacy, Competence and Innovation in Human Resource Development*. Weimar: Blandow/Dyrenfurth, pp. 166–72.

✓Barbier, J.M. and Galatanu, O. (1993) *Teacher Quality. A Study of Teacher Training Programmes*. Paris: OECD/CERI.

Barton, L., Pollard, A. and Whitty, G. (1993) Change in Teacher Education: The Case in England. In: Popkewitz, T. (eds.) (1993a) pp. 303–41.

Bastiani, J. (ed.) (1988) *Parents and Teachers: From Policy to Practice*. Slough: NFER-Nelson.

Bayer, M. *et al.* (1990) Ausgewaehlte Ergbnisse einer Untersuchung ueber strukturelle Veraenderungen in den Lehramtsstudiengaengen. In: *Erizehungswissenschaft* 1 (2) pp. 24–86.

Bazany, M. and Orbrdzalek, B. (1992) Teacher Education in the Slovac Republic. In Buchberger, F. (1992a) pp. 433–40.

✓Beernaert, Y., Van Dijk, H. and Sanders, T. (eds) (1993) *The European Dimension in Teacher Education*. Brussels: ATEE.

Bell, G. (1991) *Developing European Dimension in Primary Schools*. London: David Fulton.

Bell, P. (1970) *Basic Teaching for Slow Learners*. London: Muller.

Bell, P. (1981) *Teaching Slow Learners*. London: Macmillan.

Benner, P. (1984) *From Novice to Expert: Excellence and Power in Clinical Nursing Practice*. Reading, Massachusetts: Addison-Wesley.

Berliner, D. (1992) Some Characteristics in Experts in the Pedagogical Domain. In: Oser, F., Dick, A. and Patry, J. (eds) *Effective and Responsible Teaching: The New Synthesis*. San Fransisco: Jossey-Bass Press.

✓ Bernbaum, G., Patrick, H. and Reid, K. (1985) Postgraduate Initial Teacher Education in England and Wales: Perspectives from the SPITE Project. In: Hopkins, D. and Reid, K. (eds) *Rethinking Teacher Education*. London: Croom Helm.

Blackburn, V. and Moisan, C. (1987) *The In-Service Training of Teachers in the Twelve Member States of the European Community*. Maastricht.

Blandow, D. (1989) Training Teachers of Technology for Grades 1–6 and Technological Education in the Educational System in the GDR. In: Klerk Wolters, F. de, Mottier, I., Raat, J.H. and Vries, M.J. de (eds) *Teacher Education for School Technology*. Contributions PATT-4 conference. Eindhoven: PTH, pp. 383–401.

Blandow, D. and Ungewiss, W. (1990) Interest of Pupils – the Critical Starting Point for Effective Technological Instruction. In: Szydlowski, H. and Stryjski, R. (eds) *Technology and School*. Report of the PATT conference in Poland 1990. Zielona Gora: Pedagogical University Press, pp. 179–90.

✓Bleszynska, K., Putiewiecz, E. and Skibinska, E. (1992) Teacher Education in Poland. In: Buchberger, F. (1992a), pp. 451–69.

Blondel, D. (1991) A New Type of Teacher Training in France: The Instituts Universitaires de Formation des Maitres. In: *European Journal of Education*, 26, pp. 197–205.

Bolam, R. (1987) The Induction of Beginning Teachers. In: Dunkin, M.J., *The International Encyclopaedia of Teaching and Teacher Education*. New York: Pergamon Press, pp. 745–57.

Bolam, R., Baker, K., Davis, J., McCabe, C. and McMahon, A. (eds) (1977) *National Conference on Induction: Conference Papers*. Bristol: University of Bristol, School of Education.

Bone, T. (1992) Teacher Education in Europe. In: Kirk, G. and Glaister, R. (eds) *Scottish Education and the European Community*. Edinburgh: Scottish Academic Press, pp. 61–80.

Bone, T. and McCall, J. (eds) (1990) *Teacher Education in Europe: The Challenges Ahead*. Glasgow: Jordonhill College of Education.

Booth, R.J. (1989) A Curricular Framework for Technology Teacher Training and Education. In: Klerk Wolters, F. de, Mottier, I., Raat, J.H. and Vries, M.J. de (eds) *Teacher Education for School Technology*. Contributions PATT-4 conference. Eindhoven: PTH, pp. 107–20.

Bordas, I. and Montane, M. (1992) Teacher Education in Spain. In: Buchberger, F. (1992a), pp. 275–306.

Boreland-Vinas, H. (1991) *Teacher Mobility in the European Community: Initial Teacher Training. A Comparative Description*. Brussels: EURYDICE.

Borko, H., Eisenhart, M., Brown, C., Underhill, R., Jones, D. and Agard, P. (1992) Learning to Teach Hard Mathematics, *Journal of Research in Mathematics Education*, 23 (3), pp. 194–222.

Boud, D. (1988) Professional Development and Accountability: Working with Newly Appointed Staff to Foster Quality. In: *Studies in Higher Education,* 13 (2), pp. 165–76.

Boulton, P. and Coldron, J. (1990) Integrating Equal Opportunities: In the *Curriculum of Teacher Education (TENET) Phase II Report*, Sheffield Hallam University.

Bourdoncle, R. (1990) From Schoolteacher to the Expert. The IUFM and the Evolution of Training Institutions. In: Bone, T. and McCall, J. (eds) *Teacher Education in Europe: The Challenges Ahead*. Glasgow: Jordonhill College of Education.

Bourdoncle, R. (1993) Professionalisation of Teachers and Teacher Education. In: *European Journal of Teacher Education*, 16.

Bradley, H. (1989) Report on the Evaluation of the School Teacher Appraisal Pilot Study. Cambridge: Cambridge Institute of Education.

Bridges, E. (1979) *Education, Democracy and Discussion*. Slough: National Foundation for Educational Research.

Bridges, E. (1987) *The Incompetent Teacher*. Lewes: Falmer Press.

Brinke, S. (1990) Exploring and 'Independent Solo Flight' as Parts of the Teacher Education Curriculum: A Meta Study of Three Action Research Projects. In: Bone, R. and McCall, J. (eds) *Teacher Education in Europe: The Challenges Ahead*. Glasgow: Jordonhill College of Education.

Brown, E. (1987) *The Incompetent Teacher*. Lewes: Falmer Press.

Brown, G. and Hatton, N. (1981) *Explanations and Explaining*. London Macmillan.

Brown, S. *et al.* (1988) *Student Teachers Learning from Experienced Teachers*. Scottish Council for Research in Education Report. Edinburgh: SCRE.

Brown, S. and McIntyre, D. (1988) The Professional Craft of Teachers. In: *Scottish Education Review*. Special Issue: The Quality of Teaching. Edinburgh: Scottish Academic Press.

Bruce, M. (1989) *Teacher Education and the ERASMUS Programme*. Brussels: ATEE.

Buchberger, F. (1989) *Development of Teacher Trainers: A Neglected Issue*. Paper

198

presented to the 14 Annual conference of Association for Teacher Education in Europe, Kristianstad, Sweden.

Buchberger, F. (1992a) *ATEE Guide to Institutions of Teacher Education in Europe*.

Buchberger, F. (1992b) Teacher Education in Austria. In: Buchberger, F. (1992a), pp. 2−25.

Buchberger, F. (1992c) Educational Research and Teacher Education in Austria. In: *European Journal of Teacher Education*, 15, pp. 87−96.

Buchberger, F. (1993a) Lehrerbildung 92: Themen und Trends im internalionalen Vergleich. In: *Beitraege zur Lehrerbildung*, 11, pp. 7−20.

Buchberger, F. (1993b) Teacher Education Policies and Models in Europe. In: Karagoezoglu, G. (1993), pp. 1−13.

Buchberger, F. (1993c) *Teacher Education in Europe*. Paper, First OECD Japan Seminar, Tokyo.

Buchberger, F. (1993d) *In-Service Education of Teachers − A Comparative Analysis of Some Trends*. OAJ: Helsinki.

Buchberger, F. and Byrne, K. (1994) *Quality in Education*. Limerick.

Buchberger, F., De Corte, E., Groombridge, B. and Kennedy, M. (1994) *Educational Studies and Teacher Education in Finnish Universities*. Commentary by International Review Team. Ministry of Education, Helsinki.

Buchberger, F. and Seel, H. (eds) (1985) *Teacher Education and the Changing School*. Lin-Brussels: ATEE.

Burden, P.R. (1990) Teacher Development. In: Houston, W.R., Haberman, M. and Sikula, J. (eds) *Handbook of Research on Teacher Education*. New York: Macmillan, pp. 311−29.

Burke, P. (1987) *Teacher Development*. New York: Falmer Press.

Burn, B.B. (1992) Degrees; Duration, Structures, Credit and Transfer. In: Clark, B.R. and Neave, G., pp. 1579−86.

Busch, F. (1990) Lehrerbildung − ein Schlüsselproblem der Bildungspolitik in Europa? In: Bone, T. and McCall, J., pp. 19−40.

Buttery, T. *et al.* (1990) First Annual ATE Survey of Critical Issues in Teacher Education. In: *Action in Teacher Education*, 12, 2, pp. 1−7.

Calderhead, J. (1988) The Development of Knowledge Structures in Learning to Teach. In: Calderhead, J. *Teachers' Professional Learning*. London: Falmer Press.

Calderhead, J. (1992) *The Professional Development of Teachers in Changing Europe*. Paper presented at the 17th Annual Conference of the Association for Teacher Education in Europe. Lahti, Finland.

Caldwell, B.J. and Carter, E.M.A. (eds) (1993) *The Return of the Mentor*. London: Falmer Press.

Cameron Jones, M. and O'Mara, P. (1990) Improving Training. *Final Report to the Council for National Academic Awards*. Edinburgh: Muray House.

Carneiro, R. (1993) *The Curriculum Redefined: Schooling for the 21st Century*. Paper presented to an OECD conference, Paris, April 1993.

Castro, M.S. and Mir, M.L. (1992) *Une intervention coéducationelle á la formation due professorat*. Paper presented at the 1992 Lahti Conference of the Association for the Teacher Education in Europe.

Cels-Offermans, A. (1985) *Education and Equality of Opportunity for Girls and Women*. Strasbourg: Council of Europe. MED-14-9.

Centre for Educational Research and Innovation CERI (1990) Improving Teacher Quality (Note by the Secretariat for the Governing Board) CERI/CD90/12. Paris: OECD.

Cerna, M. and Parizek, V. (1992) Teacher Education in the Czech Republic. In: Buchberger, F. (1992a), pp. 424–32.

Christensen, J.C. and McDonnell, J.H. (1993) The Career Lattice: A Structure for Planning Professional Development. In: Kremer-Haydon, L., Vonk, J.H.C. and Fessler, R. (eds) *Teacher Professional Development: A Multiple Perspective Approach*. Amsterdam: Swets & Zeitlinger, pp. 295–315.

Churukian, G. (1993) The Policies and Models of Teacher Training in the Council of Europe Countries. Final Report. In: Karagoezoglu, G. (1993), V–VI.

Clark, B.R. and Neave, G. (1992) *The Encyclopaedia of Higher Education*. Oxford: Pergamon Press.

Commission of the European Communities (1988) *The Conditions of Service of Teachers in the European Community*. Luxembourg.

Commission of the European Communities (1991) *Memorandum on Higher Education in the European Community*. Brussels.

Coolahan, J. (ed.) (1991) *Teacher Education in the Nineties: Towards a New Coherence*. Limerick-Brussels: ATEE.

Coolahan, J. (1992a) Teacher Education in Ireland. In: Buchberger, F. (1992a), pp. 168–86.

Coolahan, J. (1992b) Educational Research and Teacher Education. In: *European Journal of Teacher Education*, 15, pp. 9–22.

Coppieters, P. (1992) Teacher Education in Belgium. In: Buchberger, F. (1992a), pp. 26–66.

Cortazzi, M. (1990) *Primary Teaching: How it is*. London: David Fulton.

Council for Cultural Cooperation CDCC (1988) Innovation in Primary Education: Final Report (DECS/EGT (987) 23) Project No. 8, Strasbourg: Council of Europe.

Council for Cultural Cooperation CDCC (1988) The Effectiveness of In-Service Education and the Training of Teachers and School Leaders. *Report of the Fifth All European Conference of Directors of Educational Research Institutions* (Triesenberg, Liechtenstein) (DECS/Rech (88) 80). Strasbourg: Council of Europe.

Council of Europe (1979) Record of the Proceedings of the 11th Session of the Standing Conference of European Ministers of Education. The Hague, 10–13 June 1979.

Council of Europe (ed.) (1981) *Sex Stereotyping in Schools. A Report of the Educational Research*. Workshop held in Honefoss, 5–8 May 1981. Amersterdam/Lisse: Swets and Zeitlinger.

Council of Europe (1982) Recommendation No. R (82) 18 of the Committee of Ministers to member states concerning modern languages. Strasbourg: Council of Europe.

Council of Europe (1984) Report of the 26th Council of Europe Teachers' Seminar on '*Young People and Advertising: The Role and the Responsibility of the School*', Donaueschingen, FRD, 19–24 November 1984. DECS/EGT (84)7.

Council of Europe (1984a) 18th Council of Europe Teachers' Seminar on '*Sex Stereotypes in Schools: The Role and Responsibility of the Teacher*'. Council of Europe: Council for Cultural Cooperation. DECS/EGT (84) 6-E.

Council of Europe (1984b) Recommendation No R (84) 18 of the Committee of Ministers to Member States on *The Training of Teachers in Education for Intercultural Understanding, Notably in the Context of Migration*. Strasbourg: Council of Europe.

Council of Europe (1985) Recommendation No R (85) 7 of the Committee of Ministers to Member States on *Teaching and Learning about Human Rights in Schools*. Strasbourg: Council of Europe.

200

Council of Europe (1986) Report of the 33rd Council of Europe Teachers' Seminar on '*Mass Media Education in Primary Schools*', Donaueschingen, FRD, 6–10 October 1986. DECS/EGT (86) 73.

Council of Europe (1987a) Documents of the Fifteenth Session of the Standing Conference of Ministers of Education, Helsinki, 1986. Strasbourg: Council of Europe.

Council of Europe (1987b) *New Challenges for Teachers and their Education.* National reports on teacher education. Strasbourg: Council of Europe. MED-15-4.

Council of Europe (1987c) *New Challenges for Teachers and their Education.* Report on the 15th Session of the Standing Conference of European Ministers of Education, Helsinki, 5–7 May 1987. Strasbourg: Council of Europe. MED-15-9.

Council of Europe (1988) *The Training of Teachers for Technical and Vocational Education.* Secretariat report. Strasbourg: Council of Europe: Council for Cultural Cooperation. CC-TE (88) 9.

Council of Europe (1989) *The Role of Appraisal in the Professional Development of Teachers.* Secretariat report. Strasbourg: Council of Europe: Council for Cultural Cooperation. CC-TE (89) 27.

Council of Europe (1990a) *The Selection and Professional Development of Trainers for Initial Teacher Training.* Secretariat report. Strasbourg: Council of Europe: Council for Cultural Cooperation. CC-TE (90) 43.

Council of Europe (1990b) *The Selection of Candidates for Initial Teacher Training in CDCC Countries.* Seminar report. Strasbourg: Council of Europe: Council for Cultural Cooperation. CC-TE (90) 47.

Council of Europe (1990c) The CDCC Teacher Bursary Scheme. Information Document. Strasbourg: Council of Europe: Council for Cultural Cooperation. DECS/EGT (90) 1.

Council of Europe (1992) Council for Cultural Cooperation: School and Out-of-School Education Section. List of documents. Strasbourg: Council of Europe: Council for Cultural Cooperation. DECS/SE (91) 3.

Council of Europe (1993a) Council for Cultural Cooperation: School and Out-of-School Education Section. List of Documents. Strasbourg: Council of Europe: Council for Cultural Cooperation. DECS/SE (93) 2.

Council of Europe (1993b) Council for Cultural Cooperation: School and Out-of-School Education Section. A Secondary Education for Europe. Progress Report 1991–1992. Strasbourg: Council of Europe: Council for Cultural Cooperation. DECS/SE/Sec (93) 22.

Council of Europe (1993c) *The European Dimension of Education: Teaching and Curriculum Content. Report on the 17th Session of the Standing Conference of European Ministers of Education, Vienna, 16–17 October 1991.* Strasbourg: Council of Europe. MED-17-7.

Council of Europe (1994) Standing Conference of European Ministers of Education, 18th Session, Madrid, 23–24 March 1994. *Resolutions on I. Education for democracy, human rights and tolerance: II, Preparation for the world of work; III The promotion of school links and exchanges in Europe; IV. Cooperation on education within the Council of Europe.* Strasbourg: Council of Europe. MED-18-6.

Corset, P. (1982) Report of the symposium on '*The secondary school and the mass media*'. Grenoble, France, 29 June–3 July, 1981. Strasbourg: CDCC.

Creager, J.G. and Murray, D.C. (1971) *The Use of Modules in College Biology*

Teaching. Washington DC: The Commission on Undergraduate Education in the Biological Sciences.

Croll, P. (1986) *Systematic Classroom Observation.* Lewes: Falmer Press.

Cumming, C.E., Kidd, J., Wight, J. and McIver, J. (1988) The quality of teaching as response. In: *Scottish Educational Review*, Special Issue on *Quality of Teaching.* Edinburgh: Scottish Academic Press.

Dahncke, H. (1989) *Educational Training: Industry and Commerce in the Future: A Contribution Concerning the Needs of School and Teacher Training.* Adelaide: South Australian Technical and Further Education (TATE) Research and Development Unit.

Dalichow, F. (1992) Degrees and other Qualifications: International Equivalence. In: Clark, B.R. and Neave, G., pp. 877–84.

Dalin, P. and Ruist, V. (1983) *Can Schools Learn?* Windsor: NFER/Nelson.

De Bolt, G.P. (ed.) (1992) *Teacher Induction and Mentoring: School-based Collaborative Programs.* New York: SUNY.

Delmelle, R. (1991) Report on the Seminar on *Training Teachers for Teaching to a Wide Range of Abilities, Interests and Backgrounds in the Classroom.* Strasbourg: Council of Europe: Council for Cultural Cooperation. CC-TE (91) 2.

DES (1988) *The New Teacher in School.* London: HMSO.

DES (1989) *Initial Teacher Training: Approval of Course.* DES Circular No. 24/89.

Dewe, B., Ferchhoff, W. and Radtke, F.O. (1992) *Erziehen als Profesion. Zur Logik professionellen Handens in Paedagogischen Feldern.* Leske & Budrich, Opladen.

DFE (1992) *Initial Teacher Training (Secondary Phase).* London: DFE Circular 9/92.

DFE and Welsh Office (1992) *Technology for Ages 5–16.* York/Cardiff: DFE and Welsh Office.

Doebrich, P. and Kodron, C. (1992) Educational Research and Teacher Education in Germany. In: *European Journal of Teacher Education*, 15, pp. 106–14.

Doebrich, P., Kodron, C. and Mitter, W. (1981) Einphasige Lehrerausbildung in Oldenburg. Gutachten für die Universitaet Oldenburg.

Doebrich, P., Kodron, C. and Nentwig, P. (1992) Teacher Education in the Federal Republic of Germany. In: Buchberger, F. (1992a), pp. 118–46.

Donn, M. and Sylfield, H. (1988) *The Careers of Teacher College Lecturers.* Wellington, New Zealand: Department of Education.

Down, B.K. (1989) 'Editorial' Studies in Design Education. In: *Craft Technology: Special Issues on Teacher Training* (1989), 21, 2.

Doyle, W. and Ponder, G. (1977) The Practicality Ethic and Teacher Decision Making. *Interchange*, 8, pp. 1–12.

Doyle, W. (1979) Making Managerial Decisions in Classrooms. In: Duke, D.L. (ed.) *Classroom Management* (78th Yearbook of the National Society for Studies in Education). Chicago: University of Chicago Press, pp. 42–72.

Doyle, W. (1986) Classroom Management and Organization. In: Wittrock, M.C. (ed.) *Handbook of Research on Teaching.* New York: Macmillan, pp. 392–432.

Dreyfus, H. and Dreyfus, S. (1986) *Mind over Machine.* New York: Free Press.

DSDE (1993) *The Training and Development of Teachers*: Interim Consultative Document. Oxford.

Dunkin, M. (1987) *The International Encyclopaedia of Teaching and Teacher Education.* Oxford: Pergamon.

Dyrenfurth, M.J. (1989) Technology Teacher Education and PATT Research: Observations, Challanges and Issues. In: Klerk Wolters, F. de, Mottier, I., Raat, J.H. and Vries, M.J. de (eds) *Teacher Education for School Technology.* Contributions PATT-4 conference. Eindhoven: PTH, pp. 279–89.

202

Egan, G. (1986) *The Skilled Helper*. Montery Calif: Brookes/Cole Publishing Co.

Eggleston, J. (1991) Editorial (special issue on teacher education). In: *European Journal of Teacher Education*, 26, pp. 195–6.

Elder, R. (1988) Improving the Quality of Teaching Through School Experience, *Scottish Education Review*: Special Issue on *The Quality of Teaching*. Edinburgh: Scottish Academic Press.

Elliot, J. (ed.) (1993) *Reconstructing Teacher Education*. London: Falmer Press.

European Commission (1991) Final Report of the Conference, *The Teaching Profession in Europe*, 3–5 October 1991, Noordwijkerhout, The Netherlands.

EURYDICE (1991) *Initial Teacher Training in the Member States of the European Community*. Brussels.

EURYDICE/CEDEFOP (1991) *Structures of the Education and Initial Training Systems in the Member States of the European Community*. Brussels.

Everston, C.M., Sanford, J.P. and Emmer, E.T. (1981) Effects of Class Hetrogeneity in Junior High School, *American Educational Research Journal*, 18.

Fessler, R. and Christensen J. (1992) *The Teacher Career Cycle*. Boston: Allyn & Bacon.

Fisher, J.S. (1989) Technology Education INSET: The Oxford Experience. In: Klerk Wolters, F. de, Mottier, I., Raat, J.H. and Vries, M.J. de (eds) *Teacher Education for School Technology*. Contributions PATT-4 conference. Eindhoven: PTH, pp. 146–59.

Foldberg, E. and Stenlev, L. (1992) Teacher Education in Denmark. In: Buchberger, F. (1992a), pp. 328–40.

Ford, J. (1969) *Social Class and the Comprehensive School*. London: Routledge and Kegan Paul.

Friere (1972) *Pedagogy of the Oppressed*. Harmondsworth: Penguin.

Fukyama, F. (1992) *The End of History and the Last Man*. New York: Free Press.

Fullan, M.G. (1991) *The New Meaning of Educational Change*. New York: Teachers College Press.

Fullan, M. and Hargreaves, A. (eds) (1992) *Teacher Development and Educational Change*. London: Falmer Press.

Furrer, W. and Wanzenried, P. (1992) Teacher Education in Switzerland. In: Buchberger, F. (1992a), pp. 328–40.

Galton, M. (1989) *Teaching in the Primary School*. London: David Fulton.

Galton, M., Fogelman, K., Hargreaves, L. and Cavendish, S. (1992) *The Rural Schools Curriculum Enhancement National Evaluation (SCENE)* Project Final Report. London: Department of Education and Science (DES).

Gambiez, C. (1981) *The Use of the Media at School to Prepare Youngster for Life*. Strasbourg: CDCC.

Gartside, P., Allan, J. and Munn, P. (1988) *In at the Deep End? Induction in Colleges of Further Education*. Edinburgh: Scottish Council for Research in Education.

Gellert, C. (1993) *Higher Education in Europe*. London: Jessica Kingsley Publishers.

Gerbex, R. (1985) Report of the Colloquy on 'The press in school' organised by the Council of Europe and APREJ. Strasbourg 20–22 March 1985. DECS/EGT (84) 7.

Gikopoulos, P. (1993) Teacher Education and Training in Greece: Current Situation and Future Perspectives. In: Karagoeszoglu, G. (1993), pp. 55–62.

Gilroy, P. (1989) Professional Knowledge and the Beginning Teacher. In: Carr, W. (ed.) *Quality in Teaching*. London: Falmer Press, pp. 101–15.

Giordan, A. and Souchon, C. (1991) *Une éducation pour l'environnement*. Nice: Z'Editions.

Gipps, C. and Murphy, P. (1994) *A Fair Test? Assessment Achievement and Equity*. Milton Keynes: Open University Press.

Girard, D. and Trim, J.L.M. (1988) *Project No. 12: 'Learning and Teaching Modern Languages for Communication'*. Final report of the Project Group. Strasbourg: Council of Europe: Council for Cultural Cooperation. CC-GP 12 (87) 11.

Glatthorn, A.A. (1990) *Supervisory Leadership: An Introduction to Instructional Supervision*. Glenview II. Scott, Foresman & Co.

Glickman, C.D. (1990) *Supervision of Instruction: A Developmental Approach*. Boston: Allyn & Bacon.

Goodlad, J.L. (1984) *A Place Called School*. New York: McGraw-Hill.

Grankvist (1992) Educational Research and Teacher Education in Norway. In: *European Journal of Teacher Education*, 15, pp. 129–36.

Griffin, G.A. (1985) Teacher Induction: Research Issues. In: *Journal of Teacher Education,* 36 (10), pp. 42–6.

Grodzka-Borowska and Szydlowski, H. (1981) Technological Literacy in the Curriculum of Polish Elementary School and Technology Teacher Training. In: Klerk Wolters, F. de, Mottier, I., Raat, J.H. and Vries, M.J. de (eds) *Teacher Education for School Technology*. Contributions PATT-4 conference. Eindhoven: PTH, pp. 416–32.

Grossman, P. (1992) Why Models Matter: An Alternative View on Professional Growth in Teaching. In: *Review of Educational Research,* 62, 2, pp. 171–80.

Grot, G. (1990) Report of Theme Technology Teacher Training. In: Sqydlowski, H. and Stryjski, R. (eds) *Technology and School. Report of the PATT Conference in Poland 1990*. Zielona Gora: Pedagogical University Press, pp. 248–51.

Gudmandsdottir, S. and Shulman, L.S. (1987) Pedagogical Content Knowledge in Social Studies. In: *Scandinavian Journal of Educational Research*, 31, pp. 59–70.

Haemaelaeinen, K. Mikkola, A. and Niemi, H. (1992) Teacher Education in Finland. In: Buchberger, F. (1992a). pp. 84–98.

Hall, G., Loucks, S., Rutherford, W. and Newlove, B. (1975) Levels of Use of Innovation: A Framework for Analysing Innovation Adoption. In: *Journal of Teacher Education*, 26, 1, pp. 52–6.

Hall, G.E. (1982) Induction: The Missing Link. In: *Journal of Teacher Education*, 33, 3, pp. 53–5.

Halsey, A.H. *et al.* (1991) *Every Child in Britain*. London: Channel 4.

Hansen, F. and Proppe, O. (1992) Teacher Education in Iceland. In: Buchberger, F. (1992a), pp. 156–67.

Hargreaves, D. (1990) Another Radical Approach to the Reform of Initial Teacher Training. In: *Westminster Studies in Education*, 13, pp. 5–11.

Harvey, R.O. (1988) Primary Science and Technology. In: Raat, J.H. *et al.* (eds) *Basic Principles of School Technology*. Contributions PATT-3 conference, 2, pp. 606–9.

Healey, C.C. and Welchert, A.J. (1990) Mentoring Relations: A Definition to Advance Research and Practice. In: *Educational Researcher*, 19, 9, pp. 17–22.

Hellawell, D. (1987) Education under Attack – the Response of European Politicians: An Informal Analysis of the Resolution on New Challenges for Teachers and their Education Adopted at the 15th Session of the Standing Conference of European Ministers of Education. *European Journal of Teacher Education*, 10, 3, pp. 245–58.

204

Hellawell, D. (1992) Teacher Education in England and Wales. In: Buchberger, F. (1992a), pp. 341–99.

Hillgate Group (1989) *Learning to Teach*. London.

HMI (1978) *Mixed Ability Work in Comprehensive Schools*. London: HMSO.

HMI (1992) Technology Key Stages 1, 2 and 3: *A Report by HM Inspectorate on the First Year 1990–91*. London: HMSO.

Hoeben, W. (ed) (1986) *In-service Education of Educational Personnel in Comparative Perspective*. Lisse.

Holmes Commission (1986) *Tomorrow's Teachers*. East Lansing.

Holmes Commission (1990) *Tomorrow's Schools*. East Lansing.

Hopkins, D. (ed.) (1987) *Improving the Quality of Schooling*. London: Falmer Press.

Hostmark-Tarrou, A.L. (1988) *The Training of Teachers for Technical and Vocational Education*. Discussion paper. Strasbourg: Council of Europe: Council for Cultural Cooperation. CC-TE (88) 1.

Hostmark-Tarrou, A.L. (1991) Teacher Education and the Universities in Norway. In: *European Journal of Teacher Education*, 14, pp. 275–86.

Houston, W.R. (ed.) (1990) *Handbook of Research on Teacher Education*. New York: Macmillan.

Howey, K.R. and Zimpher, N.L. (1990) Professors and Deans of Education. In: Houston, W.R. (ed.) *Handbook of Research on Teacher Education*. New York: Mcmillan.

Huberman, M. (1992) Teacher Development and Instructional Mastery. In Hargreaves, A. and Fullan, M., pp. 122–42.

Huberman, M. (1993) Steps towards a Developmental Model of the Teaching Carrer. In Kremer-Hayon, L. *et al.*, pp. 93–118.

Huebner, P. (ed.) (1988) *Teacher Education and Training in Europe: Present Challenges and Future Strategies*. Berlin-Brussels: ATEE.

Hunyady, G. and Kosa, E. (1992) Teacher Education in Hungary. In: Buchberger, F. (1992a), pp. 441–50.

Huling-Austin, L. (1990) Teacher Induction Programmes and Internships. In: Houston, R.W. *Handbook of Research on Teacher Education*. New York: Macmillan Publishing Co., pp. 535–49.

Jackson, B. (1964) *Streaming: An Education System in Miniature*. London: Routledge and Kegan Paul.

Jackson, P.W. (1968) *Life in Classrooms*. New York: Holt, Rinehart and Winston.

Jaroskow, R. (1993) Teacher Training: Present Situation and Prospects for Changes in Poland. In: Karagoezoglu, G. (1993), pp. 96–102.

Järvinen, A. Kohonen, V., Niemi, H. and Ojonen, S. (1992) *Educating Critical Professionals*. Paper presented to the 1992 Lahti Conference of the Association for Teacher Education in Europe.

Jenkins, E.W. (1992) Towards an Agenda for Research in Technology Education. In: Blandow, D. and Dyrenfurth, M. (eds) *Technological Literacy, Competence and Innovation in Human Resource Development*. Weimar: Blandow/Dyrenfurth, pp. 458–62.

Joyce, B. and Weil, M. (1980) *Models of Teaching* (second edn). New Jersey: Prentice Hall.

Joyce, B. *et al.* (1981) *Flexibility in Teaching*. New York: Longman.

Joyce, B. and Showers, B. (1983) Transfer of Training: The Contribution of Coaching. In: *Journal of Education*, 63, 2, pp. 163–72.

Joyce, B. and Showers, B. (1988) *Student Achievement through Staff Development*. London: Longman.

Judge, H. (1990) The Education of Teachers in England and Wales. In: Gumbert, E. (ed.) *Fit to Teach: Teacher Education in International Perspective*. Atlanta: Georgia State University, pp. 7–30.

Judge, H. (1992) Teacher Education. In: Clark, B.R. and Neave, G., pp. 1229–40.

Kagan, D. (1992) Professional Growth Among Preservice and Beginning Teachers. In: *Review of Educational Research*, 62, 2, pp. 129–70.

Kallos, K. and Selander, S. (1993) Teacher Education and Teachers' Work in Sweden: Reform Strategies and Professional Reorientation. In: Poplewitz, T. (ed.), pp. 211–61.

Karagözoğlu, G. (ed.) (1993) *The Policies and Models of Teacher Training in the Council of Europe Countries*. Izmir: Buca Faculty of Education.

Karagözoğlu, G. *et al.* (1993) Teacher Training Policies and Models in Turkey. In: Karagözoğlu, G. (ed.), pp. 126–36.

Keller, F.S. and Sherman, J.G. (1974) *The Keller Plan Handbook*. Menlo Park: Benjamin.

Kennedy, M. (1990) Choosing a Goal for Professional Education. In: Houston, W.R., pp. 813–95.

Kerry, T. (1981) *Teaching Bright Pupils in Mixed Ability Classes*. London: Macmillan.

Kerry, T. (1981) *Effective Questioning*. London: Macmillan.

Kerry, T. and Sands, M.K. (1981) *Handling Classroom Groups*. London: Macmillan.

Klafki, W. (1988) Lehrerausbildung in den 90er Jahren – Wissenschafts-orientierung und paedagogischer Auftrag. In: Huebner, P., pp. 26–45.

Klerk Wolters, F. de (1989) The PATT-Project, an Overview of an International Project in Technology Education. In: Klerk Wolters, F. de, Mottier, I., Raat, J.H. and Vries, M.J. de (eds) *Teacher Education for School Technology*. Contributions PATT-4 conference. Eindhoven: PTH, pp. 290–5.

Klerk Wolters, F. de, Raat, J.H. and Vries, M.J. de (1990) Assessing students' attitudes towards technology. In: Layton, D. (ed.) *Innovations in Science and Technology Education*, 3. Paris: UNESCO.

Kimbell, R. *et al.* (1991) *The Assessment of Performance in Design and Technology*. London: Schools Examination and Assessment Council.

Kiss, S. *et al.* (1990) Teaching of Technology in Primary Schools and Teacher Training in Hungary. In: Szydlowski, H. and Stryski, R. (eds) *Technology and School*. Report of the PATT conference in Poland 1990. Zielona Gora: Pedagogical University Press, pp. 191–8.

Kodron, C. (1993) European Dimension, Multiculturalism and Teacher Training. In: *European Journal of Teacher Education*, 16, 1, pp. 69–77.

Kommission der Europäischen Gemeinschaften (1993) Ausblick auf das Hochschulwesen der Europäschen Gemeinschaft. Reaktion auf das Memorandun. Brussels.

Kremer-Hayon, L., Vonk, H. and Fessler, R. (1993) *Teacher Professional Development; A Multiple Perspective Approach*. Amsterdam: Swers & Zeirlinger.

Lacey, C. (1977) *The Socialization of Teachers*. London: Methuen.

Laderriere, P. (1990) *Open Europe and its Teachers: Open Europe and Educational Policy*. In: Michaelsson, P.E. (ed.) *Perspectives for Teacher Education in an Open Europe*. Kristianstad-Brussels: ATEE, pp. 24–9.

Lampert, M. and Clark, C. (1990) Expert Knowledge and Expert Thinking in Teaching: A Response to Floden and Klinzing. In: *Educational Researcher*, 19, 5, 21–3.

206

Lanier, J.E. and Little, J.W. (1986) Research on Teacher Education. In: Whitrock, M.C. (ed.) *Handbook of Research on Teaching* (third edn). New York: Macmillan.

Lawton, D. (1991) The Future of Teacher Education in England and Wales. In: Coolahan, J., pp. 181–9.

Le Metais, J. (1990) *The Impact on the Education Service of Teacher Mobility.* Slough: NFER.

Le Metais, J. (1991) *Initial Teacher Training in the European Community.* Slough: NFER.

Lemosse, M. (1989) The Professionalism of Teachers: The English Perspective. In: *Recherche et Formation*, Paris: L'Institut Nationee de Recherche Pedagogique, 6, pp. 55–67.

Letvin, E. (1992) Induction. In: Fessler, R. and Christensen, J.C. *The Teacher Career Cycle.* Boston: Allyn and Bacon, pp. 59–87.

Levine, S.L. (1989) *Promoting Adult Growth in Schools: The Promise of Professional Development.* Boston: Allyn and Bacon.

Liégeois, J.P. (1987) *Gypsies and Travellers.* Strasbourg: Council of Europe: Council for Cultural Cooperation.

Liégeois, J.P. (1994) *Roma, Gypsies and Travellers.* Strasbourg: Council of Europe: Council for Cultural Cooperation.

Liston, D. and Zeichner, K. (1991) *Teacher Education and the Social Conditions of Teaching:* New York: Routledge.

Long, P. (1986) *Performance Appraisal Revisited: Third IPM Survey.* London; Institute of Personnel Management.

Louvet, A. (1991) *The Newly Qualified Teacher: A Survey of European Policy and Practice.* (CC-TE(91)) Strasbourg: Council for Cultural Cooperation. CC-TE (91) 1 rev.

Lugoviv, V.I. (ed.) (1992) *Development of Teacher Education in Ukraine in 1990–1991.* Kiev: Institute of Pedagogy.

Lundgren, U.P. (1977) *Model Analysis of Pedagogical Processes.* Stockholm: Stockholm Institute of Education.

Lundgren, U.P. (1986) *New Challenges for Teachers and Their Education.* M/ED-15-HF-41. Strasbourg: Council of Europe.

Lutherdt, M. (1990) On an Approach to an Innovation Methodology in the Course on the Training of Technology Teachers. In: Szydlowski, H. and Stryjski, R. (eds) *Technology and School.* Report of the PATT conference in Poland 1990. Zielona Gora: Pedagogical University Press, pp. 218–29.

Maanen, M. van (1991) *The Tact of Teaching.* Ontario: The Althouse Press.

Macbeth, A. (1989) *Involving Parents.* London: Heinemann.

Mackay, H. *et al.* (1991) *Understanding Technology Education.* London: Falmer Press.

MacAlpine, A. *et al.* (eds) (1988) *New Challenges for Teachers and Teacher Education.* A report of the Fourth all-European Conference of Directors of Educational Research Institutions, Eger, Hungary, 13–16 October 1986. Amsterdam/Lisse: Swets & Zeitlinger; and Berwyn, Pa.: Swets North America.

McCormick, R. *et al.* (1987) *Technology in Schools.* 4 modules. Milton Keynes: Open University.

McCormick, R. (1993) Design Education and Science Practical Implications. In: Vries, M.J. de, Cross, N. and Grant, D.P. (eds) *Design Methodology and Relationships with Science.* Dordrecht: Kluwer Academic Publishers, pp. 309–19.

McIntyre, D. and Morrison, A. (1967) The Educational Opinions of Teachers in Training. In: *British Journal of Social and Clinical Psychology*, 6. pp. 32–7.

Magrath, C.P. and Egbert, R.L. (eds) (1987) *Strengthening Teacher Education*. London: Jossey-Bass.

Man in't Veld, M. (1992) A Teacher Training Course on Gender Inclusive Strategies for Teaching Science and Technology. In: Alting, A. *et al.* (eds) *Ten Years GASAT Activities in a Changing Europe*. Contributions to the conference October 25–29 1992. Eindhoven: University of Technology.

Marklund, S. (1990) *Teacher Education Within or Outside Universities?* Stockholm: University of Stockholm.

Martin-Bletsas, J. (1989) *Initial Training of Foreign Language Teachers*. Brussels: EURYDICE.

Masterman, L. (1980) *Teaching about Television*. London: Macmillan, Chs 3 and 4.

Masterman, L. (1983) Report of European Teachers' Seminar on '*Mass Media Education*' Kristianstad, Norway, 8–14 August 1983. DECS/EGT (83) 82.

Masterman, L. (1990) *The Media Literacy Resource Guide*. Toronto: Ministry of Education.

Maurer, M. (1992) Teacher Education in Luxembourg. In: Buchberger, F. (1992a), pp. 194–8.

Mayor, F. (1992) Teacher Education in an Era of Global Change. In: *ICET Teacher Education in an Era of Global Change*, Arlington: ICET, pp. 15–19.

Mescheder, S. and Steinhüfel, W. (1989) In *Begabungsforschung: Positionen und Berichte*. Berlin: Akademie der Pädagogischen Wissenschaften der DDR.

Mialaret, G. (1992) Place et role de la recherche en education dans la formation des ensignants. In: *European Journal of Teacher Education*, 15, pp. 33–44.

Miller, S. and Taylor, P. (1992) *The Teacher Education Curricula in the Member States of the European Community*. Brussels: ATEE.

Millman, J. and Darling-Hammond, L. (1990) *Second Handbook of Teacher Evaluation*. San Francisco: Sage.

Ministere de l'Eseignement et de la Science (1992) *L'Enseignement en Roumanie*. Buchurest.

Ministry of Education (Russia) (1992) *The Development of Education*. Moscow: National Report from the Russian Federation.

Ministry of Education and Science (Bulgaria) (1992) *The Development of Education*. Sofia: National Report of the Republic of Bulgaria.

Mitter, W. (1984) Eastern Europe. Editorial in: *European Journal of Teacher Education*, 7, pp. 227–32.

Mitter, W. (1992a) Comparative Education. In: Clark, B.R. and Neave, G., pp. 1788–96.

Mitter, W. (1992b) Current Trends in Educational Research in Europe. In: *European Journal of Teacher Education*, 15, pp. 53–64.

Moerk, H.O. (1992) Teacher Education in Norway. In: Buchberger, F. (1992a), pp. 229–60.

Moermas, A. and De Voogd, E. (1992) *Women Only Groups and Career Planning*. Paper presented to the 1992 Lahti Conference of the Association for Teacher Education in Europe.

Montero, M.L. and Vez, J.M. (1989) Professional Development of Teacher Trainers: A Case Study. In: *European Journal of Teacher Education,* 13, 1/2, pp. 25–34.

Montesinos, T. (1990) La Formacion Inicial Del Profesorado Como Base Para La

Formacion Permante. In: Bone, T. and McCall, J. (eds) *Teacher Education in Europe: The Challenges Ahead*. Glasgow: Jordonhill College of Education.

Moon, B. (1993) Patterns of Control: School Reform in Western Europe. In: Moon, B. (ed.) *New Curriculum: National Curriculum*. London: Hodder and Stoughton.

Morgan, C., Hall, V. and McKay, H. (1983) *The Selection of Secondary School Headteachers*. Milton Keynes: Open University Press.

Morgenstern de Finkel, S. (1993) Teacher Education in Spain: A Postponed Reform. In: Popkewitz, T. (ed.), pp. 87–121.

Morrison, R.T. (1988) Technology Education in Scotland. In: Raat, J.H. *et al.* (eds) *Basic Principles of School Technology*. Contributions PATT-3 conference, 2, pp. 580–6.

Mottier, I. (1989) Opportunities for Women in Technical Teacher Training. In: Klerk Wolters, F. de, Mottier, I., Raat, J.H. and Vries, M.J. de (eds) *Teacher Education for School Technology*. Contributions PATT-4 conference. Eindhoven: PTH, pp. 366–74.

Mottier, I., Raat, J.H. and Vries, M.J. de (1993) *Technology Education and the Environment*. Proceedings PATT-6 conference. Eindhoven: PATT-Foundation.

Müller-Fohrbrodt, G. and Cloetta, B. (1978) *Der Praxisschock bei jungen Lehrer*. Stuttgart: Klett.

National Commission for Excellence in Teacher Education (1985) *A Call for Change in Teacher Education*. Washington DC: American Association of Colleges for Teacher Education.

National Curriculum Council (1992) *National Curriculum Technology: The Case for Revising the Order*. Yorke: NCC.

National Foundation for Educational Research in England and Wales (NFER) (1990) *The Selection of Candidates for Initial Teacher Training in CDCC Countries* (final report). (CC-TE (89) 26) Strasbourg: Council of Europe: Council for Cultural Cooperation.

Neave, G. (1987) Challenges Met: Trends in Teacher Education 1975–85. In: *New Challenges for Teachers and Their Education*. CDCC Study Conference of European Ministers of Education (M.Ed.-IT-4). Strasbourg: Council of Europe.

Neave, G. (1991) *Change and Challenge. The Mobilization of Europe's Teachers*. Noordwijkerhout. Netherlands: Council of Europe.

Neave, G. (1992) *The Teaching Nation. Prospects for Teachers in the European Community*. Oxford: Pergamon.

Nettle, E., Conners, R. and Placing, K. (1990) Learning to Become a Teacher: Student Teachers' Understanding of Subject Matter. In: Bezzina, M. and Butcher, J. (eds) *The Changing Face of Professional Education*. Collected papers. Sydney: AARE.

Neumeister, H. (1987) *Les systems de formation des enseignants dans des etats membres*. Strasbourg-Geneve.

Newman, S. (1990) *The Council of Europe and Teacher Education*. Strasbourg, Mimeo.

Nicholson, B. *et al.* (1992) Planning. In: Down, B.K. *et al. Design and Technology in the National Curriculum*; Coordinators Handbook (Secondary). Runnymeade Publications.

Novoa, A. (1993) The Portugese State and Teacher Education Reform: A Socio-historical Perspective to Changing Patterns of Control. In: Popkewitz, T. (ed.), pp. 53–85.

OECD (1989) *Schools and Quality*. Paris: OECD.

OECD (1990) *The Teacher Today: Tasks, Conditions, Policies*. Paris: OECD.

OECD (1991) *Alternatives to Universities*. Paris: OECD.

OECD (1992) *New Technology and its Impact on Educational Buidlings*. Paris: OECD.

OECD/CERI (1990) *The Training of Teachers*. Paris.

OECD/CERI (1992) *Teacher Quality*. OECD/CERI (92)8.

OECD/CERI (1993) *Teacher Quality. Teacher Education and the Quality of Schooling*. Working document.

Ooms, C. (1991) Dropout of Beginning Teachers. In: Voorbach, J.T. Vonk, J.H.C. and Prick, L.G.M. *Teacher Education 7: Research and Developments on Teacher Education in the Netherlands*. Amsterdam/Lisse: Swets & Zeitlinger.

Page, R.L. (1989) Teacher Training for Technology in the UK. In: Klerk Wolters, F. de, Mottier, I., Raat, J.H. and Vries, M.J. de (eds) *Teacher Education for School Technology*. Contributions PATT-4 conference. Eindhoven: PTH, pp. 225–37.

Pascal, C., Bertram, T. and Heaslip, P. (1991) *Comparative Directory of Initial Training for Early Years Teachers*. Brussels: ATEE.

Passow, A.H. (1985) The Education of Gifted and Talented Pupils. In: Hudson, T. (ed.) *Pergamon International Encyclopaedia of Education*. Oxford: Pergamon.

Patten, J. (1992) Letter to NCC: National Curriculum Technology. 2 June 1992.

Paun, E. (1992) Teacher Education in Romania. In: Buchberger, F. (1992a), pp. 470–82.

Peck, B. (1992a) Teacher Education in Northern Ireland. In: Buchberger, F. (1992a), pp. 400–4.

Peck, B. (1992b) Teacher Education in Scotland. In: Buchberger, F. (1992a), pp. 405–12.

Peck, B. (1993) Konzeptionen der Leherausbildung und Weiterbildung im Hinblick auf die europaeische Integration. In: Schleicher, K., pp. 152–72.

Penfold, J. (1988) *Craft, Design and Technology: Past, Present and Future*. Trentham Books.

Perrin-Naffakh, A.M. (1993) Teacher Training in France. In: Karagoezoglu, G. (ed.), pp. 46–9.

Peters, R.L., Verhoeven, H. and Vries, M.J. de (1989) Teacher Training for School Technology at the Dutch Pedagogical Technical College. In: Klerk Wolters, F. de, Mottier, I., Raat, J.H. and Vries, M.J. de (eds) *Teacher Education for School Technology*. Contributions PATT-4 conference. Eindhoven: PTH, pp. 238–42.

Petracek, S. (1989) *Regional Seminar Paper in Teacher Education*. Arlington: UNESCO-ICET.

Pivavarov, V. (1990) Teacher Education in the Soviet Union: Processes and Problems in the Context of Perestoika. In: Gumbert, E. (ed.) *Fit to Teach: Teacher Education in International Perspective*. Atlanta: Georgia State University, pp. 87–104.

Plate, N. (1992) Teacher Education in the Netherlands. In: Buchberger, F. (1992a), pp. 199–228.

Pollard, A. and Tann, S. (1987) *Reflective Teaching in the Primary Classroom*. London: Cassell.

Poole, P. and Shepard, T. (1992) Implementing the National Curriculum Design and Technology: The Challenge for Primary Teacher Training. In: Blandow, D. and Dyrenfurth, M. (eds) *Technological Literacy, Competence and Innovation in Human Resource Development*. Weimar: Blandow/Dyrenfurth, pp. 186–92.

Popkewitz, T. (ed.) (1993a) *Changing Patterns of Power. Social Refulation and Teacher Education Reform.* New York: SUNY.

Popkewitz, T. (1993b) U.S. Teacher Education Reforms: Regulatory Practices of the State, University and Research. In: Popkewitz, T. (ed.), pp. 263–301.

Popkewitz, T. and Pereyra, M. (1993) An Eight Country Study of Reform Practices in Teacher Education: An Outline of the Problematic. In: Popkewitz, T. (ed.) pp. 1–51.

Portmann, P.A. (1993) Barriers to Change in Teacher Education. In: *Action in Teacher Education*, 15, 1, pp. 14–21.

Postlethwaite, N. (1988) *The International Encyclopaedia of Comparative Education and National Systems of Education.* Oxford: Pergamon.

Proppe, O., Myrdal, S. and Danielsson, B. (1993) Change and Regulation in Ocelandic Teacher Education. In: Popkewitz, T. (ed.) pp. 123–59.

Rendle, P.C. (1981) *Scrutiny of Her Majesty's Inspectors of Schools in Scotland.* Edinburgh: Scottish Office.

Rey, M. (1986) *Training Teachers in Intercultural Education?* Strasbourg: Council of Europe: Council for Cultural Cooperation.

Reynolds, M. (ed.) (1989) *Knowledge Base for the Beginning Teacher.* Oxford: Pergamon.

Ritzen, J. (1992) Opening Address. In: Vonk, H. (ed.), pp. 11–15.

Roeder, M. (1990) *On Coping with Individual Differences in the Classroom.* Berlin: Max Planck Institut.

Ryan, K. (ed.) (1975) *Teacher Education: The Seventy-fourth Yearbook of the National Society for the Study of Education Part II.* Chicago: University of Chicago Press.

Samodaev, V. (1993) The System of Teacher Training in the Russian Federation. In: Karagoezoglu, G. (1993), pp. 11–115.

Sander, T. (1993) Discussing the Meaning of the European Dimension in Teacher Education – Crieria, Problems, Implications. In: Beernaet, T. *et al.*

Schleicher, K. (1993) *Kukunft der Bildung in Europa.* Nationale Vielflt und europaeische Einheit. Wissenschaftlich Buchgesllschaft, Darmstadt.

Schmidinger, E. (1988) Wie Planen Lehrer/Innen Ihren Unterricht? In: Buchberger, F., Schwartz, L. and Sperrer, E. (eds) *Lehren and Lernen in der Lehrebildung Padagogische Akademie des Bundes in Oberosterreich.* (Summary in EUDISED R. and D. Bulletin No. 37, p. 23.)

Schmidinger, E. (1993) *The Mobility of Student Teachers during their Practice Periods in Preservice Teacher Training in the Twelve Member States of EEC and other European Countries.* Brussels: ATEE.

Schön, D.A. (1983) *The Reflective Practitioner.* London: Temple Smith.

Schön, D.A. (1987) *Educating the Reflective Practitioner. Towards A New Design for Teaching and Learning in the Professions.* London: Jossey-Bass.

Schriewer, J. and Holmes, B. (eds) (1992) *Theories and Methods in Comparative Education.* Frankfurt: Lang.

Seel, H. (1988) Die schulprakische Ausbildung im Rahmen der Lehrerausbildung an den oesterriechischen Universitaeten. In: *European Journal of Teacher Education*, 11, pp. 49–58.

Sekretariat der Staendigen Konferenz der Kultusminister der Laender in der Bundesrepublik Deutschland (1992) Bestandsaufinahme zur Lehrerausbildung in den Mitgliedsstatten der Europeaeischen Gemeinschft. Bonn.

Selby, C.C. (1989) Women in Technology Education. In: Klerk Wolters, F. de, Mottier, I., Raat, J.H. and Vries, M.J. de (eds) *Teacher Education for School*

Technology. Contributions PATT-4 conference. Eindhoven: PTH, pp. 335–42.

Sergiovanni, T.J. and Starratt, R.J. (1993) *Supervision: A Redefinition* (5th edn). New York: McGraw Hill.

Shield, G. (1991) Industrial Awareness: A Curriculum Experiment. In: Mottier, I., Raat, J.H. and Vries, M.J. de (eds) *Technology Education and Industry*. Contributions PATT-5 conference, pp. 344–53.

Sheils, J. (1991) *Communication in the Modern Languages Classroom*. Strasbourg: Council of Europe: Council for Cultural Cooperation.

Shennan, M. (1991) *Teaching about Europe*. London: Cassell.

Shulman, L.S. (1986) Those Who Understand: Knowledge Growth in Teaching. In: *Educational Researcher*, 15, 2, pp. 38–44.

Shulman, L.S. (1987) Knowledge and Teaching: Foundations of the New Reform. In: *Harvard Educational Review*, 57, pp. 1–22.

Simola, H. (1993) Educational Science, the State and Teachers: Forming the Corporate Regulation of Teacher Education in Finland. In: Popkewitz, T. (ed.), pp. 161–209.

Skilbeck, M. (1992) The Role of Research in Teacher Education. In: *European Journal of Teacher Education*, 15, pp. 23–32.

Smith, J. (1992) The European Teaching Force: Conditions, Mobility and Qualifications. In: *European Journal of Teacher Education*, 16, 2, pp. 137–46.

Smithers, A. and Robinson, P. (1992) *Technology in the National Curriculum*. London: The Engineering Council.

Soedijarto (1976) *The Modular Instructural System*. Jakarta: UNESCO.

Solity, J. and Raybould, E. (1988) *A Teacher's Guide to Special Needs*. Milton Keynes: Open University Press.

Standing Conference of European Ministers of Education (1987) *New Challenges for Teachers and their Education*. Strasbourg: SCEME.

Stefanov, C. (1992) Teacher Education in Bulgaria. In: Buchberger, F. (1992a), pp. 418–23.

Steffens, H. (1992) Re-training Teachers for the New Technology Programmes in Ireland. In: *International Journal of Technology and Design Education*, 2, 2.

Stenhouse, L. (1975) *An Introduction to Curriculum Research and Development*. London: Heinemann.

Stoddart, T. and Floden, R. (1990) *Traditional and Alternative Forms of Teacher Certification*. Paper, AERA-conference. Boston.

Sutherland, M.B., (1990) Teacher Education in Northern Ireland. In: Thomas, J.B. (ed.), pp. 106–24.

Szymanski, M. and Piwowarski, R. (eds) (1992) *The Development of Education in Poland in 1990–1991*. Warsaw: ATEE.

Taylor, W. (1990) The Institutional Context: Continuity and Change. In: Bone, T. and McCall, J. (eds) *Teacher Education in Europe: The Challenges Ahead*. Glasgow: Jordonhill College of Education.

Teichler, U. (1988) *Changing Patterns of the Higher Education System: The Experience of Three Decades*. London: Jessica Kingsley.

Teichler, U. (1993) Structures of Higher Education Systems in Europe. In: Gellert, C. (ed.), pp. 23–36.

Thomas, J.B. (ed.) (1990) *British Universities and Teacher Education: A Century of Change*. London: Falmer Press.

Tickle, L. (1989) New Teachers and the Development of Professionalism. In: Holly, M.L. and McLoughlin, C.S. (eds) *Perspectives on Teacher Professional Development*. London: Falmer Press, pp. 93–115.

Tisher, R.P. (1980) The Induction of Beginning Teachers. In: Hoyle, E. and Megarry, L. (eds) *World Yearbook of Education 1980: Professional Development of Teachers*. London: Kogan Page, pp. 69–84.

Tisher, R.P. (1984) Teacher Induction: an International Perspective on Provisions and Research. In: Katz, L.G. and Raths, J.D. *Advances in Teacher Education*, 1. New Jersey: Ablex.

Tisher, R.P. and Wideen, M.F. (eds) (1990) *Research in Teacher Education: International Perspectives*. London: Falmer Press.

Todeschini, M. (1992) Teacher Education in Italy. In: Buchberger, F. (1992a), pp. 187–93.

Trim, J.L.M. (1988) *Consolidated Report on the Programme of International Workshops for Trainers of Teachers of Modern Languages (1984–87)*. Strasbourg: Council of Europe: Council for Cultural Cooperation. CC-GP 12 (88) 1.

Turney, C., Cairns, L.G., Eltis, K.J., Hatton, N., Thew, D.M., Towler, J. and Wright, R. (1982) *Supervisor Development Programmes: Role Handbook*. Sydney: Sydney University Press.

Turney, C. and Wright, C. (1990) *Where the Buck Stops: The Teacher Educators*. Sydney: Sydmac Academic Press.

Tzepoglu, S. and Moutzouri-Manoussou, I. (1992) Teacher Education in Greece. In: Buchberger, F. (1992a), pp. 147–55.

Uzdzicki, K. (1992) The Present System of Technology Teacher Training in Poland and Developments in this Respect. In: Blandow, D. and Dyrenfurth, M. (eds) *Technological Literacy, Competence and Innovation in Human Resource Development*. Weimar: Blandow/Dyrenfurth, pp. 196–200.

Valchev, R. (1993). Initial and In-Service Training in Bulgaria. In: Karagoezoglu, G. (ed.), pp. 26–30.

Valente, M.O. (1992) Teacher Education in Portugal. In: Buchberger, F. (1992a), pp. 260–74.

Vandenberge, R. (1988) School Improvement: A European Perspective. In: Parkay, F. (ed.) *Improving Schools for the 21st Century: Implications for Research and Development*. Gainsville, Florida: University of Florida.

Van Dijk, H. and Beernaert, Y. (1993) Promoting the European Dimension in Teacher Education – a Bottom-up Approach. In: Beernaert, Y. *et al.*

Van Horebeek, G. (1992) La Formation des Enseignants et les Universites en Belgique. In: *European Journal of Teacher Education*, 15, pp. 173–90.

Vaniscotte, F. (1989a) 70 Million Pupils. L'Europe de l'education. Hatier, France.

Vaniscotte, F. (1989b) La Formazion del Foruetim di Insegnanti. In: *Innovation in Primary Education*. Publications de l'IRRSAE de Florence. pp. 62–73.

Vaniscotte, F. (1992) Teacher Education and the Europe of Tomorrow. In: Buchberger, F. (1992a), pp. XIII-XX.

van Vught, F. and Westerheijden, D. (1993) *Quality Management and Quality Assurance in European Higher Education*. Commission of the European Communities, Brussels.

Veenman, S.A.M. (1984) Perceived Problems of Beginning Teachers. In: *Review of Educational Research*, 54, 2, pp. 143–78.

Verbruggen-Aelterman, A. (1990) The Relation between Supervision and Learning to Reflect in the Post Initial Training of Teachers in Upper Secondary and Higher Education. In: Bone, T. and McCall, J. (eds) *Teacher Education in Europe: The Challenges Ahead*. Glasgow: Jordonhill College of Education.

Vonk, J.H.C. (1982) *Opleiding en Praktijk*. Amsterdam (VU-Uitgeverij) (diss)

(Abbreviated version in English: Vonk, J.H.C. (1984a) *Teacher Education and Teacher Practice*. Amsterdam: Free University Press.

Vonk, J.H.C. (1983) Problems of Beginning Teachers. In: *European Journal of Teacher Education*, 6, 2, pp. 133–50.

Vonk, J.H.C. (1984b) The Professional Socialization of Teachers. In: Busch, F. and Spelling, K. (eds) *School Life Today*. Proceedings of the 8th Annual Conference of the Association for Teacher Education in Europe (ATEE). Copanhague/Oldenburg/Brussel: ATEE Publication.

Vonk, J.H.C. (1985) *Leraar worden, ga er maar aanstaan*. Amsterdam: VU-Uitgeverij.

Vonk, J.H.C. and Schras, G.A. (1987) From Beginning to Experienced Teacher: A Study of Professional Development of Teachers During Their First Four Years of Service. In: *European Journal of Teacher Education*, 10, 1, pp. 95–110.

Vonk, J.H.C. (1989) *Beginnend leraarschap*. Amsterdam: VU-Uitgeverij.

Vonk, J.H.C. (1991) Some Trends in the Professional Preparation of Primary and Secondary School Teachers in Europe: A Comparative Study. In: Coolahan, J., pp. 68–106.

Vonk, J.H.C. (1991a) Becoming a Teacher, Brace Yourself. In: Ho Wah Kam and Wong, R.J.L. *Improving the Quality of the Teaching Profession: an International Perspective*. Singapore: Institute of Education, pp. 3–82.

Vonk, J.H.C. (1991b) The Professional Preparation of Primary and Secondary School Teachers in Europe. In: Voorbach, J.T., Vonk, J.H.C. and Prick, L.G.M. *Teacher Education 7*. Lisse: Swets & Zeitlinger, pp. 161–89.

Vonk, J.H.C. (ed.) (1992) *New Prospects for Teacher Education in Europe*. Amsterdam-Brussels: ATEE.

Vonk, J.H.C. (1992a) New Prospects for Teacher Education in Europe. In: Vonk, J.H.C. and Van Helden, H.J. *New Prospects for Teacher Education in Europe: A Symposium Report*. Amsterdam: Vrije Universiteit, Department of Teacher Education, pp. 43–57.

Vonk, J.H.C. (1992b) *Begeleiding van beginnende docenten*. Amsterdam: VU-Uitgeverij.

Voorbach, J.H. (1992) *Some Trends in Teacher Education in Europe*. Paper to the 12th International Seminar on Teacher Education, Armidale, New South Wales, Australia, May 1992.

Vries, M.J. de (1990) *Technology in Perspective*. Eindhoven: PTH/Open Tech.

Vries, M.J. de (1991) What do Students in Dutch Technology Teacher Programmes Think of their Subject? In: *Research in Science and Technological Education*, 9, 2, pp. 173–9.

Vries, M.J. de (1992) The Role of Technology Education as an Integrating Discipline. In: Hacker, M., Gordon, A., and Vries, M.J. de (eds) *Integrating Advanced Technology into Technology Education*. NATO ASI Series F 78. Berlin: Springer Verlag.

Vries, M.J. de (1993a) Technology Education in Western Europe. In: Layton, D. (ed.) *Innovations in Science and Technology Education*, 4. Paris: UNESCO.

Vries, M.J. de (1993b) Green Design in Technology Education. In: Mottier, I., Raat, J.H. and Vries, M.J. de (eds) *Technology Education and the Environment*. Contributions PATT-6 conference. Eindhoven: PATT-Foundation.

Wagner, A. (1991) Educating Teachers. In: *OECD-Obersever*, 169, pp. 17–19.

Wagner, A. (1994) The Economics of Teacher Education. In: Husen, T. and Postlethwaite, N. (eds) *International Encyclopaedia of Education*, Oxford: Pergamon.

214

Walthert, K. *et al*. (1989) L'enseignante et l'enseignant vus par 750 parents. Berne: Direction de l'Instruction Publique de Canton de Berne (Summer in EUDISED R. and D. Bulletin No. 38, p. 15).

Whitehead, D. (1992) Teacher Trainers' Perceptions of Technology. In: Blandow, D. and Dyrenfurth, M. (eds) *Technological Literacy, Competence and Innovation in Human Resource Development*. Weimar: Blandow/Dyrenfurth, pp. 201–5.

Wilkin, M. (ed.) (1992) *Mentoring in Schools*. London: Kogan Page.

Wilson, G.M. (1991) Selection and Induction of Teaching Staff in Teacher Education Institutions. In: Bone, T.R. and McCall, J. (eds) *Teacher Education in Europe*. Proceedings of a Conference in Jordanhill College of Education, Scotland, September 1990.

Wilson, J.D. (1988) *Appraising Teacher Quality*. Sevenoaks: Hodder and Stoughton.

Wilson, J.D. (ed.) (1989) *The Effectiveness of In-service Education and Training of Teachers and School Leaders*. Report of the Fifth All-European Conference of Directors of Educational Institutions. Triesenberg (Lichtenstein) 11–14 October 1988. Amsterdam/Lisse, and Rockland, Md/Berwyn, Pa: Swets & Zeitlinger.

Wilson, J.D. (1989a) *The Role of Appraisal in the Professional Development of Teachers: Some Issues*. Strasbourg: Council of Europe: Council for Cultural Cooperation. CC-TE (89) 1.

Wilson, J.D. (1989b). *The Selection and Professional Development of Trainers for Initial Teacher Training: Some Issues*. Strasbourg: Council of Europe: Council for Cultural Cooperation. CC-TE (89) 16.

Wilson, J.D. (1990). *The Role of Appraisal in the Professional Development of Teachers*. European Trend Report. Strasbourg: Council of Europe: Council for Cultural Cooperation. CC-TE (90) 33.

Wilson, J.D. (ed.) (1990) The Selection and Induction of Staff for Initial Teacher Training. *Special Issue European Journal of Teacher Education*, 13, 1/2.

Wilson, J.D., Mitchell, L.H., Jenkins, D., Barclay, A.W., Macay, B.R. and Turner, D.L. (1985) *Initial Selection Procedures: A Review of Current Approaches by Some Professional, Public, Commercial and Voluntary Organisations in the UK*, mimeo.

Wilson, J.D., Thomson, G.O.B., Millward, R.W. and Keenan, T. (eds) (1989) *Assessment for Teacher Development*. London: Falmer Press.

Wilson, M. (ed.) (1991) *Girls and Young Women in Education: A European Perspective*. Oxford: Pergamon.

Wilson, S.M., Shulman, L.S. and Richert, A. (1987) '150 Different Ways' of Knowing: Representations of Knowledge in Teaching. In: Calderhead, J. (ed.) *Exploring Teachers' Thinking*. London: Cassell.

Winter, R. (1989) *Learning from Experience. Principles and Practices in Action-Research*. London: Falmer Press.

World Confederation of Organisations of the Teaching Profession (1989) *Report on Appraisal of Teaching*: Joint Seminar WCOTP – Council of Europe Strasbourg, mimeo.

Wragg, E.C. (1981) *Class Management and Control*. London: Macmillan.

Wragg, E.C. (1989) *Classroom Teaching Skills*. London: Routledge.

Wragg, E.C. (1990) *Training Teachers for Teaching to a Wide Range of Abilities, Interests and Backgrounds in the Classroom*. Strasbourg: Council of Europe: Council for Cultural Cooperation. CC-TE (90) 45.

Wubbels, T. (1992) Teacher Education and the Universities in The Netherlands. In: *European Journal of Teacher Education*, 15, pp. 157–72.

Zay, D. (1992) Teacher Education in France. In: Buchberger, F. (1992a), pp. 99–117.

Zeichner, K.M. and Gore, J.M. (1990) Teacher Socialization. In: Houston, W.R. (ed.) *Handbook of Research on Teacher Education*. New York: Macmillan, pp. 329–49.

Index

220

teacher trainers 116, 120, 121, 122, 124
technology education 160, 162–3
enrichment groups 60, 62
environmental issues, and technology education 161–2
equal opportunities 11–13, 182–3
ERASMUS programme 29, 163, 174, 175–6
ethnic background, and bias 66
European Community
  impact on TE 29
  and teacher mobility 165–6, 170–1
  The Teaching Profession in Europe conference 86
European Cultural Convention (1954) 4
European Journal of Teacher 25, 112
EURYDICE programme 25, 28, 37
evaluation
  by mentors 105
  definition 77
  of media education 140–1
Evertson, Carolyn 67
expectancy, and mixed ability teaching 58
expectations, of new teachers 94, 107
expertise
  characteristics of expert teachers 192–3
  research into 191–3

Fessler, R. and Christensen, J. 88, 91
financing of TE 31
Finland 27, 31, 42–3
  educational research 36
  INSET provision 46
  reflective practice 183
  system of TE 38–9, 44
  Teacher Education Act 123
  teacher trainers 116, 118, 119, 120, 121
Fisher, J.S. 162
Foldberg, E. and Stenlev, L. 38
Ford, J. 62
formalisation of TE programmes 23–4
France 27, 42–3
  INSET provision 35, 46
  reforms of educational system 27, 190–1
  system of TE 27, 38–9, 44
  teacher appraisal 70–1, 78

friendship and ability 62
Friere, Paulo 145
Fullan, M. and Hargreaves, A. 33, 47
Fullan, M.G. 91, 101
Furrer, W. and Wanzenied, P. 15, 19
future trends in education 57

Galton, M. 188, 189
Galton, M., Fogelman, K., Hargreaves, L. and Cavendish, S. 185
Gartside, P., Allan, J. and Munn, P. 122
Gellert, C. 32
Germany 20, 22, 24, 42, 42–3
  grouping policies 54
  INSET provision 46
  mixed ability teaching 61
  TE for vocational education 42
  teacher appraisal 71
  teacher mobility 171, 174
  teacher trainers 118, 119, 120, 121, 122
  technology education 160, 161
gifted children
  curriculum for 62
  definitions 61–2
  identification of 62
  and mixed ability teaching 53, 54, 57–8
Giordan, A. and Souchon, C. 162
Gipps, C. and Murphy, P. xiv
Girard, D. and Trim, J.L.M. 11
Glatthorn, A.A. 86
Glickman, C.D. 87, 100, 101
Goodlad, J.L. 81, 110
government role in teacher education 187
Grankvist 27
Greece 32, 42–3
  teacher mobility 174
  teacher trainers 117, 121, 124
Grodzka-Borowska and Szydlowski, H. 160
Grossman, P. 193
Grot, G. 157
group work, and mixed ability teaching 60, 61
grouping policies 54–6
  banding 55
  and co-education 56
  mixed ability 55–6
  setting 55

222